❇   ❇   ❇ Calypso Calaloo

CALYPSO

Donald R. Hill

CALALOO

Early Carnival Music in Trinidad

University Press of Florida

Gainesville

Tallahassee

Tampa

Boca Raton

Pensacola

Orlando

Miami

Jacksonville

Hill, Donald R.
Calypso calaloo: early carnival
music in Trinidad / Donald R. Hill.
p.   cm.
Includes bibliographical
references and index.
ISBN 0-8130-1221-X (cloth: acid-
free paper).—ISBN 0-8130-1222-8
(pbk.: acid-free paper)
1. Calypso (Music)—Trinidad
and Tobago—History and criticism.
I. Title.
ML3565.H54   1993
781.64–dc20   93-14862

The University Press of Florida is the
scholarly publishing agency for the
State University System of Florida,
comprised of Florida A & M
University, Florida Atlantic
University, Florida International
University, Florida State University,
University of Central Florida,
University of Florida, University of
North Florida, University of South
Florida, and University of West
Florida.

University Press of Florida
15 Northwest 15th Street
Gainesville, FL 32611

*This book is dedicated to a pair of writers,
one musician, four anthropologists, one
strongman, two folklorists, two historians,
one humanities professor, and one play-
wright; they were the first, other than the
calypsonians themselves, to research and
write down the histories of Trinidadian
folklore and calypso:*

Charles Espinet and Peter Pitts,

Melville and Frances Herskovits,

Daniel Crowley and Andrew Carr,

John La Rose and Gordon Rohlehr,

Andrew Pearse and Mitto Sampson,

John Cowley and Bridget Brereton,

J. D. Elder, Errol Hill, *mi dife!*

Sandimanite

＊　　　＊　　　＊

✳   ✳   ✳ **Contents**

✳ Figures

✳ Tables

✷ Preface

N Trinidad, calaloo is a thick soup made of crab or pigtail, okra, dasheen leaves, and seasoning all mixed into coconut milk. It is a blend of unlikely ingredients. The word also refers to a "confusion," a "fix," or a "stew" of the sort in which a person may become entangled. In a more positive way, it may even refer to Caribbean culture, with its many different ethnic groups and their special histories.

Calaloo is a good metaphor for calypso, that special kind of topical Carnival song that developed in Trinidad almost one hundred years ago. English-language calypso is calaloo—it is made up of contrasting ingredients. Calypso displays diversity in form, in lyric content, and in performance context.

My first contact with the American version of this calypso calaloo came when I was a teenager in the late 1950s. I liked the songs of Harry Belafonte, Stan Wilson, and the Gateway Singers. When I discovered the Trinidadian original—my introduction to the real thing came through recordings of songs from the late 1930s and 1940s by Lord Invader and Lord Beginner—I realized that I loved that calypso more than its American copy. I liked the peculiar logic of the lyrics, the way the words were pronounced, and even the singer's names: "Atilla the Hun," "Lord Invader," "the Roaring Lion," "Houdini," "Lord Beginner."

Fifteen years later, while living in Carriacou (Grenada) and Trinidad, I renewed my interest in calypso. I discovered that there was more substance to the original calypso than I had imagined during my youthful period of intoxication with the words, names, and catchy tunes. That substance in calypso was a robust sense of life tempered by fatalism. I wanted to find out all I could about these intriguing songs in their creative context.

So that is the subject of this book: classic calypso as it developed from Carnival and moved through various social contexts and media environments, including the Carnival streets; Carnival tents where calypsos were sung; phonograph records of calypso and related songs and dances; shows, theaters, and clubs where the songs were performed; and films in which calypso was featured. This study is organized around these media; it is not a chronological survey per se but examines each venue separately in chronological order. Short sketches of important singers and others in calypso's history are included along the way. Whenever possible, this work uses extended quotes from the people involved in the calypso story or from contemporary accounts. This method of focusing on both media and situational explanations of events results in a chronological overlap from one chapter to the next as calypso is examined in different contexts. In each context, calypso took on a different character, depending on the media and on who was describing that setting.

Chapter 1 is the introduction. From the beginning, more attention is devoted to the context of calypso performance than to a tight definition of the genre. Chapter 2 consists of a brief review of Trinidad's history from the late eighteenth century. This section is not an attempt to give a complete history; rather, it focuses only on what seems important with respect to the development of calypso. For example, very little attention is paid to the East Indian population of Trinidad, although surely it is as important as the populations covered. This is not an oversight, however, because by and large the cultural contributions to calypso came from other groups. When people with an East Indian cultural background contributed to calypso, they did so as Creoles, not as East Indians. Calypso singer the Roaring Lion and others have introduced some East Indian–

derived tunes into calypso, and quite a number of the promoters and
others who contributed to calypso were of East Indian descent. But
the contributions they made largely reflected their Creole cultural
heritage, not their East Indian one. The significant facts that many
East Indians replaced Creoles on sugar plantations from the 1840s on
and that sugar was a reason so many different people came to
Trinidad are not central to this study. The historical sketches simply
set a context for the real subject, the development of the calypso tent
and the subsequent development of calypso until about 1950.

Chapter 3 focuses on calypso as music for outdoor events, especially Carnival—that is, calypso for "the road." Chapter 4 covers the
the development of the fancy masquerade Carnival at the close of the
nineteenth century.

Chapter 5 centers on the calypso tent, that peculiarly Trinidadian
institution that developed at the beginning of the twentieth century
and that is so important to all subsequent forms of calypso. Chapter 6
concerns the first two generations of tent singers early in the twentieth century. Chapter 7 centers on calypsos that were commercially
recorded on phonograph records. Most of the recording took place in
New York City or in Trinidad. In New York, calypso joined other
musical styles in shows, at dances, at clubs, and on the stage. This is
the focus of Chapter 8. Chapter 9 concentrates on calypso outside
Trinidad and on the people who promoted calypso and related
Caribbean music in New York.

Chapter 10 examines the censorship of calypso and the evolution
of the steel band. Censorship was an important issue over the entire
scope of this study. The struggle to combat censorship of calypso in a
way serves as a metaphor for the struggle for political independence
in Trinidad. Similarly, the grass-roots struggle to develop the steel
band as a form of Carnival entertainment in the 1940s involved more
than music: it was also a kind of political development in a social
climate of economic depression and unrest. The steel band was a new
medium for calypso; its development moved Carnival to a new phase,
one radically different from the tent-based calypso of the earlier era.
This study closes at about the time the steel bands became respectable, around 1950.

Chapter 11, the conclusion, constitutes a curious coda to this
study; it is in the metaphorical style used now and again to convey
what would otherwise take another study to express. In it the

significance of this seemingly frivolous calypso, which has held the attention of so many different people, is addressed.

Appendix 1 consists of calypso lyrics transcribed from records with a brief history of some of the songs. Appendix 2 is a descriptive list of readily available calypso recordings. There is also a glossary, listing words related to calypso that are frequently used or are of great significance.

I hope this study finds readers among Caribbeanists, anthropologists, ethnomusicologists, folklorists, and record collectors. Although by training I fit roughly into the first four categories, it was really my love of calypso, especially the old calypso in 78-rpm records, that drove my research through the many years it took to complete it.

Many people have aided me in preparing this book. For various reasons, both personal and intellectual, the following stand out: Bert Belasco, Kevin Burke, John Cowley, Dan Crowley, Raphael De Leon (the Roaring Lion), Ray Funk, Anthony Hill, Blanche Hill, Errol Hill, Rosamond Hill, Ron Kephart, Alex Leader, Hollis Liverpool (Chalkdust), Neville Marcano (the Growling Tiger), Walda Metcalf, Leonard de Paur, Richard Price, Gordon Rohlehr, Michael Senecal, Steve Shapiro, Jean Simonelli, Randolph Span, Dick Spottswood, Bill Starna, Stephen Stuempfle, Joseph Taubman, Keith Warner, Maureen Warner-Lewis, Ralph Watkins, and Lise Winer. I also thank calypsonians Lion and Sir Lancelot for the use of the song material attributed to them in these pages.

❊   ❊   ❊ Calypso Calaloo

1 ✳ Introduction

*These satirical songs spring up
like poisonous fungi.*

Henry Edward Krehbiel, referring to
Martiniquean Carnival songs

OR me, there are just two kinds of music in this
world, calypso and everything else. In Trinidad, where it took shape,
calypso was Carnival music. There were songs for singing on the
open road during pre-Lenten Carnival, songs for Carnival dances,
and songs performed in calypso tents, those special arenas originally
located on the grounds where Carnival masquerades were assembled.
Some calypsos, which gained popularity during Carnival, were sung
in stage shows or as a part of vaudeville productions meant to amuse
patrons between movie reels. Outside Trinidad, calypsos were sung
in clubs in many cities that touched or are near the Atlantic Ocean: in
New York, London, Accra, or Lagos. Some calypsos were put on
78-rpm phonograph records and sold in shops in Trinidad and
around the world.

All these calypsos are the subject of this book, as they were
developed in the first half of the twentieth century in Trinidad. So
when I write about calypso, I mean calypso from this classic period.[1]

Many calypsos are topical songs. Calypso lyrics are a bible of
Creole thought, though the core idea is often obscured through layers
of indirection or abstruseness. Calypsos tell about everyday life, the

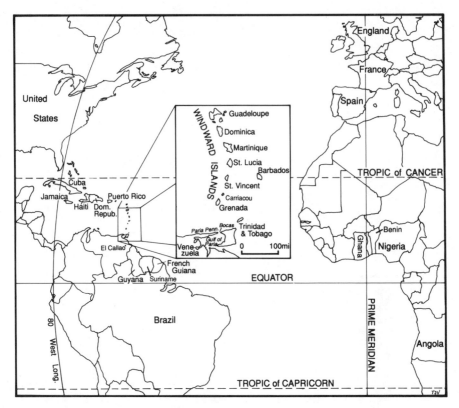

1 ✳ Trinidad's place in the Western Hemisphere. Cartography by Timothy J. VanVranken.

human predicament. In Trinidad, calypso lyrics are quoted in conversation in much the same way proverbs or biblical passages might be. The lyrics tell about personal problems and about the calypsonian's attitude about life in colonial Trinidad.

The term *calypso* as a name for Carnival songs appears in print by 1900.[2] This passage from the *Port of Spain Gazette* gives a good indication as to what was meant by *calypso* during Carnival 1903: "The music of various 'calypso' etc. is an improvement on last year's and a noticeable feature is that the songs are not composed in order to ridicule any persons in the community, as is the case with other bands, but the words are merely based on local events of importance and in praise of their union."[3]

As the *Gazette* implies of "last year's" calypsos, the songs sometimes presented a less-than-respectable, oblique, or blunt perception of people. Calypso, especially as a part of Carnival, comments on people's problems with each other. By pinpointing interpersonal difficulties, the calypsonian draws attention to a discrepancy between an ideal form of living and actual life. Corruption, unusual sexual appetites in men, the breakdown of communication between men and women, or the supposed characteristics of ethnic groups or classes are all singled out as causes of problems mentioned in the songs. Through wit, humor, and hyperbole, the calypsonian raises issues that are in the air. When reacting to a song one is by extension thinking about the problem raised in the song.

There is a progression of issues taken up in calypso, from the specific and personal to the abstract and universal—from self-depreciation, to family criticism (except mothers, who are praised), to ridicule of one's female companion, to ridicule and criticism of all women, to a longing for better behavior by the members of one's own group, to finding fault in other groups, to class antagonisms, to singling out individuals of high social status (with occasional praise), to critical comments about the social system (slavery, colonialism, the mother country), to criticisms of all humanity or inclusion of the calypsonian and his group in the human condition, and finally, to comments on the meaning of life or death (often put as an acceptance of fate or, somewhat contrarily, as existential stances, which allow for many unusual behaviors).

Strong attitudes expressed in calypso have a cathartic value. More than that, differences and similarities among social groups are defined and a bizarre sense is made out of a complicated society. Most calypsonians came from the lower class. In their songs, they could size up their position vis-à-vis other classes.

Singers of classic calypso were usually men. Early calypso almost always portrayed a male, Creole perspective, even when the singer took the role of a woman in a song.

Types of Calypso

Calypso, narrowly defined, is any song that after about 1898 was sung at Carnival time in Trinidad, either in the streets by revelers or in staged performances by semiprofessional and professional singers. These songs were called calypsos by participants in Carnival and in the press. Some of these songs were known by other names when they were sung in a different context but were renamed when sung for Carnival. For example, a lavway (a litanous tune sung informally in outdoor festivals) becomes a special sort of calypso during Carni-val. Other genres that contributed songs to calypso were belairs (nineteenth-century topical songs in French Creole), calindas (songs for stick fighting), and bongos (wake songs). Traditional Carnival speeches and masquerades have also influenced calypso lyrics. Tunes from other Caribbean islands and from England, Africa, the United States, or India were borrowed for use in Carnival as calypsos. Between the 1890s and the 1930s the Venezuelan-style string band was used to accompany calypso, and some melodies from there were adapted as calypso.

After 1900, several names were loosely given to calypso subtypes. The lavway predates calypso, but the term came to be nearly synony-mous with outdoor calypso; indeed, the modern term for the lavway is *road march*. The lyrics of lavways often referred to Carnival itself and especially to the feting, dancing, and sexual activity associated with Carnival. One type of lavway was the leggo, a street song for people who "let go" toward the end of Carnival, from Tuesday evening to midnight.

Some calypsos praised the singer or his Carnival organization. Some lauded politicians or businesses. The songs could be sung outdoors in the calypso tents, which grew up alongside the camps where Carnival masqueraders assembled their costumes and prac-ticed their routines.

"Oratorical" calypsos may have originated from ritual boasts or insults (picong) spoken by costumed characters as they made their rounds during Carnival.[4] "Ballad" calypsos told a story.

An informal and not entirely consistent terminology was used to describe the musical form of many calypsos. Most lavways were single tone, with *tone* meaning tune, not musical tone. A single-tone calypso is a calypso with one melody with a four-line verse. A double-tone calypso has two melodies, a verse of perhaps eight lines, sometimes sung in the oratorical style, and a chorus with a different melody, which was four lines long.

These definitions of calypso do not tell us much; for one thing, participants and experts do not agree on terms. For another, this study is not an examination of the formal characteristics of the genre as much as of the context in which calypsos were sung. Before Carnival Monday each year, calypsos were sung at practices or rehearsals, when a group of masqueraders would get together in the evening, make their costumes, and go over their musical routines. After a few years, the musical performances separated from the masquerade activity and were confined to a corner of the masquerade camp and covered with a tarpaulin. This was the calypso tent, and it was there that the longer, storylike calypsos developed; lavways were usually restricted to the close of the show as a mimic of street Carnival.

In the early 1900s, then, calypso was performed in two settings, the street Carnival and the tent, resulting in outdoor and indoor calypso.[5] The two social contexts tended to create different kinds of music: the former included catchy melodies and allusions to abandonment (bacchanal), sexual activity, excessive drinking and eating, heightened power assuming almost mystical proportions (the stick fighters' calindas are especially strong on this score), identification with Africa, use of Patois, and a clear antiestablishment (anti-British) tone. The characteristics of the indoor calypsos included emphasis on lyrics over melody; storytelling; broad choice of subject matter; use of standard English (some masters of double-tone and ballad calypsos were schoolteachers, although calypso singers came primarily from the lower class) or at least mastery of hyperbole (if hyperbole is ever a virtue, it is in the hands of a good calypsonian); selective use of Patois, or nonstandard English; critical commentary on the social order expressed with a debatelike clarity; and, finally, sometimes elaborate praises of the mother country (Great Britain).

The audience for outdoor calypso is the Carnival reveler. The audience for indoor calypso included the singer's sponsoring organization (such as a masquerade band or a group of stick fighters) or eventually the ticket-buying public, which consisted of Creole Trinidadians of all classes, and tourists.

Among the first singers of the new topical songs in English were lower-class chantwells (singers) from calinda bands (such as Myler the Dentist and One Man Bisco). Their calindas and road marches were adapted to encompass broader themes. These became single-tone and double-tone calypso. Songsters from the middle class (the Senior Inventor, Executor, Norman le Blanc, and Julian Whiterose) were especially noted for double-tone calypso. Some individuals—Whiterose is an important example—participated in the evolution of both indoor and outdoor calypso; that is, the road marches and the double-tone form. Other singers—Railway Douglas stands out here—were known for ballads. Ballad calypsos were appropriate only for tent performances.

There were other songs that cannot easily be described, particularly at the beginning of the period (1900), when formalized, double-tone rhyming had not yet developed, and toward the end of the period (1930s and 1940s), when a variety of forms from other countries was incorporated into calypso.

The earliest calypsos were an assortment of many song forms. Here is the chorus of one of Whiterose's songs. It was labeled as a double-tone on the 1914 Victor phonograph record from which it is transcribed:

> Iron Duke in the land Fire Brigade!
> Iron Duke in the land Fire Brigade!
> Bring the locomotive just because it's a fire botheration
> Bring the locomotive just because it's a fire botheration
> Sandimanite.[6]

The eight-line verse of this song was sung in speech tones.

Later, during what calypsonian Atilla called the golden era of calypso (roughly 1920 to 1950), we find the interjection, often by the calypso singer called Lion, of themes from American popular culture:

> Of all the famous singers that I have seen
> On the movie screen
> Of all the famous singers I have ever seen
> On the movie screen
> Lawrence Tibbit, Nelson Eddy
> Donald Novice and Morton Downey
> Kenny Baker and Rudy Vallee
> But the singing prodigy is Bing Crosby.[7]

Lion used a new tune for these lyrics. His choice of topic is unusual in that it applies to American popular singers, but his verse can be set in the customary eight lines.

Calypso Composition

At the beginning of this century, many calypsos had their origins in a handful of Africanlike call-and-response tunes. Different lyrics were set to these tunes, in the manner described by Albany, a school-teacher-calypsonian.

When the tent was all set up, and the leaders [were] in the carnival spirit, [chantwells] came on the scene. Every band had their chantwell who would take up any topic [in] his song. At the night's practice, the women members òf the band would be the choristers. When the chantwell sang out his refrain, they in turn would take it up. [This] gave a wonderful display of real good singing. For music, the clarinet, flute, bass, quatro, guitar, and violin. In those days calypso held more meaning than today, and one of the best features was the giving of picongs [insults].[8]

Although the same melodies were used over and over again, certain singers eventually became associated with particular lyrics, even though the lyrics were often composed by several "hands." The chantwell or calypsonian made the song his own in performance. A particular song was thought of as Inventor's song, Executor's song, or Atilla's song.

The legal device of copyright did not matter much for the chantwells and the older generation of calypsonians—that became an issue with the pianist and orchestra leader Lionel Belasco and the American-based calypsonian Wilmoth Houdini. Belasco held the copyright on well over one hundred songs. He probably did not write most of them, however, but rather transcribed them and perhaps slightly modified the lyrics.

Some songs were written by well-known ghostwriters who

came into prominence in the 1920s. In the 40s [they] became an indispensable adjunct in kaiso [calypso] presentations. . . . Among famous kaiso writers were a proof-reader at the "grand old lady of St. Vincent Street," the "Port-of-Spain Gazette," an ex-Deputy Mayor of the city, and an ex-minister of the Trinidad government. The art of kaiso writing by non-kaisonians seems to have always been practiced, though not acknowledged. The proud boast of the kaisonian, even to this day when it is fairly well known that there is a plethora of kaiso writers, is that he is the sole composer of music and lyric. Any acknowledgment of other sources of creative genius lessens his stature, unlike his fellow artistes in other fields such as the concert pianist, singer, or actor.[9]

The Growling Tiger, a singer who came into prominence in the mid-1930s, mentions a merchant helping him with lyrics to several songs. Lion mentions asking permission from others to use their songs. Pretender, who first sang calypso in the late 1930s, states that his contemporary, the Lord Invader, used Pretender's "And God Made Us All" when appearing at Carnegie Hall in the late 1940s without much recognition for the author. (This song was borrowed by the American entertainer Huddie Ledbetter, better known as Leadbelly.) Calypso scholar Steve Shapiro has probably done more than any other person in tracking down attributions of songs, and he has found that scores of important songs were not written by the calypsonians who made the songs famous.[10]

Many calypsos were coauthored by Reynold Wilkinson, a government clerk and tent manager. Sometimes the actual composer wanted to remain anonymous, but in other instances he received a fee from the calypsonian who then claimed the song as his own, with tacit approval of the composer. Most of the songs by the established singers, however, seem to have been either composed or thoroughly reworked by the calypsonian himself.[11]

Song Origins

Calypso singers have borrowed songs from a wide range of sources. Many tunes and lyrics came from other islands or from the South American mainland. After emancipation, Afro-French songs drifted in from Grenada, Carriacou, St. Lucia, Dominica, and Guadeloupe. British Creole migrants brought songs from Barbados, St. Vincent, and Tobago. And late in the nineteenth century, the sound of the string band blew in from the Spanish Main. There is ample evidence of the contribution of Patois and French songs to calypso in the 1890s and 1900s. For example, both chantwell Patrick Jones and calypsonian Atilla the Hun point to Martinique as the source of "L'Année Passée."[12] The Haitian tune "Chaconné" is another well-known song borrowed by chantwells in the 1890s (from the melody of a song about a hot-air balloon that flew over Trinidad).

Songs in English were common, too, especially after 1900—"Tobo Jestina" from Tobago in 1909 ("Tobo Jestina who go married to you for your face like a whale and you just come from jail"), "Sly Mongoose" from Jamaica ("Sly Mongoose, Dog know your name!"),

"Payne Dead" from Barbados ("Hoy, I ain't kill nobody but me husband"), "Mama No Want No Rice" ("no coconut oil; All she want is brandy handy all the time") from the Bahamas, and some of the best from Carriacou and the Grenadines: "They Want Fo Come Kill Me," "Mathilda" ("take me money and run Venezuela"), and "Brown Skin Gal."[13] Songs came from the lips of migrants, merchant seamen, and Antillean mariners in sloops and schooners. Atilla the Hun had been a merchant seaman; so was Houdini for a time. King Radio learned songs from Carriacouan sailors longshoring the docks of Port of Spain.

Calypso is Carnival music, and throughout the Caribbean, wherever there were Africans, their descendants, and French, there were topical songs with a family resemblance. It seems most likely that calypso's oldest roots lie in West Africa and in France. This position is both parsimonious and logical.[14]

Many song genres have influenced calypso or have been renamed calypso when played in the context of Carnival. For example, several important song genres have had different histories in Trinidad and in nearby Carriacou, Grenada. The differences found in belairs and calindas on the two islands are especially instructive, because the different course taken by traditional topical music on the two islands may tell us something about a similar dialectic in music found elsewhere in the Americas.

Both Trinidad and Carriacou share a baseline Creole culture that is Afro-French. Both islands shared the Afro-French song form (or forms) called belair. Although several kinds of belairs are found in Trinidad and in Carriacou (migrants brought some of the Trinidadian belairs from Carriacou after 1838, and vice versa), all belairs are topical songs in the same sense that calypsos are topical. On both islands belairs are sung in French Creole (Patois).

In Carriacou, belairs are still sung at the opening of a Big Drum Dance, an Africanesque ritual with many creole overlays in which the ancestors are supplicated or thanked.[15] In Trinidad (and in the French islands), belairs were associated with creoleness and with mixed Afro-European origins. Even in Carriacou, a case could be made that some types of belairs were originally parodies of French ballroom dances.

The belair took different routes on these two islands. In Carriacou, these Creole songs and dances were attached to an essentially Afro-

Caribbean religious ritual. In Trinidad, the belairs remained secular and were transformed into English calypso. In Carriacou, the Big Drum Dance is a creolized, West African–derived religion of the type analogous to the Macumba or Candomblé of Brazil. It is island-wide and coexists with Christianity. In Trinidad, Carnival is an island-wide festival—except in East Indian villages—parallel to the Big Drum of Carriacou but secular rather than sacred. Carnival, with transformed belairs and all, celebrates a British (transformed Afro-French) Creole culture, one in which religious institutions are more clearly separate from everyday life than in Carriacou.

Significantly, the opposite was the case for the calinda: As the accompaniment for stick-fighting songs, sung in French Creole, calinda has always been associated with the African portion of Afro-French Creole culture. In Carriacou, calinda, being African, is a natural part of the Big Drum. In Trinidad, it was brought into calypso as a jamet (underclass) or African activity. In short, the Carriacouan Creole synthesis has an African flair; even today, older Carriacou people call themselves Africans. In this they are nearly unique in the British Caribbean. This African Creole synthesis, Carriacou people say, includes various African nations that established family lines. The songs of these nations are played at each Big Drum performance (the Ibo, Mende, Yoruba, Moko, and so forth).

In Trinidad, calypso (as Carnival music) is the synthesis. It is essentially a Creole synthesis, a British version of Afro-French culture. Calinda is brought into that synthesis.

While the African and French influence on the customs of Trinidad were more or less continuous in the nineteenth century,[16] the Spanish flavor came into calypso and Carnival late in the century and then more or less continuously through the 1930s. This influence seems to have occurred mostly in instrumentation in certain dance pieces. It is less pronounced in lyrics. The string band, popular from around 1890 through the 1920s, seems to be of Venezuelan origin. It consists of violin, one or more guitars and cuatros (a four-string guitar), and maracas. Probably reflecting French Creole influence, the clarinet was sometimes added to this group. Strolling musicians were the vogue of the new, middle-class Creole Carnival at the turn of the century. String bands were the basic accompaniment of the earliest single-tone and double-tone calypsos, and the terms *paseo* and *castillian* came to be nearly synonymous with calypso.

Outdoor Carnival music has been heavily influenced by the music associated with seasonal activities, such as Christmas, Easter, local harvest fetes, and Emancipation-Day celebrations. Genres of outdoor songs that have influenced or have been entirely incorporated into calypso are lavways, leggos, calindas, bongos, and belairs.

Indoor music has also influenced Carnival music. Many of the indoor songs may be traced to European dances such as contra dances, reels, and couples dances in addition to the aforementioned Venezuelan (and Colombian?) castillians and paseos. These are known in Trinidad as lancers, quadrilles, reels, jigs, and paseos.

This introduction is intended to help sort out the complex origins of calypso. The rest of the book will put this complexity in a social and cultural context and make some sense of it all.

2 ✳ A Historical Sketch of Trinidad

These dances are stupendous.

Friedrick Urich, a merchant's clerk,
referring to Carnival dances of 1831

THE first people to inhabit Trinidad were American Indians. Their influence on calypso was slight.[1] In 1498, Columbus sailed into the Bay of Paria, claimed the Indians' land for the Spanish Crown, and named it Trinidad (fig. 2). Years later, the Spaniards settled in the north and established their capital at St. Joseph. For several centuries the population of Trinidad consisted of the few Spanish colonialists, small communities of runaway slaves, and American Indian settlements in the south. But toward the end of Spain's rule of Trinidad, policy changes were initiated that would help determine the composition of nineteenth-century Trinidadian society.

Class and Ethnicity in the Nineteenth Century

In 1776 King Charles II of Spain issued the first of two "Cedulas de Poblacion." Under its terms any Catholic, of whatever nationality, could settle in a Spanish colony. However, as table 2–1 shows, this decree had little effect on the population. Although the non-Spanish population did not increase as the Spanish Crown had hoped as a

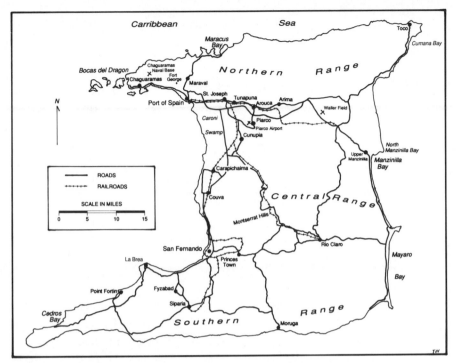

2 ✳ Places in Trinidad. Cartography by Timothy J. VanVranken.

result of the 1776 cedula, a French-Grenadian colonial, Phillipe-Rose Roume de Saint Laurent, looked over Trinidad. He intended to encourage fellow French colonials to establish plantations. In 1783 he traveled to Spain and convinced Charles II to issue a new cedula, expressly for settling Trinidad by Catholics with sympathies toward the Spanish Crown. As a result of St. Laurent's efforts, a new cedula was issued in that year.

Often called "the Cedula" in Trinidad, the Decree of Population of 1783 was an attempt to encourage whites, free people of African descent, and colored Roman Catholics from friendly nations to establish residence in Trinidad by offering land grants.[2] Whites received twice the land granted to the others, and each settler received import, trade, and tax benefits.

Table 2–1 shows the population of Trinidad in 1797, the year the island was captured by the British. The free French population (white and colored) outnumbered the free Spanish population (white and colored) by almost twenty to one. Thus, at the moment the British took control of the island, the baseline was set for Afro-French

Table 2-1. Population of Trinidad as a Spanish colony by nationality and ethnicity, 1783 and 1797

		White	Colored[a]	Slave	Indian
1783	Spanish	126	245	310	2,000
1797	Spanish	150	200	300	1,127
	French	2,250	4,700	9,700	
	Total	2,400	4,900	10,000	1,127

Source: Based on Pearse 1956a:175.
a. The term *colored* was widely used in the eighteenth and nineteenth centuries to refer to people of mixed African and European descent. By the second half of the nineteenth century in Trinidad, the term tended to refer to people with some African descent who were of the middle class or the elite.

Creole[3] culture to become the most important cultural complex in a colony with many layers of cultural complexity. The elite persons of this culture were either white or colored and culturally more French Creole than Afro-French Creole. The slaves were of West African descent and were culturally West African or Creole (that is, their culture combined several important West African cultures with French culture adapted to slave life in the Caribbean).

St. Hilaire Begorrat was an estate owner who immigrated to Trinidad from Martinique with his father, Pierre, and their slaves.[4] In the late 1700s, he told a British commission about the migration of French Creole planters and slaves to Trinidad: "I am sure that on my arrival in 1784 [slaves] did not amount to 1,000. [The 10,000 slaves now present] were introduced by the House of Barry and Black, English merchants, from the islands of St. Vincent and Grenada, and the revolutionary troubles in Martinique in 1792,[5] brought an immigration of between three and four thousand slaves in this colony with their proprietors."[6]

The census of 1797 also illustrates the cultural, legal, and social categories in which Trinidadians were placed. Such divisions, firmly etched in the minds of the British colonial rulers and most other Trinidadians for nearly a hundred years, formed the basis of a complex sense of identity on which rested rights and obligations.

One legal distinction was that between free and slave. Elaborate rules separated the two groups and defined how masters were to treat slaves and the conditions under which slaves could be bought, sold, or freed. The Spanish and French tended to view slavery as more basic than color; that is, the status of being a slave was more significant than one's color. They operated under the provisions of Roman law, on which the Spanish law of Trinidad was based.

Table 2–1 illustrates this point: Within the free French planter class, the colored French outnumbered the white French by more than two to one. From the point of view of the aristocratic white French planters, the colored French planters were superior to many of the non-French whites and, of course, to all other nonwhites.

It was within that Creole mix, seen as French by the white aristocratic planter class but as Afro-Creole by the French Creole-speaking slaves on the estates of the French, that Trinidadian (Creole) culture as we know it today originated. As a group these Creoles looked to France for high culture and to the dialectic between the estate and the slaves' quarters for local Creole culture.

When the British[7] consolidated their rule over Trinidad, the British population of the island increased, but not to the point where the Afro-French culture was in danger of losing its dominance (table 2–2).

In the view of the expatriate British rulers and the Creole—that is, Trinidad-born—British, this legal division between the free and the slave came to be judged as part of a practical separation between white and nonwhite. They sought to restrict rights that had been granted to the free coloreds under Spanish law.

Two decades after the Capitulation, planters, merchants, and top government officials formed two separate but related elites: Most of the merchants and the officials were British and most of the planters were French Creoles (see tables 2–3 and 2–4). In the nineteenth century, the former group was sometimes called the "English party,"[8] and they supported British colonial rule and English cultural ways. They tended to be English-speaking Anglicans. Many were English-born or English Creoles. In contrast, the "French party" consisted of Roman Catholics, many of them French speakers. Yet this group contained some non-French Catholic plantation owners who some-times sympathized with the French. This group included Madeirans, Irish, Catholic Scots, Corsicans, Germans, and the original Spanish.

Color was a complex issue for the white planters. The aristocrats among them were endogamous and sought to retain racial purity by

Table 2–2. Population of Trinidad as a British colony by nationality and ethnicity, 1803

	White	Colored	Slave	Indian
Spanish	505	1,751		
French	1,093	2,925		
British	663	599		
Total	2,261	5,275	20,464	(?)

Source: Based on Pearse 1956a:176.
Note: There is no breakdown for the number of slaves held by free Spanish, French, or British.

excluding the colored elite as potential marriage partners. Yet a few African ancestors were to be found within the genealogies of some of the white French, and, although not acknowledged, rumors persisted of other African progenitors. Thus, at their edges, the colored and white planter classes overlapped: it was better to be an elite French colored planter than to be a white artisan, especially an English-speaking artisan.

The color issue was even more Byzantine for the colored estate owners and professionals. Dark complexion did not automatically exclude one from the colored group, although here, too, the colored elite tended to be endogamous. Although it is true that some colored aristocrats sought to be white, if not in appearance then in culture, an increasing number of them in the nineteenth century found value in their special status and in Afro-Trinidadian heritage. Their involvement in Carnival and their translation of the customs of the poor blacks[9] is the single most important modification in the development of Carnival and calypso as part of the national culture of Trinidad and Tobago.

This division based on color extended through the class system. In the early nineteenth century one was not simply a member of the elite—one was white British, colored British, white French, or colored French. Other divisions within the elite existed among occupational groups (such as planters, merchants, or major government officials) or political orientations (for example, the French were divided into Royalists or Jacobins). An elite person could be ethnically French, English, Scottish, Portuguese, Spanish, and so on.

Table 2-3. Population of Trinidad as a British colony by nationality and ethnicity, 1825

	White	Colored	Slave	Indian
Native	1,410	6,844	14,526	
British	985	1,181		
Spanish	365	2,108		
French	417	1,187		
Corsican	20			
Italian	21			
German	29			
American	56	1,028		
African		947	8,547	
Chinese	(12)			
Total	3,303	13,295	23,073	783

Source: Based on de Verteuil 1984:3–4.
Note: There is slight variation between these totals and those given in de Verteuil. *Native* refers to Trinidad-born, who are mostly French and Spanish. Indentured ("free") Africans are listed as *colored*. Chinese are not included in the *white* or *colored* categories.

These differences were mirrored in the other classes. For example, the lower class was composed of either French Creole or English Creole slaves, a very heterogeneous population. Above them in status were free fishermen and peasants. They encompassed the (colored) Spanish peons, Creole yeoman farmers or laborers, and American Indians.

Cultural divisions among all these groups was exacerbated by physical isolation (fig. 3). This separation extended well into the last third of the nineteenth century. In the north, settlements stretched a few miles east and west of the old Spanish capital of St. Joseph to Arima and Port of Spain. The latter community became the British capital and was the center for the British civil service. After the sugar crisis of the 1830s and 1840s, when many French planters converted their assets to cocoa, British planters tended to live on the sugar estates south of St. Joseph and in the Naparimas surrounding the coastal community of San Fernando. In the early 1800s free colored (French) planters were centered in the Naparimas,[10] but by midcentury the French elite, although also found in Port of Spain, was centered in the cocoa-growing areas in the valleys of the northern and

Table 2-4. Estimate of the population of Trinidad by "party," 1825.

	Free	Slaves	Total
English Party	2,166	(3,692)	(5,858)
French Party	15,277	(19,381)	(34,658)
Total	17,443	23,073	40,516

Source: Table 2-3.
Note: The total free "English Party" equals British white plus British colored. The total free "French Party" equals all other white and colored, including Africans, Chinese, and American Indians. The estimated totals for the slaves of the English and French parties are based on the following formula: The number of free English is divided by the number of free French (13,535, a number that excludes the Chinese, Africans, and Indians, groups that did not hold slaves). This ratio (.16) is multiplied by the total number of slaves (23,073) to give the estimated number of slaves in the English party (3,692). The remaining slaves are estimated to be in the French party.

central mountains or in the coconut plantations on the east coast between Manzanila and Mayaro.[11] The surest route to the coconut estates from Port of Spain was not overland, but by steamer. Similarly, boats were the best method of travel between the communities near the extremities of the island—Port of Spain, Toco, Moruga, San Fernando.

In 1870 a telegraph line connected St. Joseph with Port of Spain, in 1876 a railway line connected Port of Spain and Arima, and in 1882 a second line connected the capital and San Fernando. These technological improvements helped to bring towns into contact with one another and facilitated migration from traditional and isolated small communities to Port of Spain, to San Fernando, or abroad.

Although most of the population of the island lived either on the estates or in greater Port of Spain or San Fernando, there were also isolated pockets of maroons (runaway slaves) in the northern mountains, Spanish fishermen in coastal villages, and Spanish peons (subsistence farmers) on marginal lands in the northern mountains and elsewhere.

This complex cultural pluralism yielded a curiously simple structure of opposing social forces. Power and influence came from above—power from the free British and high culture from the free French. The free coloreds had their own version of British and French metropolitan cultures, as did the slaves. From another direction came the cultural impact of the African in bondage: slaves dominated these

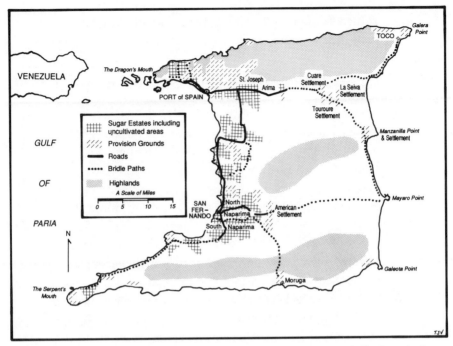

3 ✳ Trinidad in the early 1850s, based on Basanta's 1853 map. Cartography by Timothy J. VanVranken.

other groups in terms of population, at least until the arrival of the East Indians after emancipation. Creoles of African descent also put the fundamental stamp on Trinidad's expressive culture.

Unlike other slave colonies, late-developing Trinidad was never completely dominated by slavery.[12] In 1810, two-thirds of the island's population were slaves, much lower than the proportions in other colonies. Slaves lived on comparatively small estates (60 percent on estates with fewer than fifty slaves, compared with 24 percent for Jamaica). More slaves were African-born than West Indian-born and many were urban: nearly 25 percent lived in Port of Spain in 1813, half lived on sugar estates, and most of the rest lived on other estates. Although African-born slaves tended to come from many spots in Africa, one-third came from the Bight of Biafra (including many Yorubas). African slaves tended to marry other Africans rather than Creole slaves, and stable unions were common. Mortality greatly exceeded fertility, and the slave population gradually declined in the years preceding emancipation. In sum, although the population of Trinidad was diverse, the French and their African and Creole slaves created the dominant Creole culture of the countryside from the last years of Spanish rule until emancipation in 1833.

Carnival and Other Annual Celebrations before Emancipation

Carnival, as a festival of the French Catholics, was imported into Trinidad after the Decree of Population by planters and slaves from the French Caribbean.[13] Carnival consisted of masquerade balls and visiting by parties of the elite from estate to estate. Wealthy citizens, in particular Sir Ralph Woodford, governor from 1813 to 1828, gave elaborate masked balls, and in the evening during Carnival the leading members of society would don masks and drive through the streets of Port of Spain, visiting houses thrown open for the occasion. The free colored developed their own means of joining in the festival, as did slaves, although theoretically prohibited from participation except as onlookers or by special favor.[14] Slave involvement in Carnival varied from estate to estate; slaves were usually allowed more latitude for entertainment on the French estates.

The diary of Friedrick Urich, a merchant's clerk, shows clear evidence of slave, colored, and free African participation in Carnival. He writes about Port of Spain's Carnival in 1831:

> Sunday 13th Feb. After dinner we went to see the negroes dance.
> Monday 14th Feb. I went to call on the Bocks but he told us that she was getting ready to attend the disguised ball. Entrace [sic] fee $8.00. We follow various masked bands. The dances are usually African dances, and the enthusiasm of the negroes and negresses amuse us very much, for these dances are stupendous. We play smart and look on at the ball for a short time from the street, and then return home and go to bed.
>
> Tuesday 15th Feb. I feel very weary after running around so much. The noise of the masked bands however, banishes this feeling and gives me the wish to go out, but my boots are wet and I cannot get them on, so I have to be lazy and stay at home.[15]

Christmas, not Carnival, was a more important occasion in (Protestant) British-dominated urban Trinidad.[16] Participants in feting and serenading included whites and free coloreds. Celebrating coincided with a period of martial law, which was invoked annually during this season to keep slaves from plotting revolts. All free men were expected to participate in military drills.[17] Activities included dancing, parades, and singing. More license was allowed than at other times of the year.

By end of the first quarter of the nineteenth century, members of the English party assimilated many French Carnival customs, grafting pre-Carnival rehearsals (costume making, speech practicing, and, eventually, calypso singing) to the New Year's side of Christmastime festivities. In Port of Spain, Governor Woodford celebrated Carnival by holding masquerade balls, and the British and French elite rode around town in costume. Others walked from house to house.[18] According to Anthony de Verteuil, "in the early 1830s [Carnival] was accepted as the celebration of the whole community."[19]

Slaves had other celebrations, which when practiced in the open seemed pure entertainment. Yet these diversions included secret elements unknown to the planters. Slaves established a "network of secret societies through which the slaves created an existence entirely separate from the world of the plantation."[20] On a Diego Martin estate a French planter overheard slaves singing in Patois. Their song referred to the successful slave revolt in Haiti:

The bread is the flesh of the white man, San Domingo [Haiti]!
The wine is the blood of the white man, San Domingo!
We will drink the white man's blood, San Domingo!
The bread we eat is the white man's flesh.
The wine we drink is the white man's blood.[21]

Slaves formed themselves into regiments, complete with kings, queens, and so forth. Feasts were held, including mock communions (of which the above song may have been a part). There were competitions, and obeah (magic) was practiced. Many of these customs were also incorporated into Carnival.

By 1834, slavery in British possessions was coming to an end. In that year, slaves were indentured for a four-year contract; in 1838 they were freed. Some freedmen sought to work land they bought. Others squatted on land and farmed. Many moved to Port of Spain or San Fernando. Work once performed by slaves was taken over by workers imported from nearby islands or from abroad, particularly from India. Outdoor culture, especially Carnival, gained the freedman's mark, as the next chapter will illustrate. And the British set down policies that eventually made their mark on the island's Afro-French Creole culture.

3 ✳ The Yard
and the Road

We march! We are on the march and we are marching!

Lionel Belasco, referring
to the Carnival rioters of 1882

CALYPSO developed in late-nineteenth-century Port of Spain, when former slaves mingled with other Creoles and once-indentured Africans in an emerging urban Carnival. That proletariat calypso owed a lot to the rural nineteenth-century slaves of Trinidad and the Lesser Antilles. If calypso is envisioned as a bag full of many different rocks, each rock could stand for a song genre performed on estates all over Creole rural Trinidad. This chapter will briefly sketch that estate setting in which songs ancestral to calypso lived, look at the social environment of urban Port of Spain, and describe Carnival after emancipation.

The Yard

The focal point of the slave's workaday life consisted of a triangle made up of the yard, the plantation, and the garden plot allowed most slaves for their own subsistence. The slave's house was on one side of the yard, but slaves were rarely at home. The hut usually had one or two rooms and served mostly for sleeping. The hut was, then, a bit of indoors stuck in an outdoor arena, the yard. The house and garden were located on the master's land. One day a week was given to slaves to work their own crops, thus saving the owner from feeding his property.

In the Big House—the estate house—lived the proprietor and his family. Large and pretentious, the house was the center of power on the plantation. Although the estate owner sponsored plenty of out-door amusements, dinners and dances for the free elite population were held indoors. The guests at these parties were landowners, merchants, and government officials. Household slaves were cooks and servants, and some doubled as musicians. The entertainment might consist of quadrilles, lancers, and other European-style dances. The most important instruments played indoors were the violin (for dances) and the piano (a parlor instrument).

African-derived entertainment took place in the yard. Music was made on African instruments, especially the drum, when allowed. Sometimes creolized versions of the master's dances, accompanied by the violin, also took place in the yard. The African-style entertain-ment consisted of formation of a ring, with musicians, singers, would-be dancers, and spectators forming a circle around a small space left for the dancers. At any one time, either women or men would dance. When a man and a woman danced as a couple touching or holding onto one another, perhaps together with other couples, that dance represented a creolization of the European Big House lancers, quadrilles, or reel dances.

After emancipation, the notions of house, yard, and garden were easily adapted to the freed people's own land. The yard-house-field configuration became ubiquitous among yeoman farmers and squat-ters. Their progeny were to be found in the yards whenever a fete, game, or ritual transformed the yard from a woman's mundane work place to an ideal world of song, dance, or communication with the dead.

Yards were the hub of the everyday world for rural Creole families and the center of local activity for denizens of barrack houses in urban Port of Spain. A rural yard was bounded by a house, an oven, and outbuildings (a shed or a kitchen). People lived in the yard; they only retreated indoors to sleep or when it rained. Yards were for chores, socializing, and other diversions and for ritual. Some of the traditional yard-based activities even to this day include washing, shelling corn, cooking, gossiping, playing cards and dominoes, and holding prayer meetings, wakes, and other funerary or propitiatory rituals that asked the living to support the dead.

The Road

If the yard was a woman's domain, the road—especially crossroads—and the rum shop were man's domain.[1] When the African-style Creole entertainments moved out of the yard, they took to the road. Liming (loafing, not especially an African practice), stick fighting, serenading, and Carnival bacchanal happened outside rum shops or general stores, at crossroads, or on the road. When serenaders were brought inside for rum or food, it was as if the outside came inside, and the formality and privacy of the home were broken by the spirit of the road.

In most Caribbean islands—and Trinidad is no exception—another rough distinction is made between the countryside and the town. The former consists of plantations, villages, and gardens, whereas "town" is usually the major port. In Trinidad, "town" is greater Port of Spain and perhaps a bit to the east; the rest of Trinidad is "South."

> You could stay in the South and try all you want
> You have to go to Town to become important
> The 'ting that North want to put to you,
> While you in South you en have any value.[2]

This distinction between country and town, like that between yard and road, is readily expanded into metaphor. Country is provincial, town is cosmopolitan. Country is a closed world and gossip-laden; town is more open and gossip is less personal and more group oriented. Yard and house, garden and yard, road and yard, country and town: these are words often paired in the West Indies.

Before emancipation, Port of Spain was bounded by the Queen's Wharf to the south, the Queen's Park Savannah to the north, French Street to the west, and St. Anns river to the east (figs. 4 and 5). Beyond those boundaries was the country: St. James Barracks to the west, the Botanical Gardens to the north, and Belmont and Laventille to the east. Moving to the major part of the island, that is, east through Corbeau Town to the old Spanish capital of St. Joseph and then south to San Fernando and beyond, all that was "South."

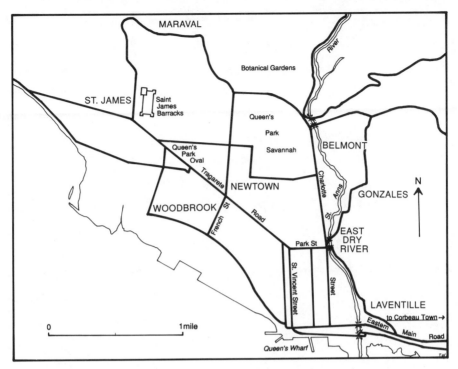

4 ✳ Greater Port of Spain, Trinidad. Cartography by Timothy J. VanVranken.

Although the mental map of Port of Spain was extended west and later east, the image of town versus country continues to the present day.

The Calinda

In Trinidad today and in the recent past, calinda means stick fighting and the songs played for this sport. Centuries ago, from New Orleans to British Guiana, calinda was a dance. In 1724 Labat wrote the first known account of calinda. "The dance which pleases them [the slaves] greatly, and which is their most customary is the calinda. It comes from the coast of Guinea, and according to all appearances from the Kingdom of Arrada [the present-day Bénin Republic, formerly Dahomey]. The Spanish have learned it from the Negroes and dance it all over America in the same way as the Negroes."[3] The exact connection between this calinda dance and stick fighting is not known, although the latter appears in a lithograph entitled "Stick Fighting among Slaves," dated 1779 (fig. 6).[4] Nevertheless, the

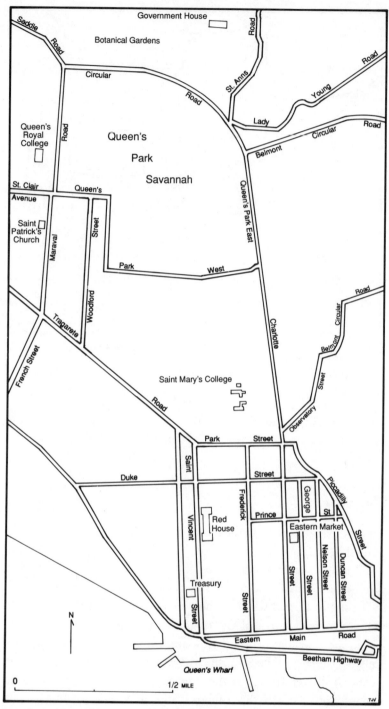

5 ✳ Central Port of Spain, Trinidad. Cartography by Timothy J. VanVranken.

6 ✶ "Stick Fight among Slaves." Lithograph by A. Brunias, 1779. From the Barbados Museum.

French elite mimicked their slaves and danced the calinda and fought with sticks. They wore the neg jardin jersey (fig. 7), which usually consisted of a fabric shirt covered with triangles of colored garment and an appliqué heart on the chest of the costume. The whole outfit was covered with small mirrors.

Stick fighting was part of the canboulay festival. After emancipation, former slaves adapted the canboulay to commemorate the August 1 event and for other times as well.[5] Canboulay included a ritual burning of cane fields, together with stick fights and dances. Around 1843, canboulay was grafted to the opening of Carnival, on Sunday evening.

From the eighteenth century on, estates rivaled each other in stick fighting. This idea of territoriality was taken into the towns after emancipation, and so, at Carnival and on other occasions, intense hostilities occurred among barrack yards. In 1879, the attorney general of Trinidad described the bands of stick fighters in the barrack yards: The bands included "persons without any settled occupation, subsisting by theft or by the favour of the prostitutes whose wages they share. They have no charitable, political or other definite object, but are called into operation only for the purpose of fighting with other bands."[6] A yard served as the home for a band of

7 ✳ Stick fighter outfitted in a neg jardin jersey, a mirror-covered fabric shirt with an appliqué heart on the chest, early 1900s. Courtesy of *Shell Trinidad* magazine.

stick fighters. Jacob D. Elder has located some sixty-four yards in two areas of Port of Spain, dating from the late 1800s until the 1940s.[7] Hell Yard, Newtown, and Toll Gate were some of them. Each band had internal rivalries from which emerged the king, leading the others on holidays or other festive occasions. Female backers, followers of the stick fighters, were led by an older woman called a matador. As the band moved through the village traces or the streets of Port of Spain, open competition occurred among the rival groups. Calinda was more than a game, more than a folk-sport.[8]

A stick fighter called a "retired warrior" in an interview published in the *Trinidad Guardian*[9] gives a firsthand account of the practice as it existed in the 1870s:

I am not of the elite[10] but an ordinary working man and [can] . . . tell you of some of the doings of my particular claim—the stick fighters. The two great factions were the Bakers and the Freegrammers.

The former, who were always dressed in white, "ruled" the eastern part of the town, their auxiliaries being the Corailia band, composed of "decent" fellows, store clerks and the like; "De Leon" made up of "jacketmen," cartmen and shop clerks. These bands were from East of

the Dry River. West of the Dry River bridge, that is from Duncan to
Henry Streets, better known as the French Quarter of the town, were
the Young Bakers [or] . . . "Tai-Pings," brave and reckless fellows.
From L'Hospice bridge up to Belmont the "Maribones" held sway. This
band consisted of the worst and toughest element anywhere: the men
and even their boys and women always dressed in burlap. They were
considered the most dangerous of all the fighting bands, caring
nothing about the lives of others and little about their women; the
safety of the onlookers mattered little to them, and when broken
bottles and showers flew thick and fast, everyone had to seek shelter.
The alarm, "Maribones coming down," would fill everyone with terror,
doors and windows were quickly closed and the inmates of the houses
along their line of march would kneel and pray; they would utter a
genuine sigh of relief when the dreaded "Cocoa-bagged" Devils had
gone by and were well out of sight. Sticks, knives, missiles of every
kind that could hurt, maim, or even kill their antagonists were used by
this murderous band with utter recklessness. From midnight on
Sunday they began to gather their men by means of conch shells and
cattle horns blown at short intervals, and when they started out on the
warpath, woe be to those who opposed them.

. . . The Freegrammers . . . chief king was Ernest Auguste, the
second king being that notable stick fighter One Man Bisco. The
auxiliary bands of this faction [included] "Corbeau Town," made up of
fishermen, boatmen, butchers. . . .

The dividing line was Henry Street and any Baker who dared
venture west of that line was properly beaten. Similarly, any
Freegrammer bold enough to cross Henry Street was at risk of [being]
beaten to death by the Bakers. This rule applied not only during the
two days of Carnival, but on any and all times during the year. . . . The
king of his band was always dressed as a pierrot and led his men to the
fray; he was generally noted for his fearlessness and because of his
powers as the best stick fighter of the band. He always started out with
a whip, but when the battle was well on, discarded it for a stick, usually
carried by his paramour. . . .

On meeting his opponent, the pierrot [fig. 8] would deliver a
wonderful oration, dwelling principally on his own prowess, his
invincibility and the dire things in store for his enemies. The "enemy
king" was entitled, of course, to reply which he did by impressing the
first speaker that he would conquer him, overrun his dominions and,

8 ✳ Stick fighter "Pierrot," leader of a stick fighting faction, early 1900s. Courtesy of *Shell Trinidad* magazine.

in a word, utterly annihilate him. Then began the whipping. Immediately behind the pierrot there were usually three leaders—the best fighters in the band—one in the middle of the street, and one on each side of him, a few yards off, closely followed by their men. The "battle-song" enthused the whole group, especially when reinforced by a few good shots of rum. If the leaders fell, the band would feel discouraged but their places were soon filled by other warriors. The wounded men would be quickly picked up by their women and friends and hurried home, attended to as quickly as possible in the hope of rejoining their bands without unnecessary delay. When a leader fell, the slogan was: "Coule, sang moen ka coule" [Flowing, my blood is flowing]. That dirge-like utterance would cheer them up and they would redouble their efforts at trying to vanquish their opponents.[11]

Stick-fighting bands that roam the streets are virtually extinct in Trinidad's Carnival today, but they continued to exist into the 1970s in Carriacou, Grenada.[12]

Stick fighting was ritualistic: Defeating the opponent was impor-   31
tant but acting out (performing) was also valued by participants and   *
observers. The symbolic content of the songs and the stick fight was   The Yard
significant. There was a magical part to this stick fighting. Special   and the
sticks, said to be more effective, were mounted. They contained   Road
supernatural qualities because they were cut at a certain phase of the
moon, were cured in a special way, or had magical substances rubbed
on them. Apprentice stick fighters were formally trained. In one
technique, stones were thrown at the apprentice, who had to fend
them off with his stick. In the fight itself, a blow to the opponent's
head had top priority. To draw blood was the aim and the blood of
the victim was drained into a blood hole. Wounds were treated by a
second, the "doctor." A typical stick-fighting competition with a
series of fighters might last from eight o'clock at night until dawn.
Accompanied by drums or the tamboo bamboo (bamboo stamping
tubes hit against the earth and struck with a stick to give percussive
effects) the battoniers fought one on one. To fight "a la trois" was an
interesting variation in which three stick fighters formed a triangle, all
fighting against each other. Names for the blows or moves included
casabal, *carre*, *chopper*, and *dentist*, the last made famous by Myler
the Dentist, who was said to be capable of extracting an opponent's
tooth with a single sharp blow. When the battoniers roamed away
from their home yard into the territory of another band, fights or even
riots sometimes developed between the rival bands. When the police
entered the picture, hostility was turned toward them and, sometimes, against the system itself (such as when fires were set).

Stick fights were accompanied by songs (calindas). Sometimes the
stick fighter himself was a noted chantwell. Before fighting, he would
boast of his intrepidity: "I am Joe Talmana and I challenge all
comers!" The lyrics of the songs were thought to have special power.
This quality of calinda was a leftover from the time when the songs
were part of pre-emancipation rituals; it was to influence the
speechifying of oratorical calypsos popular in the 1910s. Musically,
many calindas consisted of alternating lines of verse and refrain that
articulated between lead vocalist and chorus. A lead line would be
followed by a chant sung by the chorus. This would be repeated to
varying lines sung by the chantwell.

Elder notes that during breaks in the fighting women sang carisos,
which were similar to the songs sung by the men.[13] While Elder

maintains that carisos eventually evolved into the calindas sung by men, it is likely that both kinds of songs existed side by side and that both influenced calypso. By the 1930s, recorded calypso included unaltered calindas (except in accompaniment, where a string band generally replaced the drums or tamboo bamboo) and boasts based on calindas. Still other calypsos grew out of calinda by doubling and doubling again the number of lines in each verse.

Christmastime Celebrations

For the British, the wild flavor of Christmastime celebration paralleled that of Carnival:

> When X-mas came in former days
> The time for Martial schoolery
> Three guns from Fort George battery were
> The signal for tomfoolery.
> Then all our town folk turned as red
> As lobsters in hot water:
> And, had there been an enemy
> There might have been much slaughter!
> But after vapouring a week
> The scarlet fever vanished
> Until next Christmas Martial thoughts
> Were from each bosom banished.[14]

Although the annual martial law period was suspended in 1846,[15] the drills of the military regiments became a model for many Carnival masquerade bands. This yielded the dominant theme for masquerading for the rest of the nineteenth century. Military themes continue to the present day, although now the American military is burlesqued, not the older British Militia. The Royal Dragoons, the Royal Battalion, and the Royal Artillery were the names of some of the military masquerade bands. The Carnival band, Artillery, predates 1834 and continued into the twentieth century.[16]

Carnival in 1845

In an article in the *Trinidad Standard*, John McSwiney described the street Carnival of 1845:

The streets are thronged by parties and individuals in every variety of national and fanciful costume, and in every possible contortion and expression of "the human face divine." Some are gay and noble—some are as ignoble as rags and uncouth habiliments can make. Some are marching to the sound of well-played music—the violin, the guitar, the castinet, the drum, and the tambourine strike the ear in every direction. Some delight themselves in the emission and production of sounds of the wildest, most barbarous, and most unearthly description imaginable, and their instruments are as extraordinary as the sounds they make. Now we observe the Swiss peasant, in holiday trim, accompanied by his fair Dulcima—now companies of spanish [sic], Italians, and Brazilians glide along in varied steps and graceful dance. . . . But what see we now?—goblins and ghosts, fiends, beasts and frightful birds—wild men—wild Indians and wilder Africans. Pandemonium and the savage wilds of our mundane orb are pouring forth their terrific occupations. It would seem as though the folly and madness fitful vagaries of the year had been accumulated in science and solitude to burst forth their exuberant measures and concentrated force in the fantastic revels of the Carnival.[17]

Town

After emancipation, many freed slaves moved from plantation to town, augmented by migrants from other islands and by indentured Africans. These groups formed the core of the grass-roots urban Creoles.[18] Although they enriched Trinidad's Carnival, Carriacouans, Grenadians, Vincentians, and especially Barbadians were resented. Unlike the then-despised East Indians, who had been coming to Trinidad since 1845 as indentured laborers, the Antilleans had the advantage of being Creole. Still, they were immigrants and were perceived as foreign. As police they were hated and feared. Some were resented because they became small landowners, crafts specialists, small-time entrepreneurs, and teachers. The Patois spoken by many small islanders—a slur sometimes used by native Trinidadians to refer to the immigrants from nearby islands—further exacerbated the linguistic complexity of the island. A calypso popular one hundred years after emancipation expresses a long-held opinion: "Small Island go back where you really came from."

Port of Spain grew rapidly in the mid-1900s.[19] Settling in the center of town and in the suburbs of Laventille, East Dry River, Corbeau Town, and Belmont, the Creoles and Africans worked as domestics, porters, and longshoremen or in the crafts. An unknown number became an underclass—petty criminals, prostitutes, and vagrants. Many lived in barrack houses located out of the sight of passersby behind or adjoining middle-class houses or street-fronted businesses. Barrack houses were cut out of a long shed that was attached to a back wall.[20] The house's only door let out into a narrow yard that sometimes was bounded by another barrack range. Each apartment was about eleven feet square and was partitioned by a wooden wall that did not reach the ceiling. Each row had a single water tap and toilet. In some lower-class neighborhoods endemic diseases were common, and epidemics of cholera and smallpox hit the population more than once. Although migration to Port of Spain continued throughout the period, unemployment and crime increased.

Out of the squalor of the barrack yards a new, vibrant culture germinated, centering on the canboulay and on that part of the canboulay that later came into its own, calinda.

The Africans

After emancipation, between 1838 and 1871, over 6,000 liberated slaves and indentured Africans settled in Trinidad.[21] The former slaves had been freed by the British navy, enforcing British law against the slave trade. The others were indentured workers brought from Africa, including Creoles from Sierra Leone (that is, previously freed slaves who had lived for a time in Sierra Leone), Radas from Dahomey, Yorubas from Nigeria, and people from Angola ("Congos").[22] According to a travel writer of the time, Charles Kingsley,

> The south-west corner of Montserrat is almost entirely settled by Africans of various tribes—Mandingos, Foulahs, Homas, Yarribas, Ashantees, and Congos. The last occupy the lowest position in the social scale. They lead, for the most part, a semi-barbarous life, dwelling in miserable huts, and subsisting on the produce of an acre or two of badly cultivated land, eked out with the pay of an occasional day's labour on some neighbouring estate. The social position of some of the Yarribas forms a marked contrast to that of the Congos. They

inhabit houses of cedar, or other substantial materials. Their gardens are, for the most part, well stocked and kept. They raise crops of yam, cassava, Indian corn, etc; and some of them subscribe to a fund on which they may draw in case of illness or misfortune.[23]

As Kingsley notes, Africans and Creoles formed voluntary associations, some of which evolved into stick fighters' bands and other Carnival groups.[24] The outlying districts were dominated by wattle and daub huts, not by barrack houses. Many Africans lived in Belmont, where even today the Shango (Yoruba) religion survives, as did a Rada religious organization as late as the 1950s.[25] Donald Wood suggests that some Carnival bands, as voluntary associations, may have been the lineal descendants of indentured African secret societies. Other bands may also have evolved from the estate-based secret societies. Whatever their origin, bands differed from each other. Some had members who claimed descent from a particular African group, while others were based on occupation. Still others may have counted membership strictly within the jamet or underclass.

The Africans and the jamets both had an impact on Carnival. It was believed that bands of toughs ruled the streets and that the police dared not enter Belmont. Africanesque rituals were common; for example, wakes lasted until dawn, complete with bongo dancing and singing. Wood recounts the story of Joseph Allen, a member of a Congo society.[26] Allen was charged by the police with disorderly conduct for holding dances several times a week. Neither the police nor the society's middle-class neighbors liked the Congo society's all-night wakes, with bongo songs sung in Patois.

Class Battle Lines Drawn: The Carnival Crises of 1858, 1881, and 1884

In 1858 the governor outlawed masquerading, an order that was disobeyed.[27] The police arrested masqueraders and their backers, but a crowd of approximately 3,500 celebrants armed with hatchets, axes, cutlasses, bludgeons, and knives defied the police and noisily congregated in front of the station house. As a result of this émeute and the law against group masquerading, showy Carnival atrophied. Individual traditional outfits, such as pierrot, continued, as did canboulay. For the British, Carnival from the 1850s through the early 1880s represented the antithesis of respectability.

Carnival had been co-opted by the rude jamets, and the British authority did not like it. Antipathy between the British government and the masses, together with the innate exuberance of Carnival itself, boiled over to encompass more than the usual demonstration of narcissism and social symbolism. It was a time to even scores, for men to prove their masculinity in stick fighting, and for the lower class to express their symbolic—if not real—power.

Relationships among classes came into sharp focus with the riots of 1881 and 1884, crises that shook the colony itself. In 1881, a depression hit Trinidad, and unemployment in Port of Spain was severe.[28] The British feared potential Carnival riots and replaced Inspector L. M. Fraser—considered weak by many in the English camp—with the tougher A. W. Baker, who had kept Carnival under control in 1878 and 1879.[29] In 1880, Baker had succeeded in having participants hand over their torches, sticks, and drums. Revelers felt that Baker wanted to stop jamet Carnival, however. The English-language press (the New Era, Fair Play, the Port of Spain Gazette, the Chronicle) all backed Baker and found the jamet Carnival repulsive.[30]

Before the Carnival of 1881, it was rumored that participants planned to torch Port of Spain, which had once before burned down.[31] Furthermore, there is some evidence that the jamets were receiving encouragement from middle-class backers who were miffed by an allegation that a colored policeman was left in stocks by the Irish-born Sergeant J. N. Brierly.[32] However, an investigation of the incident determined that this rumor was spread to cover up Brierly's obtaining evidence against two civil servants for forgery and extortion.[33] Of course, the Crown supervised the investigation and backed the activities of the police against the Carnival revelers.

Meanwhile, Baker was said to have bragged to friends that he could stop canboulay altogether, although he had no such instructions from the governor, Sir Sanford Freeling.[34] Furthermore, Baker had not received a message from the governor to put out the torches, although he had clearly intended to do so.

Father Anthony de Verteuil's meticulous account of the incident reflects his dual stations as priest and as a member of an elite French estate-owning family:

> The whole of the week before Carnival was a time of rumours and counter-rumours in Port of Spain. Some of them spread in the usual

way, at the market, in the barrack yards, through the marchands—
itinerant vendors of sweets, fish, oysters, vegetables—among the
domestics in the houses of the rich; the wife of A. Bernard, an official of
the Colonial company, learned from her servants that the street lamps
in the town would be smashed; R. Wilson, J. B. Payne and E. H.
Manoll, merchants of Port of Spain got it on the grapevine that an
attack would be made by the people on the police. But along with this
rumour-mongering there seems to have been a deliberate attempt by a
number of middle class coloured, "the respectable class" and their
agents, to stir up trouble, to convince the "cannaille" that the very
existence of Carnival was being threatened; that not alone would the
carrying of torches be stopped but all masking and carnival itself
would be destroyed. . . . It is even very probable that an organisation
was formed to resist any police interference with carnival, and
particularly by ensuring that the bands acted in concert.[35]

This year, the usual Carnival revelry would become something
more—political action. The Maribone, Diamaitre, and Baker leaders
got together and decided to fight the police, not each other.[36]

Then, during the weekend before Carnival, an anonymous an-
nouncement was posted:

NEWS TO THE TRINIDADIANS
Captain Baker demanded from our just and noble Governor, Sir
Sanford Freeling, his authority to prevent the rite of Can Boulay, but
Our Excellency refused.[37]

On Carnival Sunday night, with about 150 men at his command,
Baker moved to extinguish the torches as masqueraders entered
town. The jamets Lucretia, Sarah, Peg Top, Bullinder (a transvestite),
and Sarah Jamaica were ready for action.[38] Along with the men, they
gathered in Homer Yard between Duke and Park streets. Carrying
their own *pouis* (sticks), the men wore their pants backwards and
they put pots on their heads as helmets to block blows from the
balata-sticks the police had made for themselves in the government
sawmills. As the midnight bell sounded in the Royal Gaol, units of
negs jardin lit their torches, broke into calinda songs, and began their
march through town.

Lionel Belasco, Trinidadian pianist and calypso entrepreneur, was
told about the march by his mother:

This happened just opposite her house. They were so scared the windows were all closed [as] the fighting went on. Captain Baker charged [the Freegrammers. A famous fighter called] "One Man Bisco" met Captain Baker and Captain Baker told him to stop.

And One Man Bisco said, "Stop? We march! We are on the march and we are marching! If you cross this line, I am sorry for you!"

Captain Baker was backed by police, you know. And he had [his sword and] his white charger. He charged Bisco and his followers. And Bisco had this big stick and he struck the horse and the horse reared up. The horse and Bisco had a little fight before they subdued him [in front of] this crowd. You can't fight with sticks against horses and swords. And that was about the end of the canboulay. And after that the government banned it.[39]

Another view comes from this recollection of a battonier:

The Chief of Police certainly had his hands full, but he was a brave man, and, always at the head of his men (from 50 to 100 sometimes). He and his force had many a serious fight with the different bands and many a brick was hurled at them. . . . It looked as if he had a charmed life for . . . the bands fought for blood and with the utmost viciousness, whether with other bands or with the police. The policemen were armed with bayonets and [balata?] sticks but were no match man-for-man with the stick men. You talk of rapiers and broadswords, but these are as child's play compared to good stick fighting, which is an art that takes long practice, a quick eye and fine judgment in order to excel.[40]

Thirty-eight policemen were injured in the melee, eight of them seriously.[41] From fourteen to twenty-one of the Carnival revelers were arrested and eventually put on trial.[42]

On Monday morning, Captain Baker rode through the town and found it to be quiet.[43] Nevertheless, when he reported the riot to Governor Freeling, he requested use of regular soldiers from the barracks in St. James. Fifty men were moved to police headquarters and forty-three local residents were made special constables. The mayor called an extraordinary meeting of the Port of Spain council. They asked the governor to do all he could to prevent more rioting. Then, eleven members of the city council were deputized, including the mayor, Joseph Emanuel Cipriani, father of future labor leader A. A. Cipriani, who was later to play an important role in the development of calypso; and Ignacio Bodu, who, within a few years, would spearhead a drive to convert Carnival into a middle-class fete.[44]

Cipriani criticized Baker's scheme to break up the bands with balata-stick-wielding irregulars.[45] Most deputies did not want Carnival suppressed. Furthermore, damage to the borough streetlamps was a direct result of the rioting brought on by the police attack. The deputies believed that the governor and perhaps even Baker should meet with the revelers and the police should be left in barracks. In short, many from the French party did not want interference in Carnival.

The governor acted on Cipriani's advice and decided to address the people in Eastern Market, with the police well in the background. The governor told the people that although he did not want to stop the celebration, he ordered a ban on carrying torches in town. He said he would withdraw the police and soldiers if the citizens would behave in an orderly manner. The crowd was apparently with him and, according to Gertrude Carmichael, cries of "We promise not to carry torches" were heard.[46]

The governor, against Baker's wishes, confined the police to barracks until after Carnival. Revelers held a mock funeral for Captain Baker—in true Carnival fashion—outside the police barracks, and some torches were seen in the jeering crowd. The protesters taunted in song: "The police can't do it" (i.e., stop the celebration).[47] Nevertheless, the instruction to the police to take no action remained in force. After this demonstration by the mob, the police attempted to resign en masse, but the governor convinced them to remain.[48]

There were no more problems in Port of Spain, but in Couva in central Trinidad the Couva Savanna and Exchange bands clashed several times during Carnival, and on Carnival Tuesday fourteen revelers were arrested.[49] Although there was no more ruction, the authority of the police had been weakened and, for a while, they had to patrol the town in pairs.

Baker, not satisfied with the governor's actions, wrote to Freeling and asked that a commission be established to investigate the causes of the riot.[50] The commission, led by R. G. Hamilton, met, and its recommendations, the Hamilton Report, resulted in greater restriction of Carnival:

> Up to this year, although disturbances from time to time occurred
> from persons paying off old grudges under cover of the Carnival, the
> conduct of the people generally appears to have been comparatively
> harmless, their performance being mainly of a low and stupid style
> buffoonery, but since 1868 certain bands of ruffians have come into
> existence, who take advantage of Carnival to muster in force to fight
> with each other, and to carry riot and disorder throughout the town.
> These bands which are composed of persons of the lowest character,
> many of them being immigrants from other islands, appear to exist for
> no other purpose than that of fighting against each other, and of
> creating riot and disorder. They are thus of quite modern date and
> have no connection with the old Carnival. From the time these bands
> took part in the carnival, the riot and disorder greatly increased as well
> as the obscenity and indecency attending these exhibitions. It is
> common during Carnival for the vilest songs, in which the names of
> ladies of the island are introduced to be sung in the streets, and the
> vilest talk to be indulged in while filthy and disgusting scenes are
> enacted by both sexes, which are beyond description and would be
> almost beyond belief were it not that they were vouched for by
> witnesses of unimpeachable credibility.[51]

Trinidadian newspapers, in a modification of their earlier views, objected to the Hamilton Report and hinted that Hamilton exhibited color prejudice.[52] The working and jamet classes of Port of Spain openly hated Hamilton and Baker: a new police barracks in town on St. Vincent Street was burned to the ground and people in the crowd remarked, "If only this pig could roast."[53]

In 1882 Carnival was quiet, partly as a result of the two British men-of-war anchored in the Port of Spain harbor.[54] As a result of the earlier riots, an attempt was made to push a musical ordinance through the Legislative Council. This ordinance called for "appropriate punishment" for those who played drums or chac chac near public roads and even for those who played the piano after ten o'clock at night.[55] As no one seconded the ordinance, it failed to pass.

In 1883, riots broke out in Belmont and Eastern Dry River involving the Newgate band, a group of immigrants from the English-speaking eastern Caribbean. The French-speaking bands subsequently sought revenge on Carnival Tuesday, and Captain Baker seemed unwilling to do anything to bring the situation under control. There was more trouble in San Fernando, Arima, and Arouca. According to de Verteuil, these incidents caused "a revulsion of feeling among the middle class supporters of the festival who had supported the lower classes for the past two years."[56] Freeling sensed that the colored middle class was turning against some of the Carnival baccanalists—at least his invocation of small-island prejudice seems to blame the Newgates and not the French bands. As a result, he sent this message to the Legislative Council:

> Gentlemen of the Legislative Council, I regret to have to inform you that it has been reported to me that the carnival of this year was more disorderly than any known for many years except that of 1881.
>
> Fighting, throwing stones and bottles, and obscenities prevailed more or less, and bands of disorderly persons unmasked and armed with long sticks marched through the town to the alarm and danger of the inhabitants.
>
> I am induced and I am glad to believe that no large number of Trinidadians belong to these bands, but they are principally composed of bad characters from the neighbouring islands.
>
> I had hoped that the good order which characterized the Carnival last year would have prevailed at this, but such not having been the case, it has become imperative that steps should be taken as will effectually for the future, quell any disorder by ensuring the immediate apprehension and severe punishment of offenders.
>
> In framing measures for this purpose, I shall endeavour not to deprive the community during the day time of the amusement they apparently find in masquerading so long as such privilege is not abused; and I am convinced that if Legislation is required for the ends I have in view, I shall receive your cordial cooperation and support.[57]

The way was now open for the co-opting of Carnival by the middle class, which was then in the process of forming from disparate ethnic elements (Catholics of various nationalities, descendants of free blacks, formerly indentured Africans, and even colored English-speaking Antilleans and Trinidadians). Freeling and many English expatriates seemed unaware of the social process taking place. Just as Trinidadians were becoming British Creoles, the English metropolites continued to see the color line first and restrict true Englishness to

Anglo whites. The result was the beginnings of a rump British ethnicity that de facto excluded the English themselves, by their own doing. This new English-speaking Trinidadian—of Afro-French, Catholic, and Antillean Afro-English culture and of mixed race— would eventually include the Chinese, the Syrians, a minority of the East Indians, and others. This group developed Carnival as their premier cultural expression. After years of turbulence, a moderate Carnival developed, one that mediated between the raucous canboulay and the older, still cherished, elite Carnival.

On January 21, 1884, the Legislative Council passed an ordinance that backed Freeling's statement the previous year.[58] As the jamet bands and Baker's police postured at the opening of Carnival '84, Freeling had a new proclamation posted in Port of Spain:

PROCLAMATION

Whereas owing to the disturbance that occurred at the Carnival last year, it has now become necessary for the preservation of the public peace and order, that the time of the Carnival should be restricted and that other provisions should be made for enforcing law and order during the continuance thereof:—

Now therefore, I, Sanford Freeling, Governor as aforesaid, do hereby proclaim and make known as follows:—

1. The Carnival of the year 1884 shall not commence until 6 o'clock in the morning of the 25th day of February and shall end at 12 o'clock midnight of Tuesday the 26th day of that month, during which time persons will be permitted to appear masked or otherwise disguised.

2. The procession generally known as the Cannes Brulées or Canboulay shall not be allowed to take place and further regulations for giving effect to this provision will shortly be promulgated.

3. Measures will be taken for the rigid enforcement of the law and all persons are warned and cautioned accordingly.[59]

Then, on January 25, the Legislative Council was called into session again and upon the advice of some of the legislators the ordinance was revised to give "the Governor power to prohibit by proclamation, public torch processions, drum beating, any dance or procession, and any disorderly assembly of ten or more persons armed with sticks or other weapons."[60] On January 27, a suspicious fire burned the Union Club, the Ice House, a hotel, the New Era Printing Office, and several other buildings.[61] Rumors spread that the government intended to

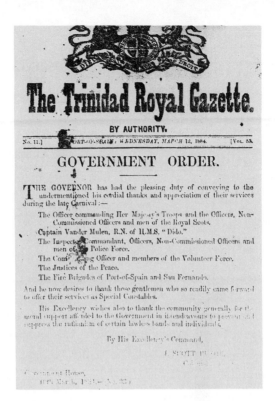

The Trinidad Royal Gazette.

BY AUTHORITY.

No. 11.]   PORT-OF-SPAIN: WEDNESDAY, MARCH 12, 1884.   [Vol. 53.

GOVERNMENT ORDER.

THE GOVERNOR has had the pleasing duty of conveying to the
undermentioned his cordial thanks and appreciation of their services
during the late Carnival:—

The Officer commanding Her Majesty's Troops and the Officers, Non-
Commissioned Officers and men of the Royal Scots.

Captain Vander Mulen, R.N. of H.M.S. "Dido."

The Inspector Commandant, Officers, Non-Commissioned Officers and
men of the Police Force.

The Commanding Officer and members of the Volunteer Force.

The Justices of the Peace.

The Fire Brigades of Port-of-Spain and San Fernando.

And he now desires to thank these gentlemen who so readily came forward
to offer their services as Special Constables.

His Excellency wishes also to thank the community generally for the
moral support afforded to the Government in its endeavours to prevent and
suppress the ruffianism of certain lawless bands and individuals.

By His Excellency's Command,

J. SCOTT BUSHE,
Col. Sec.

Government House,
10th March, 1884.—No. 22.)

9 ✳ Government
decree following
Carnival disturbances.

ban Carnival entirely. The social atmosphere reached near panic. But as hundreds of special constables were armed with long staves, Port of Spain's Carnival passed uneventfully.

In the south, it was a different story. In Montserrat and Oropouche there were disturbances, the riot act was read in Couva, and in Princes Town a band of five hundred people with sticks, stones, bottles, and a few guns advanced on town. Freeling wrote of the chaos to Lord Derby, the secretary of state of the colonies: "At Princes Town . . . it was found necessary to read the riot act and for the Police to fire upon the mob who attacked them. Two deaths occurred and two or three people were wounded. One of the men shot was, I understand, a king or leader of the bands."[62]

Freeling thanked his forces for suppressing the Carnival rioters (fig. 9). More proclamations against obscenity were issued in 1891, 1893, and 1895.[63]

The riots and subsequent restrictions broke the back of the jamet Carnival. The new Carnival that emerged belonged to the Creole middle class.

4 ✳ Fancy Masquerade and Calypso

Not a soul to be saved on the day of carnival
When the dragon appear.

King Fanto

THE last chapter traced a mix of musical genres found in the rural yards, the urban barrack yards, and in the Carnival-time streets of Port of Spain and other towns of late-nineteenth-century Trinidad. Upset by this music and the people who produced it, Governor Freeling, in concert with town officials, circumscribed jamet Carnival and thereby paved the way for the development of a new, fancy masquerade Carnival. This chapter will examine that new Carnival.

Anglicization and the Rise of the Middle Class

Colonial Trinidad posed special problems in the early years of British rule. Most of the island's population was not Protestant and English. Furthermore, the superstructural institutions were not British either; they were inherited from the Spanish. The British were foreigners in this conquered land.

For the British, this became an intolerable position.[1] They feared the Republican French, and the loyalty of all French Creoles was doubted by some. The British did not trust the Catholic church in

Trinidad, with its internationalist flavor and its secular extension of different nationalities called the "French party."

After 1838, the British sought to anglicize this society, as a midcentury governor noted. "In the year 1840, this colony was Spanish, French and English for it was governed by the laws of Spain, the general feeling and languages were French, and now trial by Jury, the Criminal and a greater part of the Civil Code is English, and the language is fast spreading. In short every nerve has been strained to reverse the order of nations as shown above and to render this an English colony, not only in name but in reality."[2]

Anglicization was not an orderly process. Nevertheless, the institution of English law in the 1840s set the island's population under a single legal system (Spanish law had allowed much local autonomy). Attorney General Charles Warner pushed anglicization between the 1840s and 1870, and he lost his post.[3] A Francophobic anti-Catholic racist, he "became easily the most unpopular public figure in nineteenth-century Trinidad."[4]

Under the administration of Governor Arthur H. Gordon, who had forced Warner to resign, the anglicization process was relaxed, and more tolerance was shown toward French culture, the Catholic church, and Carnival.[5] Paradoxically, this liberalization was accompanied by a weakening of French Creole culture, not a strengthening of it. French influence had traditionally been strongest on the sugar estates. But Gordon established more liberal land policies that favored small, English-speaking planters and, as a result of a fall of sugar prices in the 1870s, many French Creoles sold their sugar plantations and turned to cocoa. In addition, by 1890 the importance of sugar in Trinidad declined as a result of competition with other cane sugar colonies and European countries that produced beet sugar.[6] Although some sugar estates in Trinidad were capital-intensive, more advanced industrial production in Cuba and elsewhere made it more efficient to produce sugar there than in the technologically backward British colonies. These changes meant that sugar and other plantation crops would never again dominate Trinidad's economy. Trinidad became more economically diversified and the bucolic French life on the sugar estates lost its culturally dominant position.

The British were slow to start an educational system based on English as the language of instruction.[7] But government schools for ex-slaves were gradually established, and both the Catholics and

Anglicans set up many church-run, low-cost grammar schools. Elite French Creoles did not want a British education at all, and so before the 1870s they sent their children to France to be educated. But their loyalties gradually changed, and by the early 1900s many French Creoles were educated at Catholic schools in Britain and many middle-class children received grammar-school education in English in Trinidad.

More than any other institutional change, the steady growth of English literacy among the Creoles directly influenced the development of calypso in that language. Gordon Rohlehr quotes J. H. Collens, a secondary-school teacher of the time, on one side effect of the increasing prestige of English. "In my capacity as Dominie I have continually had to check the disposition of my pupils in Trinidad to use long-winded words and high-flown phrases. Boys and young men spend hours poring over dictionaries, simply to try and master the meanings of words which for length may be measured by the yard. They positively do not believe in the sweet simplicity of the Saxon tongue."[8]

Trinidadian culture began to reflect British influence as British infrastructure was implanted and as spoken English replaced French in public forums. Yet anglicized Trinidad was a special case of creolization: Trinidad did not become culturally English. For example, the French Creoles pushed for more tolerance of Catholicism, one result of which was the Marriage Ordinance of 1863.[9] Furthermore, the small English elite was folding into the French Creole elite, not the other way around. Although British expatriates and even many British Creoles considered England as their home, French Creoles—indeed, most Trinidad natives—considered themselves Trinidadian. The soul of this culture was Afro-French.

Trinidadian Creoles could easily be distinguished from their counterparts in Barbados, to give an example of a society that developed almost completely from British and West African antecedents. They were also different in culture from the Creoles of, say, Martinique, a society dominated by a French and African cultural mix. Although Afro-Latin in the subjective areas of music, in patoisisms found in everyday speech, in dance, and in most other cultural qualities, Trinidadian Creole culture now was British in its politics, its economy, and in its written and spoken word.

It was at this time—the last decades of the nineteenth century—that two limited reform movements fermented in certain elite circles of Creole Trinidad. The first attempt at reform was led by white landowners from the French party. The second attempt at political reform represented an early move on the part of Afro-Trinidadian Creoles to gain greater influence as Creoles in general rather than as French Creoles or English Creoles in particular. Colored and black lawyers led this effort to establish political enfranchisement for themselves, the educated Creoles.[10]

Both these reform movements began as moves to obtain some local elective representation in the island's Legislative Council. Both movements failed.[11] Not until 1924 did Trinidadians achieve elective representation for certain male property holders.

On another front, there was movement toward wider cultural expression for a group of middle-class male Trinidadians as some Port of Spain merchants, artisans, and others began to wrest Carnival from the working and jamet classes.

Carnival in the 1890s

From the perspective of old-time aficionados of fancy middle-class Carnival in the 1930s, the jamet Carnivals of the 1880s and the early 1890s invoked an unpleasant nostalgia of turbulence, with their calinda-based violence and raucous Patois songs. In the last years of the century, two new Carnival institutions were created by some of these same Creoles: the fancy masquerade band and the calypso tent. This "fancy Carnival," as it was called, would dominate the pageant for forty years. Performances of Carnival songs in English came to replace or supplement the earlier Patois lavways and calindas.

Ignacio Bodu, a Port of Spain merchant, author, petitioner, and teetotaler, played an important role in this development. Bodu was sympathetic to the jamet Carnival, except for its excesses. In a deliberate effort to "upgrade" Carnival, he offered a cup for the winner of a competition between the new-style fancy masquerade bands. "His main object in offering a prize for competition was to elevate the tone of the Carnival here and thus banish from it the obscenities that formed one of its chief characteristics in years gone by. He was gratified to find that he had been successful to a great extent. In conversation with a few merchants he learnt that next year they too would offer prizes for competition and then a regular committee would be formed to make the necessary regulations for the competition."[12] The efforts by Bodu and others were not appreciated by everyone in Trinidad's diverse middle class, as noted in this anonymous letter published in *Argos* more than twenty years after Bodu's initial efforts. The letter refers to Bodu's efforts, as a member of Port of Spain's city council, to contain the jamet Carnival of 1881: "Papa Bodu and others of his ilk, the then City Fathers were very sympathetic and used to lay down loose stones upon streets . . . so that the Burgesses of the Town could amuse themselves in their Ancient and Honourable method, and when fearless Police Inspector [Captain Baker] undertook to stamp out the nuisance, great was their indignation at his daring to interfere with the only Amusement of the People."[13]

Bodu's masquerade competitions merely formalized what had been taking place in the years since the riots of the 1880s. Carnival came to be dominated by the Creole middle class in a tenuous balance with the jamets on the one hand and the British political structure on the other (fig. 10). The governor and Lady Jerningham, with others of their station, perused Carnival from decorated carriages (as the elite had been doing for years). Meanwhile, the calinda of the jamets continued in the yards of Eastern Dry River and elsewhere in Trinidad, away from the town centers. And the middle class expanded the fancy masquerade bands.

The Carnival bands of this era were called social unions. Perhaps the most important social union was the White Rose organization. This band was founded in 1894 (with Bodu's financial support) by a man known variously as J. Resigna, Henry Julian, the Iron Duke (after Wellington), or, taking his appellation from the band itself, Julian Whiterose. Whiterose once made a phonograph record in which he staked his claim as leader of the White Rose Social Union:

> At my appearance upon the scene
> Julian the devil [?] play the Cord
> And still I am the head of fraternal order [White Rose Social Union]
> Calling, sweeping to all the agony
> Achieving my surprising majesty
> In blending, beaming and swaying
> Jumping this way, bawling, "Clear de way, Whiterose joli" [Handsome
>   Whiterose]
> "*Djab re-re-o*" [The devil masquerader—e.g., Whiterose—was out of
>   control][14]

10 ✳ Carnival on Frederick Street, 1888. Drawing by Melton Prior, *Illustrated London News.*

Another social union was the No Surrender band, founded in 1899. Its members were Patois-speaking, grass-roots Creoles who borrowed the slogan used by the colored and black middle class to articulate their opposition to the abolition of the Port of Spain Borough Council. It is possible, even likely, that this band of jamets was financially supported by middle-class backers in an attempt to further their aims of limited suffrage.

The year 1900 marks the first reported use of banners to front masquerade bands. They were apparently modeled after those that headed religious processions. The *Mirror,* in a lengthy article dated February 29, 1900, makes brief reference to this practice as well as to other features of turn-of-the-century Carnival:

> In 1900, Carnival Monday was better than many of the previous
> years [as] the Police succeeded in maintaining order and, considering
> the dense crowds that moved through the streets, there was
> comparatively few arrests. There was hope that better behavior would
> take place on Tuesday and Mr. Bodu offered a cup for the best Band
> that day.
>
>   . . . Carnival Tuesday 1900, the second and last day of the carnival

season in Trinidad, fully justified all expectations of a splendid masquerader show. Crowds from the country came up by train and swelled the dense masses that thronged the streets. . . .The costumes surpassed everything seen for some years.

Two or three bands were easily ahead of the others in that respect. The opinion of the majority of the people was that the Brigade Union was easily first. Their banner was excellently made; it was light blue silk with words "Brigade Union" in dark letters neatly place [sic] across it. The members were dressed in light blue; males with tightly fitting tunics, knickers and socks to match. Their slouched hats were trimmed with light blue ribbon.

"White Rose Social Union" was next in order of merit. The members of that band wore very beautiful costumes of white and light green. Their banner which was of light green had a white rose in the centre, the rose branch forming a wreath outside them. On the banner were the words "White Rose Social Union established in 1894." . . .

On the whole, Carnival 1900 was a decided success from every point of view. The orderly behaviour of the vast crowds was remarkable and the patriotism of the people found expression in cheering for the Queen and the singing of patriotic songs.

White Rose Social Union had won the first cup offered by Bodu; it was always one of his favorites. This Carnival was very different from the jamet Carnival, and the reporters from the *Mirror* and the *Port of Spain Gazette* liked it. "Now, what we maintain is that if the new departure started by Mr Bodu be kept up in the future, and other liberally-minded gentlemen follow this good example, the people will be inspired with something better in their aims on Carnival days than that of getting drunk and behaving in a manner disgraceful to all ideas of civilization."[15]

Social unions were actually clubs. They were partly the outgrowth of the African and grass-roots Creole voluntary associations that existed decades earlier and partly the new creations of middle-class Creoles, perhaps based on ethnic associations, in their attempts to upgrade Carnival. Social unions, like the calinda bands before them, tended to draw members from friendship groups based on class, color, and ethnicity (e.g., ethnic associations, immigrants from one particular island, people who worked together, Yorubas, Radas, or other Africans, and so forth).

Following Queen Victoria's death in 1901, Councillor Bodu tried
to persuade Julian Whiterose not to appear with his band. Although
Whiterose had apparently signed a letter sponsored by Bodu that
recommended that Carnival not be held, Whiterose wanted to have
Carnival anyway:

To The Editor Of The Port-Of-Spain Gazette

Sir,—Please allow me space in your valuable paper to state as
follows:—

In defence of myself and the Leaders of other various bands whom
Mr Ignacio Bodu has so conspicuously placed before the eyes of the
public, that we have really consented with him and requested the
interview with his Excellency for the postponement of the coming
carnival, I beg to say that such an assertion we all most unanimously
deny. We do not yet see the necessity or the objection from legal
grounds, that will cause us to combine with Mr Bodu as to such
conference with His Excellency. As we told him on the afternoon of the
meeting, we think ourselves as Loyal (though poor) as the high
authorities who will soon take part in very many recreations soon after
the burial of her Majesty Queen Victoria.

The whole community, leaders and members of various bands were
totally down against the director of the White Rose Social Union, as it
was rumoured that I had consented with Mr Bodu as to the conference
with His Excellency on the subject, which in defence of myself and the
welfare of my Union I must deny. I can only state that I was compelled
to sign the letter dated 29th January, 1901.

Believe me with fidelity,

yours truly,

Henry Julian.

Director of the White Rose Social Union.[16]

Homage to the Queen notwithstanding, Carnival took place, although the *Gazette*'s reporters from Maraval, Mayaro, and other
country districts wrote that Carnival was dying. Any drop in Carnival
activities outside the major towns was probably more likely a result of
the better transportation system that took celebrants to Port of Spain
or San Fernando than of the death of the Queen, a letdown after the
centurial celebration, or because of a moribund Carnival. Here is how
Tiger sang of the event in the mid 1930s:

Queen Victoria died in 1901
And as usual Carnival went on
I mean there wasn't a greater ruler than she
She caused the abolition of slavery
And she reigned 63 long years
When she died the whole universe shed tears
And although we played our Carnival
We were not recognized as Carnival.[17]

Calypso and the Water Riots of 1903

The year 1903 seemed to unfold with just another fancy masquerade Carnival, as both the middle class and the elite enjoyed their pleasures. The February 4, 1903, issue of the *Gazette* had an article entitled "Fete Champetre," which noted that this gala was again being organized by a Mr. Bowan. It was scheduled for the Queen's Park Oval under the patronage of Lady Maloney, the wife of the governor, Sir Alfred Maloney. The vocal and instrumental music was to be provided by the Police Band and by Belasco's String Band. The fete was to conclude with a dance and was to cost five shillings for members and ten shillings for nonmembers. This was an elite dance, distinct in character from the middling fancy masquerade band rehearsals.

Less than two months later, one of the worst riots in Trinidad's history erupted. Many factors led to the riot and the burning of the main government building—the Red House.[18] Opposition to the Crown Colony government had increased since the 1890s, an opposition that went hand-in-hand with the rise of Creole influence. After the abortive attempts at reform a decade earlier, Trinidad continued to be governed by an appointed body.

The secretary of state for the colonies, Joseph Chamberlain, was against any move for partial suffrage in instances when non-Europeans constituted a majority of the groups envisaged to vote, as was the case in Trinidad. In 1896 he wrote, "Local government . . . is the curse of the West Indies. In many islands it means only the rule of a local oligarchy of whites and half-breeds—always incapable and frequently corrupt. In other cases it is the rule of the negroes, totally unfit for representative institutions and the dupes of unscrupulous adventurers."[19]

In 1896, after the failure of the reform movements, Chamberlain moved to reduce the influence of elected representatives in the island council (the "Unofficials"). The Port of Spain Borough Council, an elected body originally set up in 1853, now became a forum for blacks, coloreds, and white radicals. The Borough Council represented the voting ratepayers. They felt their powers should be increased, not reduced or abolished. The council refused to allow Chamberlain to control their budget, and so, in late 1898, he abolished it. In January 1899, the council met for the last time and issued a formal protest: "This Council, at its last meeting and on the eve of its abolition, wishes to place on record its strongest protest against the injustices and unfair treatment they have received from the Government of this Island."[20]

The Legislative Council, a body appointed by the governor, and the Borough Council, it must be remembered, represented the middle class, not the working or lower classes, the island's majority. Their views were better represented by two new organizations, the Trinidad Workingmen's Association (TWA) and the Pan-African Association, an organization founded in London by a colored lawyer in 1897. The leader of the TWA was H. Sylvester Williams, a Trinidadian. He attempted to form an alliance between the Afro-Trinidadian and colored masses and the middle class. A member of the Trinidad branch of the Pan-African Association, Emmanuel Lazare, began a third group, the Rate-Payers Association (RPA), in 1901. The members of the RPA were Afro-Trinidadian, colored, and white. They were middle-class merchants and professionals who intended to "supervise" the disbursement of public funds in lieu of council representation. This group, though small, became influential.

The RPA took up the issue of the public waterworks. Water had been piped directly into the homes of the middle class and wealthy, but communal standpipes served the working and jamet classes. The director of public works, Walsh Wrightson, attempted to control waste by making unannounced visits to homes and cutting off leaking taps:

Wrightson pas vlai ba nous g'leau
Maloney pas vlai nous entre
[Attorney-General] Vincent Brown fair un l'ordinance
Pour tax nous, sans humanity.

(Wrightson wouldn't give us water
Maloney don't want us to enter
Vincent Brown make an ordinance
To tax us without humanity.)[21]

The ratepayers took Wrightson's act as an infringement of their rights. They forced the government to postpone metering water piped into the houses. The RPA organized demonstrations outside the Red House, where the Legislative Council met to discuss the issue. On March 23, 1903, RPA spokesmen seemed to incite the crowd as rioting began. Soon the Red House went up in flames:

> Fire brigade water the road
> Mama, the Red House burning down
> Tell them it spreading all over town.[22]

The police fired on the rioters: sixteen people were killed and forty-three were wounded. The victims were demonstrators, the poor people of Port of Spain, not the militant middle-class members of the RPA.

A story circulated in Trinidad that the riot was instigated by a street character known as Greasy Pole:

> While Henry Forbes over at the Artillery kaiso tent was singing[, a] terrible price was paid by one of the rioters known as Greasy Pole. He had been sent to prison [on the allegation] that he had broken up the Governor's carriage and had instigated the burning of the Red House. He had suffered terribly from incarceration: [he] had gone to prison a slim and stately young man but had left the hovel of horrors big, swollen . . . like Lollote Borde—Lollote was an extremely stout female. . . . Henry Forbes [sang]:

> Ce Vrai Ce Vrai la jol dangereau,
> Ce vrai ce vrai la jol dangereau,
> A fuss la jol, dangereau,
> Johnnie See See ea [he?] semantay,
> Greasy Pole sortie la jol
> Ee gros con Lollote Borde,
> Sans humanity.

> (It's true, it's true,
> the jail is dangerous

It's true, it's true,
the jail is dangerous,
Johnnie Zee Zee, swear not to go back.
Greasy Pole come out of jail,
He is as big as Lollote Borde,
Without humanity.)[23]

Antigovernment feeling followed the riot, and the British sent a warship with two hundred troops to Trinidad. A commission of enquiry found the police action justified except for a few instances of police brutality. The heart of the matter, however, missed by the commission, was middle-class disenfranchisement, especially for colored and Afro-Trinidadians.[24] It was not until independence (August 31, 1962) that enfranchisement was achieved.

For many years following the riot, the No Surrender Band supported the RPA and their policies. Calypsos against Governor Jerringham were popular. As the new governor, he was Chamberlain's messenger in abolishing the Borough Council. There was also a spate of calypsos on the burning of the Red House. No doubt the Creole middle class was as classist as the English, but unlike the latter, they were not racist. The growing alliance between grass-roots Creoles and the middle class strengthened.

The water riots of late March 1903 may have put a damper on Carnival 1904. According to "Chiney" Patrick Jones, an Afro-Chinese Creole and one of the important turn-of-the-century calypsonians, Carnival 1904 was not as good as in previous years. "Now three years they [had] played with banner and beautiful costume . . . but the ministers of religion got themselves together and criticized the banners. They say it is more suitable for religious processions and so on. The bands, the following year, 'resigned' and carnival went down to jamet—shirt and pants mask—no costume. Calypso went away—all the songsters resigned. They started playing the great stick bands [again]."[25] Jones's view was a middle-class one. Now, although middle-class fancy masquerade bands had temporarily abated, their involvement continued on several other fronts. They visited and sometimes participated in ribald shows in barrack yards and brothels. They continued as jacket men (gentlemen stick fighters). They joined the jamet chantwells in singing Patois Carnival songs, although their forte was calypso in English.

Carnival in 1905 and 1907

In 1905, the fancy masquerade bands were back in force. Street calypsos, which included many lavways with their typical African-style call-and-response melodic lines, seemed degenerate to the *Gazette*'s reporter:

> Another complaint lay in the direction of the carnival songs. Although it is not expected that the effusion [of] the carnival bards should excel in literary attainment, yet in many past instances, they have abounded with at least some degree of originality and local pointedness; which cannot fairly be said to have been the case with those under review. Despite the labour of months devoted [by] the various bands to the practicing of what is known in the masquerade world as "calypsos," the entire carnival muse seemed to have degenerated into meaningless fragments of verse, occasionally broken by the refrain of "one bois"—a sentiment which we learned found its origin with a masquerade celebrity on being defeated in a course of stickfighting.[26]

This comment suggests that calinda-type lavways dominated the street celebration, probably with the "no surrender" chant of the ratepayers and the Red House fire as themes.

The *Gazette*'s reporter also described "wild Indians" (a Carnival masquerade) and a "neg jardin" band that was considered "disgrace-ful."[27] As usual, various masquerade bands competed for prizes, and wealthier people paraded the streets of Carnival in carriages. There was a "free engagement" between rival bands in which several "cases had to be sent to the hospital for treatment." There appeared to be fewer organized masqueraders and ballad-type calypsonians than in prior years.

In 1907, Carnival preparations were not extensively reported but fancy masquerade bands continued. The *Gazette* was preoccupied with Carnival violence, especially that associated with stick fighting. They mused over the "bad" influence all this had on children. Carnival was "regressing" once again.

The February 12, 1907, issue of the *Gazette* includes an article entitled "Tourists and Visitors," which notes that 348 tourists, pri-marily from the United States, had arrived the Sunday before on a

German steamer: "Yesterday the tourists were to be seen about the town taking snapshots of the masqueraders and otherwise enjoying themselves immensely." Lionel Belasco, at that time a young entrepreneur and leader of Belasco's String Orchestra, which played for various carnival dances, felt that tourism was the reason for an "improvement" in Carnival and for the switch from Patois to English: "With the coming of the tourist they anglicized them for commercial purposes."[28] It is possible that more calypsos were sung in English to appeal to the tourists, although it is unlikely that tourists could fully understand calypsodic English.

In 1907, Port of Spain continued to exert its dominance over Carnival, reflecting the urbanization of the Creoles and an improved train service that carried more than 3,500 passengers during Carnival. The town versus country dichotomy was exacerbated as town Carnival lost its connection with the traditional seasonal constraints of the rural plantation Carnival. "The Gazette reported a harangue against a song with a monotonous chorus of ribaldry, and meaningless jargon to the strains of which the maskers of the feminine sex in particular, wrought themselves into contortions, sufficient to explode the already accepted theory of the vertebrae and the human machination."[29] The same article also reported on the value of Carnival in advertisement: "Some of the local merchants however availed themselves of the opportunity of advertising, and in this direction [decorated a] well got up car with an attendant band of music proclaiming the excellence of 'Tennant's Stout,' the agents of which are Messrs. G. R. Allston."

Improvement in Carnival was equated with expurgating Patois songs and Carnival rumpus and participating in fancy masquerade bands and English calypso that praised the Crown. Because the unfavorable elements were integral to grass-roots life and the favored elements were approved by the middle class, Carnival represented an acting out of class-based opposition, a secular ritual concerning tensions inherent in the society. As rules for appropriate behavior changed and as the colony came under the influence of British superstructural institutions, a dialectic within the Creole group emerged. The Creoles developed the arenas of Carnival and calypso, in which class and cultural differences were subjects for symbolic commentary. But Carnival remained a Creole creation, excluding some (Creole) English white Protestants and rural East Indians.

Composition of the Carnival Bands

Most fancy masquerade bands were similar in form, although each had its own jealously guarded persona. During its peak, the White Rose Social Union consisted of "about 23 or 30 persons."[30] As the band danced up the streets, they were fronted by a banner held by two costumed members. Then came the chantwells (singers), who would lead the chantlike lavways composed in the masquerade camps specifically for the band. The chantwells were usually also dressed as major characters in the band. In 1902 the following male characters led the White Rose band: "Henry Julian (Lord Iron Duke), H. Mans (Second Lord Advocator), Daniel Todd (Duke of York), L. Storey (Prince of Orange), A. Nurse (Edward the Confessor), A. Joseph (Lord Chancellor), John De Freitas (Brutus), G. Martin (Julius Caesar)."[31] Whiterose later sang of his progression through a cast of characters in the White Rose Social Union:

Remember '94 and [?] '95
When I was a Teacher and then Lord Adulator
They called to me two years later
As Second Lord and then Advocator
Advocator, they called me Advisor,
Was Advisor and now Supervisor
Me name Supervisor, and they call me
Lord of this island
[??] devirey [return].[32]

The large Carnival bands also had minor characters: warriors, sailors, Indians, imps. Usually the band would portray a theme, although liberal allowance was made for bringing together under one banner portrayals from different periods of history or a mixture of factual characters with mythological ones. In addition to the personas mentioned previously, there were also fancy sailors, great warriors, kings, pharaohs, Huns, Indians, the devil (or dragon), robbers, tourists,[33] stilt walkers (moko jumbie), bats, clowns, and borokit.[34] Some of the characterizations that seemed more common in jamet bands were djab djabs (devils or slaves), bad behavior sailors, bats, Indians, and pierrots (clowns and country kings).

The Devil Bands

Perhaps the most interesting bands of this era were the devil or dragon bands that came to dominate Carnival for a few years in the 1910s. Devil bands grew out of the various djab djab or devil masquerades that seem always to have been popular in Trinidad. Noting the decline in Carnival when fancy masquerades seemed to give way to a cluster of calinda bands, Chiney Patrick Jones, once a member of the White Rose band, decided to form a new type of organized masquerade band. "Now, you would like to know when carnival improved—that came back to a costume. In 1906 we decided to bring back carnival and in that year I and [Gilbert] Scamaroni opened a band called 'Khaki and Slate' [named for the band's colors]: that was a devil band with large wings, better than what we have today [1956], with spring wings, had the 'Imps,' 'Lucifer,' the 'Dragon' and another big costume taken from a book called 'Dante's Inferno.' "[35] The supernatural qualities of this theme have fascinated Trinidadians of all classes:

> It is interesting to note that while Patrick Jones introduced this type of mas' because of its novelty and its dramatic possibilities there is now a well established theory about dragon mas'. The theory is that the dragon band is an ambulatory depiction of Satan and his horde cast from Heaven. Theoretically he and his followers return to earth on the two days before the Lenten season commences in order during "the forty days and forty nights" to try the virtue of the faithful. It seems that though this theory is fairly wide-spread and well known, the persons who play this kind of mas' feel no reluctance in portraying the forces of evil and regard it merely as a means of enjoying themselves. Undoubtedly however, some individuals go through periods of great excitement preparing to play this type of mas' and seem to be completely absorbed during this period with thoughts of the two days of revelry to come.[36]

In 1907 Jones broke with Scamaroni and opened the first Red Dragon band,[37] the name taken from the color used in all its costumes. Then, in 1911 Jones came out with the first demonite band, a band in which the character Beelzebub (devil, lord of the flies) made its entrance.[38] These bands are still remembered and are sometimes revived in form or spirit.

There were three sets of characters in dragon bands: imps, beasts, and gownmen.[39] Beasts had a dragon's head and were covered with scales. Sometimes the tongue and tail moved. They were tied to chains held by the imps, who they attempted to attack in their thrusting dance movements. The imps wore masks with horns, tights, wings, and tails. The king imp or tempter led the other imps in a darting and skipping dance called crossing the water, which was done whenever they had to cross an open drain or a puddle in the street. The water, representing holy water, would extinguish the fire of the devil band, a supernatural possibility to be avoided at all cost by these creatures from a fiery hell. They carried bells in their hands that signaled their appearance or axes, dice, cards, or horns. The gownmen wore capes painted with a scene from the Bible and would play the crowd with flamboyant bows. Some of the gownmen included Lucifer, Beelzebub, Bookman, Queen Patroness, and Satan. Sometimes their masks were imported from Germany but, as the masquerade grew in popularity, they were made in Trinidad. Their dance was a waltz step. The music consisted of traditional tunes similar to paseos or castillians (songs from the nearby South American mainland) and were played by a string band sometimes augmented by a clarinet, saxophone, trumpet, or drums.

Dragon bands met in their masquerade camp to practice their dance routines and, under the leadership of the chantwell, their songs. Musicians were paid from contributions given by visitors to the mas' camp or by patrons. Masaqueraders bought their own costumes.[40]

Rival dragon bands competed with one another. When two bands met, the beast kings mimicked each other by copying the other's dance steps:

> Georgie was the reigning beast from whom "Willie" (Mr. William La Borde, alias Willie the Beast) captured the crown. The step that brought him victory was one which was shown to him in a dream. One night after practice at the tent of his band Willie went home to sleep. He dreamt that a man came to him dressed in a top hat and tail coat. The man suddenly turned into a "zandolie" (green lizard) and started

to wriggle on the ground. "Willie" awoke, told his wife about the dream and immediately began to practice a step in imitation of the movements of the "zandolie." He perfected this dance and by it won the crown from Georgie.[41]

Some participants thought dragon bands to be nothing more than good fun. Others liked the symbolism. A few thought that dragon bands were fraught with a stark supernatural aura.

Charles Jones on the Fancy Masquerade Bands

One of the new breed of Carnival aficionados in the 1910s was schoolteacher Charles Jones, whose Carnival name was the Duke of Albany. Writing in 1947, he described some fancy masquerade bands of the period:

> The band called "Standard" had Plummer as their chantwell. They had a king and queen, ladies in waiting, maids of honour and other members of the band, some forty or fifty in all. The beauty and grandeur of their costumes were wonderful. The king and queen r[ode] in state on a horse-drawn chariot, beautifully decorated with all the items of fancy used in the costume of the players, [all of whom] had a canopy over them. . . .With the members of the band following, the chantwell leads his band, dressed in a suit of velvet of the same colour of the others, sword in hand, with gloves, and hat turned up at one side imitating Sir Walter Raleigh (with a lovely plume at the top). He walks at the head of the band with an air of dignity, all the while singing out his refrain to be picked up by the members of the band. On meeting another band, the chantwell would advance and give out his challenge. [When they met the] Artillery [band], at the corner of Duke and Charlotte Streets, [Plummer] sang:

> Tell the Artillery to meet me by the grocery
> Tell the Artillery to meet me by the grocery
> Some of us may be wounded
> Some of us may be slain
> The balance remain will fight for victory.

> The band would take up the chorus and sing it out, giving a wonderful tone to the accompaniment. With all their grandeur these players of long ago, played around the city streets for the two days

carnival, carrying on with the discipline and respect, [and] always appreciated by the lovers of clean enjoyment. . . .

The band called Artillery had as their chantwell Henry Forbes—his singing name was "The Inventor." [This was] another band of well organised players. Like the others, they also had their King and Queen and all the members of their royal household. This band [had] the same principle of dress [as] the other fancy bands, with their costumes made of the best silk obtainable, in a beautiful "self [flesh] colour." This band had a cannon drawn by horses in place of the chariot, with their King in his fine and beautiful display of artful masquerade. Sitting by his side [was his] Queen, majestically dressed. . . .The chantwell also [wore a] lovely costume of velvet, with his sword [and] gloves. [A] cape [was] thrown over his right shoulder, and like the other chantwells a lovely plume [was] in his hat. He strutted on ahead of his band like a peacock in a farm yard, so proud was he of his high office. On meeting "Standard," he gave out his command like this:

> Charge one on them Artillery
> Charge one on them Artillery
> Artillery charge another volley to make men surrender.

On hearing the command from their chantwell, the band gave out a volley, for they used a real cannon (the practice only stopped when a woman member of the band got hurt as a result of being too near the cannon!). . . .

There was a band called White Rose with Frederick Julien as their chantwell. His singing name was "The Iron Duke," a singer of the most intellectual songs. He also was the organizer of this band, one of the loveliest that ever walked the streets of Port-of-Spain. They wore white costumes made of the best silks and satins, with gold braid, lace, ribbons, spangles, swansdown and many other decorations. . . . They sang and danced to the music of their band and the sweet refrains from their chantwell. [He was] dressed in a manner [similar] to the other chantwells—white velvet costume, his lovely white cape, gloves, [and] his sword in hand, [an] outfit befitting his office. [He] always [was] at the head of his band. [He carried the] proud appearance of a General leading his troops [as] he went on. For many years this band held sway. So great was their fame, that at one of the downtown competitions held at the "Almond Walk"—now known as

Broadway—the merchant called "Papa Bodu" always, so it is alleged, favoured this particular band causing this verse to be referred to him:

> Down on the Almond Walk Papa Bodu
> Di moun La Verite [tell me the truth].

For many years this band continued to play. Though losing some of its members, new ones took their places and fell in line with the others who knew all about the manner of carrying on [such a] band worthy of highest praise. [This is just] another feature of the old time carnival, forever gone. . . .

There was no rushing or pushing in these bands. They paraded the streets in an orderly manner without any interference from the onlookers or non-players. There was an atmosphere of real comradeship in the carnival of long ago. . . .

To hear these chantwells singing, each man doing his best to beat the other! The present day competition is in truth and fact just a display of costumes, no doubt setting the judges to sit and wonder. Imagine a competition with three or four bands, each with chantwell [who must] sing to gain his laurels. Persons who did not care to go to the tents then had the opportunity of listening to the calypso and help judge. . . .

There was a feeling of brotherly cooperation among the singers. . . . The old fellows carry an air of respectability. They [were] always well dressed and [took] pleasure in coming to the tent that way. . . . The old singers often had a car awaiting them after the show to take them to the home of one of the respectable families around Port-of-Spain. [There, they would] entertain some stranger who, having heard of their singing and not being able to visit the tent, left no stone unturned to meet the singer and hear his songs.[42]

As Carnival ruction decreased and its Dionysian elements were rendered more genteel, both masquerade and calypso became media in the expression of the cultural and even the political values of the Creole majority of the island. Just as the streets begot the fancy masquerades, the social unions begot the calypso tent, the most deliberate and contemplative medium for the expression of Carnival values. In this dialectic of masks, sticks, skits, and songs, classic calypso was born.

5 ✳ The Tent

Buy half a cigarette.

comment made by Railroad Douglas to
Young Pretender while giving Pretender
a fee of three pennies for singing in his tent

IF there is a center to the calypso wheel, it is the calypso tent. The tent was originally an informal arena set up in a masquerade camp or calinda yard for practicing a Carnival band's songs. Whatever Carnival music had been and whatever it was to become, once calypsos were made to fit this venue, all other forms of calypso could only be defined in terms of their relationship to the tent form. Just as tent calypso was the child of outdoor Carnival music, the twentieth-century lavways, recorded calypso, calypso in clubs and theaters, and calypso over the radio were the children of tent calypso.

The Early Tents

The calypso tent came into being around 1899 in the masquerade camps of the major social unions of Port of Spain and the large towns of Trinidad. The calinda yards also contributed to the tents' inception and growth, although the opinions of experts vary. Jacob D. Elder claims that "by 1899 the merchants in Port of Spain like Fernandez Co. and Sa Gomes Ltd. had begun to experiment with the organization of 'calypso tents' as a form of public recreation."[1] He also claims,

"In 1899, it is recorded that one Norman la Blanc . . . set up the first carnival tent to which he invited the Negro singers [to] compose kalinda songs which were then beginning to be called 'ca-i-so.' "[2] The Roaring Lion has written:

> The idea of the building of tents associated with the carnival, originated at the beginning of the twentieth century. According to Bennie McCollin (calypsonian Lord Persecutor) who owned the Roosevelt barbar shop which still stands on Duke Street, the first carnival band tent was built in 1901, at the corner of George and Duke Streets. Lord Executor sang there for the carnival band that year. Clemen's Dye Shop was situated at the front of the tent, facing the road. It was, as usual, a barrack yard.
>
> Chennette Alley also had a tent in those days. Julian White Rose had one erected at the top of the hill at Duke Street Quarry the same year.[3]

Establishing the identity of the first calypso tent is about as fruitful as figuring out how many angels can dance on the head of a pin: there probably was no actual first tent but rather a metamorphosis from the informal practices whereby chantwells rehearsed with a chorus in the masquerade camp to a more formal tent in which invited guests and passersby watched and heard the practices and then perhaps paid for their enjoyment.

On the calinda front, jacket men had participated in stick fights and had sung calindas in the batonniers' yards for many decades. No doubt others watched but did not participate. Intermission between stick fights was a good time to enjoy the songs. It is difficult to say just when a group of onlookers became a critical mass of patrons.

The Duke of Albany, onetime sponsor of a calypso tent, described the tents as they existed around 1900: "For the few weeks preceding carnival, folks had the pleasure of listening to real intellectual singing, so great and wonderful was their rendition of songs. And, as the songs were all sung in Patois there was single tone and other minors that are now lacking."[4] He describes tents where the language was Patois, just as it was in the Dame Lorraine show (a ribald affair that gained popularity after the crackdown on jamet Carnival in the middle 1880s). He also mentions the litanous single-tone calypsos, sung in Patois, which probably continued as the language of song in some tents, especially in calinda yards and in French districts (e.g., along Duke Street). At the same time, English was the language of government, of education, and of some commerce, especially a few blocks south and east of Woodford Square. As English became the language of prestige, calypsos sung partly or entirely in English became more popular.

Each of the early tents had their own character. Some were nothing more than a corner of a stick fighters' yard or barrack yard covered with coconut fronds. When batonniers were tired of fighting, they practiced songs in Creole (English) or in Patois. Sometimes women sang. Sometimes the chantwell would practice a song with a chorus composed of members of a stick fighter's band or a masquerade band. In a few yards, groups of Carnival "Indians" practiced their songs.

The *Trinidad Guardian* described the doings in the No Surrender yard in 1899:

> Bands of roughs were organizing like the "No Surrender Band." These bands practiced ribald songs. These songs are for the most part intended to bring certain persons into ridicule, and if rumour speaks correctly, some of the respectable persons do not think it either undignified or setting a bad example, to attend some of these rehearsals and openly evince their approval and appreciation of these mountebank proceedings which were the lovers of order and public decency they would use every effort on their part to stamp out of our midst as a disgrace and scandal to our boasted civilization. When [people] of intelligence and occupying some position in the community give their sympathetic and probably substantial support to the carnival as carried out in Trinidad by the lower classes, how can it ever be expected to improve or die out?[5]

The *Gazette* reporter seems to be describing a different sort of tent in 1903 in Arima, along Eastern Main Road:

> On Monday, Wednesday and Saturday nights the streets of the Borough are crowded with streams of people traveling from one part of town to another to attend the rehearsals in their tents of the various regularly organised carnival bands. And in many instances the treat is well worth the trouble. The tents are about as well made as they are anywhere else, and with their floral decoration of palm and croton leaves shut off against walls of matted coconut leaves, and the whole structure brilliantly illuminated with a flood of light from a number of various coloured chinese lanterns, presents a very picturesque appearance. In these tents for two or three hours at a stretch on these

nights 20 or 30 of the members of the bands assemble and rehearse the songs with stringed instrument accompaniment, which they intend to sing at the carnival. The whole tone of the Trinidad carnival has undergone a very pleasing change of late years, and not one of the least indications of it is the careful and systematic training for weeks before the carnival begins of the "Social Unions" as most of them are not inappropriately named. This year's prizes are being offered by merchants and others at Arima for the best dressed bands and the best singing band. Disinterested persons at present class the most prominent bands and the following order of merit. 1. Sweet Evening Bells, 2. Royal Britannia, 3. Brigade Union, 4. Trafalgar. The banners in which there is also promise of great improvement this year, are being made and painted by the local artist, Mr. Parades.[6]

The first tents were constructed through cooperative effort in a work group known as the "gayap," a custom found throughout the rural Caribbean.[7] A structure of bamboo posts and beams was covered with palm fronds and a tarpaulin or sail to give some protection from the rain. Benches or chairs were added and the area was lit with *bul de fe* or *flambeau*, a corked bottle filled with kerosene and topped with a wick made of paper or rag. Hurricane lamps or lanterns, made of wood and colored paper and illuminated within by a candle, were set at the entrance of the yard to attract visitors.[8] When the tent was completed, the helpers held a feast.

Chantwells were hired by the masquerade bands, although sometimes band sponsors would invite chantwells from rival bands to sing in their tents.[9] Chantwells occasionally would invite themselves into rival tents: "In the event of anyone hearing of another with much fame, he in turn would go to that tent and do his best to give out a better song to prove he could sing."[10] Although some calypsonians sang solely in certain tents for years at a time, others changed often, even during a single season.

Particular masquerade bands drew their chantwells and general membership from the same social class:

Norman Le Blanc, a store walker,[11] who earned fame as the first to sing a complete kaiso in English, was chantwell to Shamrock Syndicate, a band of whites and persons described as near-whites.[12] The Duke of Marlborough, Georgie Adilla, who was a senior shop assistant, was chantwell to Crescent, a band composed from the coloured

middleclass and persons described as near-whites, while Julian White
Rose, a self-employed cleaner and dyer, was a chantwell to White
Rose, a band of equal social status with Crescent. Kaisonians like Red
Box, Lord Baden-Powell, and Conqueror could not in their wildest
dreams aspire to become chantwells of such bands.[13]

In some tents, women dressed in the colors of the masquerade band
and circulated during the performance. Each carried a bouquet of
flowers and a tray to collect donations.[14] This custom was also found in
rural Trinidad and in nearby islands: in Carriacou, contributions were
made in a like manner for quadrilles or lancer's dances. In the early
tents in Trinidad, a chant might accompany the request for money:

Even if it's a farthing, heed my oration
The bouquet is out for your consideration;
Royalties long ago made their contribution
To perpetuate the glory of this ancient tradition,
But note, you're under no obligation
To give, even a voluntary donation,
Verily,
It's up to your generosity.[15]

Some prominent social unions gradually formalized their calypso
tent performances by adding chairs for visitors and charging a
nominal fee for attending the practices. As the calypso tents assumed
more prominence in Carnival, they gained equity with the masquerades, and the phrase *social union* was replaced by *syndicate*, which
indicated an affiliation between a tent and a masquerade band.

The idea of the calypso tent spread rapidly, according to Lord
Executor. "Soon after 1900, with the calypso gaining popularity and
competition becoming quite fierce in Port of Spain, the calypsonians
began to 'scatter.' Norman Le Blanc was the first to leave the capital for
St. Joseph, where he carried on the 'White Rose' band. 'Lord Philomel'
went to La Brea, the 'Duke of Marlborough' to Cunupia, Henry Forbes
to Manzanilla, the 'Black Prince' to Tunapuna, all opening tents in these
districts. Executor himself joined the 'Iere Belles' in St. Joseph in 1905
and this band was for long the arch-enemy of 'White Rose.' "[16] "The
most striking feature in connection with the St. Joseph [White Rose]
band was the . . . splendour [of the costume] of the principal of its
members, that of the king, young Norman Le Blanc, being said to have

cost $45. It was a wonderful sight, and although a pure invention, bore a general sort of resemblance to the dress of a dashing, courtier of the Elizabethan Age."[17] St. Joseph and Tunapuna are both located along Trinidad's Eastern Main Road and are a short distance apart. It may be that some chantwells dispersed, while others maintained a chain of tents in nearby communities. "A large number of people gathered in Madame La Rose's yard for the purpose of receiving some of the leading carnival singers from the city connected with the 'White Rose S/U.' of Tunapuna. Elaborate preparations were made by the Director, J. Fernandez and members, to give the visitors a cordial reception. The tent was prettily illuminated with lanterns and decorated with crotons and ferns for the occasion. Precisely at 7 o'clock, the well-known 'chanter,' A. Julien, took the chair, and subsequently afforded much pleasure with his recitation of the customary songs."[18]

The system of masquerade camps and calypso tents not only spread along Eastern Main Road but in the South as well, to San Fernando:

> Among the principal carnival bands practicing for the coming masquerade is White Rose Social Union whose colours are to be sea green and white as on past occasions. The coronation ceremony when the King and his Consort of the union for this year, are to be crowned, takes place on the eleventh instant at the band's marquee in Upper Hillside Street. Joseph Nimbatt and Ms. Annie Clarke are the sovereigns. The music of various "calypso" etc. is an improvement on last year's and a noticeable feature is that the songs are not composed in order to ridicule any persons in the community, as is the case with other bands, but the words are merely based on local events of important [sic] and in praise of their union.[19]

This dispersal of the idea of fancy masquerade and calypso tent helped to cement an evolving Creole identity throughout the island. Even as fancy masquerade Carnival spread, the older forms of masquerading continued: ole mas' (makeshift masquerades with simple messages written onto the costumes), traditional masks, and stick fighting persisted in most parts of the island, even in Port of Spain, and continued to evolve in their own inexorable manner.[20]

A new stage in the development of Carnival was reached in 1919 with the Guardian's "Victory Carnival" (fig. 11), marking the end of World War I. Executor, who was on the verge of becoming the elder statesman of calypso, was the most prominent singer at the time;

Houdini, who later became the first important calypsonian in New York, was starting out in the African Millionaires' band. Chiney Patrick Jones was "giving fatigue" to Executor, as they sang against each other in the calypso wars. The chantwell Douglas, just out of service with the British West India Company in Europe, was redefining the tent system. Whiterose and Le Blanc were at the close of their careers, although Le Blanc may have lived on for a decade or more.

In 1919, the *Guardian* sent a reporter to calypso tents and calinda yards, providing this full report of the pre-Carnival rehearsals:

CARNIVAL BANDS AT PRACTICE: WHAT A VISIT DISCLOSED
The respective band practices reached a satisfactory stage on Friday evening when the opportunity was taken by a representative of the Trinidad Guardian to visit the scene of operations. At Cavalry, Woodford Street, there was a marked display of enthusiasm. A large benab covered over with coconut branches and liberally decorated with flags and paper balloons had been erected on the stop opposite the A.M.E. Church. Inside the benab has been placed in neat rows along the sides several benches on which those who were privileged to gain admission were seated. A small charge of a couple of cents was exacted for entry, but this did not deter people from turning up in large numbers to listen to the airs which should prove exceedingly popular. Long before 9 o'clock, the hour fixed for the proceedings to begin, spectators made their way in Wordford Street, so that when Mr. E. Briggs and his musicians opened their programme with a lively composition fully four hundred persons surrounded the benab. The musical instrument of the band here consisted of four pieces—a violin, flute, cuatro and guitar their blending soft and low being very good indeed. Several prominent members of the community who were present expressed themselves as being quite pleased with what they had heard, theirs being principally patriotic. At George Street, where the "Bamboo Band" had also entrenched themselves under a coconut leaf hut, the crowd of spectators was not so large as in New Town, but what they lacked in members they made up for by their spirited approval of the tunes . . . which were being rehearsed. Here the musical paraphernalia were confined to the popular "instruments" of the proletariat, which consisted of lengths of hollow reeds of bamboo, a small grater operated on by a musician with a stick, a "chac-chac", and the inevitable empty gin flask with a tin spoon as the beater.[21]

TRINIDAD GUARDIAN. FRIDAY, FEBRUARY 28, 1919.

Victory Carnival

MONSTER FETE ON QUEEN'S PARK SAVANNAH.

Have your fun in the town, but don't miss the gala celebrations in the BEAUTY SPOT of Port-of-Spain.

PROGRAMME AND PRIZE LIST :

MONDAY, MARCH 3.

Bands to assemble in Marine Square 12.30 Judging for Mr. Maillard's special prize At conclusion of this ceremony percussion of bands to march up Henry Street to Queen's Park Savannah. Competitions to commence at 2.30 p.m.

THE PRIZE LIST.

Best dressed Band: 1st $60, 2nd $40, 3rd $20.
Most Original Band: $25.
Individual Masquerader. Best Fancy Dress: $10.
Individual Masquerader. Most original Costume: $10.
The best Queen of any band: Plate Prize.

Decorated Vehicles.

Best decorated Motor Cars: 1st, 2nd and 3rd Plate prizes.
Best decorated Motor Lorries and Vans: 1st $10, 2nd $5.
Best decorated Cabs: 1st $10, 2nd $5
Best decorated Bicycles: 1st $5, 2nd $2.50
Best decorated Donkey Carts: 1st $5, and $2.50
Best decorated Dray Carts 1st $5 and $2.50

Musical Competition.

Best Carnival Song by band $10
Best Topical Song by individual or band $10
Best Fancy by band $20.

Entries for these events should be sent to the Hon. Secretary Carnival Committee, 22 St. Vincent Street

TUESDAY, MARCH 4.

Presentation of prizes at the grand stand, Queen's Park Savannah, 4 o'clock. Battle of Flowers and Decorated Motor Parade.

Illumination of Savannah 8 o'clock.

Electric lights will be strung across the whole length of Queen's Park West from the Charlotte Street corner to Cipriani Boulevard. At night these will give the effect of a series of arches of light spanning this beautiful thoroughfare. Residents around the Savannah will be asked to decorate their houses with flags or in any other way that their imagination may suggest.
The following suggestions for special features in the parade are submitted.

1 A waggon representing Trinidad War Memorial.

2. Every Estate Ally to be represented; each Ally is separate car or vehicle.

3 All clubs to be represented in decorated cars or other vehicles.

4 Business firms and local agencies (such as typewriter, sewing machine and phonograph dealers) invited to enter special displays.

5. All motor car owners and other vehicle owners to be invited to take part in parade with decorated and illuminated vehicles.

SPECIAL PRIZES.

Best Decorated Vehicle 1st $50, 2nd $40.
3rd $20
Most Original Motor Car Plate Prize
Best Decorated Cab $5

For the convenience of spectators who wish to view the parade of masquerading bands in the Savannah, the Grand Stand has been kindly placed at the disposal of the Carnival Committee by the Turf Club

Grand Stand Tickets. Two Shillings.

Now on sale at the Offices of THE TRINIDAD GUARDIAN, 22 St. Vincent Street and on the GRAND STAND on Monday, March 3

Refreshments will be obtainable at a BAR run by Messrs. Stephens Ltd

ORGANISED BY

"The Trinidad Guardian" Carnival Committee.

II ✳ Advertisement for a "Victory Carnival" celebrating the end of World War I.

The " 'instruments' of the proletariat" at the George Street tent were the tamboo bamboo, lengths of bamboo that are hit as they are struck on the ground, and the bottle and spoon, still the favored instrument of the average Carnival reveler, an instrument that is the spirit of Carnival itself.

In the 1920s, the performance of lyrical calypso was gradually separated from masquerade bands and calinda tents. The by-then-classic picture of a fancy masquerade band, with banner waving and a chantwell and chorus chanting, declined as the calypso tent became a more important forum for song than chanting on the streets with a masquerade band. A few singers became primarily tent performers, masquerading for them being casual and secondary.

When calypso was associated with fancy masquerade or calinda bands, the calypsonian was called a chantwell. The defining characteristic of the chantwell was that he sang calypso while masquerading and usually while leading a band. Sometimes, he was also a stick fighter and led a band of battoniers. As calypso grew independent from masquerading, however, the singer was no longer called a chantwell, did not lead a band, and did not necessarily sing on the road. Such a person was a calypsonian, one who sang in tents separate from his Carnival activities.

The Growth of Independent Tents

Some of the important individuals in the development of the calypso tent were Whiterose, King Fanto (Fanta), Railway (Chieftain) Douglas, and a group of singers who together formed the Toddy Syndicate in the late 1920s.

After Whiterose, discussed earlier, Fanto is usually identified as the most important person in changing the way calypso was presented in practices.[22] According to Atilla, " 'Fanto' would travel from San Fernando—forty miles away—to Port of Spain, to sing with a certain 'band' called 'Red Lion' [a red dragon band]. To help defray this singer's expenses, one penny was charged as entrance fee to listen to the singers in their 'tent.' "[23] Others followed Fanto's lead, and by the end of the season "the price of admission had climbed to four cents."[24] "Sometimes the takings exceeded expectations. For example at a certain tent one night, gate receipts amounted to $40.00. A five-dollar note was a rare sight in those days and one side bore the imprint of a steamer [on the local currency]. When the money was counted and checked in the presence of the kaisonians [calypsonians], with whom the takings were shared, one keen singer queried the collector saying, 'But whey de steamer?' The collector, taking offence, retorted haughtily and indignantly, 'You are questioning my integrity!' To this the kaisonian replied, 'Ah don't know about integrity, but I ain't see the steamer.' "[25]

Fanto introduced a new, sexier calypso, performed with a little dance step, and thereby weakened the hold the older performers like Whiterose and Le Blanc had on the crowd with their *picongs* (verbal battles between two or more singers) and their boastful calypsos.

In terms of making the calypso tent a vehicle for the presentation of English-language calypso and in terms of the transition from a tent located in a mas camp to an independent tent, Chieftain Douglas played the most significant role (fig. 12). Douglas began his career as a chantwell for and leader of the Railroad Millionaires, one of the tourist bands that developed during World War I. He "dressed in

12 * Pioneer calypso tent performer Chieftain Douglas, circa 1950. Courtesy of Errol Hill.

cream flannel pants, fawn-coloured shirts, Panama hat. The women [in his band] dressed in flannel skirts, with shirts and hats similar to those worn by the men. They had handbag[s] with long strap[s] slung over one shoulder. Some [had] notes representing real money pinned on the front of their clothes looking all the while like some of the tourists who visit our shores occasionally. They had sweet music."[26]

In 1921 Douglas opened the Railroad Millionaires' tent.[27] "This was at 26 Duncan Street. Douglas forbade the traditional calinda and calinda music from his tent, and introduced the flute, cuatro, guitar, bass and violin, hoping to attract a more sophisticated audience, and corner the so-called respectable middle class citizens. Douglas was an entertainer, and organized a one-man show backed by a chorus group, reserving improvisation and picong for the end of the show."[28] Chieftain Douglas, usually known as Railway Douglas as a result of his occupation as a railroad ticket clerk,[29] was responsible for changing calypso tents from impromptu sessions held in mas' camps or calinda yards to formalized, programmed performances of calypsos composed in major keys (not the minor-key calindas). He also contributed greatly to the ballad calypso, enchanting his listeners night after night with long novelettes in song. Douglas was one of the last of the chantwells who led fancy masquerade bands and one of the first of the tent manager–calypsonians.

Some of the furnishings for Douglas's tent came from the railroad: tarpaulins to cover the ground, bamboo supports, gas lanterns. He decorated the interior of the tent with Christmas paper obtained from shops.[30] He rented chairs, printed tickets, and charged six cents for seated customers and four cents for standing room, opening on Monday, Wednesday, and Friday evenings. Performances started at eight o'clock in the evening and concluded two hours later, when all tents were supposed to close. At first, Douglas might sing for the entire two hours on a platform that also held a small orchestra; later, he invited calypsonians from other tents to sing.

By the early 1930s Douglas's tent had moved several times and was located on Nelson Street:

TO-NIGHT! TO-NIGHT!
Railroad Millionaires
44 Nelson Street
(Opposite Eastern Market School)
OPEN
COMPETITION
1st Prize $3.00, 2nd $2.00,
3rd $1.00
COME AND HEAR
Admiral Douglas
Atilla The Hun, The Lion,
Inveigler, Albany, Controller
and others too numerous to
mention.
Do not be misled by handbills. Douglas and
troupe will not be singing at 74 Henry Street in
the future, his tent is situated at the above
address.
BE EARLY AND AVOID THE RUSH!
Constables will be present to maintain order.
PRICES: 6, 18 and 24 cents.[31]

Young Pretender got one of his first jobs with Douglas, for a token payment. "I can remember singing with him and Atilla [in] 1932. I

could never forget that. Johnnie Walker and all those [were] on the
show.[32] And after the show, he [Doyles] said, 'Pretender, you gonna
be great boy.' He pat me on the back and gave me three pennies. He
said, 'Buy half a cigarette.' Never forget that. . . . I was proud that this
great man shake me hand."[33] Pay was not much better for established
singers. According to Beginner, Lion

> came out with me when he first started to sing, and he told me that he
> was singing in Bedford Lane, Belmont and he want to get between the
> big fellows. We used to knock around by singing all night in George
> Street. When morning broke, I carry him to Douglas who was living in
> Prince Street. And Douglas took him in his tent. Douglas gave me three
> shillings as a partner, and give me two shillings for my friend, Lion. I
> told Lion, "Don't grumble yet. Let me see what you have, expenses."
>
> The next night we got a few white people [as customers in the tent].
> They sit all on stones. And me have the tent in me hand [e.g., the
> audience liked his songs], you know, Douglas singing good too.
> Douglas come back with the same thing [pay]. Three shillings and two
> shillings. We say, "No, we can't tolerate that again." And we pull out
> and we went up South.[34]

Douglas did not like the jamet class's idea of fun. He did not like
the rude Dame Lorraine performances, with their double entendres,
and he preferred the string band to African instruments such as the
verra or scrapper and the tamboo bamboo.[35] Douglas helped make
English the language of choice in the "high-class" calypso tents and
so, by the early 1930s, Patois was used only in singing obscene songs
or to obscure a verse or a phrase in English calypso. Aldous Huxley,
the English writer who was apparently a calypso aficionado, describes
the scene in the tent of one of Douglas's rivals: "The Lord Adjudicator
sang almost incomprehensibly (which was the more regrettable, as
his song was evidently richly obscene) in that queer French patois
which still lingers among the negroes of Trinidad."[36]

In 1929, a group of calypsonians—Executor, Atilla, Mentor, Perse-
cutor, Trafalgar, Modern Inventor—established their own tent under
the management of Reynold Wilkinson. They named the tent the
Toddy Syndicate[37] after a popular chocolate drink that sponsored the
show and raised admission above the norm at the time. The Toddy
Syndicate differed from Douglas's tent in that it was more openly
commercial and it brought together a variety of calypsonians with

different styles. Although most songs were in English, Executor and Atilla used Patois for effect.

This set the trend for the 1930s and early 1940s, when a few individual singers became professional and achieved something of a star status. The focus of attention shifted from the venue—the spectacle of it all—to the calypsonian. But however singular a calypsonian might become, the center of his power was always the tent: "It is doubtful whether the calypso is as brilliant with any other background but the calypso tent."[38]

Calypso Competitions

Singing competitions have had a long history in Trinidad's Carnival. They were common in the late 1920s, when they outgrew the Carnival tents, just as the tents later outgrew the masquerade camps. For example, in 1927, the Carnival Improvement Association sponsored a Carnival competition in Marine Square, modeled after the *Guardian*'s Victory Carnival show of 1919.[39] The finale was held on Carnival Sunday night, March 1. Several singing contests were part of that competition: a group organized by Atilla the Hun, the rising young protégé of Executor, won as the best singing band. Albany won a special prize for singing. Judges included Miss Jeffers (who continued to judge for more than a decade), a wealthy planter and laborite, A. A. Cipriani, and musician Lionel Belasco, who by that time lived in New York and only returned to Trinidad for Carnival. Meanwhile, on Carnival Monday night at the Palace Cinema in San Fernando, a "Grand Double Programme Night" was advertised with an "Extra Special Carnival Singing Competition by Johnnie Walker and the Best Singers of Port-of-Spain and San Fernando." Also on the bill was the "Final Installment" of a silent movie, "Days of 49 (6 Reels)" and a "Comic (1 Reel)" movie.

The greatest of all calypso competitions, the crowning of the calypso king of the island, grew out of these earlier local competitions. The first island-wide competition was the crowning of Calypso King in the Victory Tent in 1939. The contest was judged by calypso-loving, elite Creoles; it was an interesting competition indeed. The contestants included Caresser, Radio, Atilla, Pretender, Lion, and Tiger. Both Pretender and Lion have written or spoken about this event. Lion recalled:

In 1939, the Victory Calypso Tent decided to give a show in the Princes Building. As an added attraction, it was agreed that for the first time, whosoever should win the calypso competition, will be crowned king. [The competition] was never intended to become an annual affair [and] was discontinued until the fifties when it was resurrected by a new generation of bards.

[The 1939 Calypso King Competition] took place on February 17. . . . I had introduced "Cavalcade of Calypsos" in 1938. In either 1936 or 1937, I also made a cavalcade of American popular songs, mostly those that Bing Crosby sung, [as] he was one of my favourites. It was titled "The Crooning Prodigy." Consequently, with two years experience in writing medleys, it was not too difficult for me to improve on the idea and embark on writing a more ambitious song of [that] kind. [That new song] turned out to be the most popular of the three, so popular that it was in great demand for five successive calypso seasons. The audience demanded, by special request, that it be sung every night throughout the entire calypso tent practice, and the cinemas were no exception. This one was called "Six Feet of Earth." It was rated as the masterpiece of the century, as far as calypso is concerned. Truly, it was the talk of the town for years [as] it never seemed to grow old. Anyone who lived during 1939 to 43 will readily testify to this fact. Every competition that I took part in and s[a]ng "Six Feet of Earth," I won as "easily as kissing hands." Yet, I made the silliest mistake when I stupidly decided to sing another song instead in one of the important competitions I entered that year. Here is what happened.

In those days, calypso competitions were plentiful. In nearly every big calypso show there used to be one, whether it was in the tent or in the cinema. Very often these competition shows were held especially to attract the fans and, more often than not, they were sponsored by business firms that gave attractive prizes in cash or kind, or both. These gimmicks drew a crowd. At times the competition was "open," meaning that a singer was free to sing a song of his choice. Other times the singers were told what to sing about—e.g. history, politics, or a particular product. This was called a "grand-calypso competition.". . .

Now I was no easy walkover in any kind of competition. Where calypso was concerned calypso lovers would have readily given fifty-to-one on me [against] anyone [in] the field. This is no boast, it is the truth. [The] only [others] to win [were] my partner, Atilla The Hun and at times, King Radio who had a wonderful voice and was liable to steal the show unexpectedly. There was nothing to fear from the others. Mind you, I am not saying that I was never beaten by a Small Fry, for even such a singer can, on the odd occasion, come forth with a winner. But whenever I did lose, it used to be a surprise to the public. . . .

However, February 17, 1939, was one of the occasions when I had victory in my hands, and for no obvious reason, I threw it away, stupidly. What took place was this: Atilla and myself decided to call [the] competition we were giving at the Princes Building, a "calypso king competition." Of course, no real importance was attached to such a competition in those days. . . . The building was packed the night of the competition. Mootoo Brothers was playing and Captain the Hon. A. A. Cipriani and Mrs. A. P. Plimmer were the judges. There was a third judge, but I can't remember who it was. The song I ought to have done was "Six Feet of Earth," the Cavalcade. Everybody expected me to sing that song. But I chose to sing new songs. When it was announced that I was going to sing a new song, the sigh that came from the audience told me that they were disappointed. But I thought I could have won with the new song. It turned out that I was not only wrong, but I was a big fool.

After the competition, the Captain openly said to me, "Lion! why didn't you sing your cavalcade of songs, 'Six Feet of Earth'? You would have won easily." Tiger placed first and Pretender came second.[40]

Pretender mentions Tiger, not Lion, in his version of that historic occasion:

I like to remember him [Tiger] and laugh at myself [about] 1939 [and] the first calypso king competition [with] me, Atilla, [and] Caresser. Atilla sang, "Help the Blind." I come and hit them with, "The Virtue of Women," people clapping at me and all. Me and Atilla down the corner there saying, "Well, it's lovely tonight." And Tiger walking in with an unknown calypso, something 'bout, "Trade Union!" From the time he hit the third verse, well, my mouth long like a flute! The man win the thing man!

Well, so help me God, me and Atilla with the usual shake hand and well done! But I wish me hand was a snake! He cut me up man, I hear he laughing a kinna' piss mouth laugh! He should remember that song![41]

This is a verse of Tiger's winning song:

> I'm advising every worker as a West Indian
> Try and join a labor union
> I'm advising every worker as a West Indian
> Try and join a labor union
> It's the only way you can achieve your rights
> And stop the oppressive man overnight
> To be a lawyer or a progressive man
> To be an inspiration to the rising generation.[42]

After World War II, calypso, masquerade, and steel band competitions were central features of Dimanche Gras. After 1962, the competitions were government sponsored.

Tent Sponsors and Advertisement

The Victory Tent was managed by Reynold Wilkinson, a government bureaucrat who worked in the new Red House (the central government building in Woodford Square, Port of Spain).[43] He typified the managers of the establishment tents—those that drew patrons from all classes but that catered to the middle class, to the elite, and to foreigners (especially tourists). These tent managers were the logical heirs to the jacket men (gentlemen stick fighters who were intrigued by the jamet Carnival in the 1880s) and to Bodu and other shopkeepers who developed the tent idea before World War I. Wilkinson's peers included the contractor Sylvester Talyor, schoolteacher-calypsonian Charles Jones, Railway Douglas, Guyanese advertising man and entrepreneur Johnny Khan, planter and labor leader A. A. Cipriani, importer Isidore Smart, ship chandler Cecil Voison, bank accountant A. E. James, customs broker Sonny de Silva, and accountant Jimmy Smith.[44] Although they put on the shows to make profits, many did not. They often tightly managed the program and picked singers they thought would be popular or who had something important to say to the public. A few tent managers were calypsonians (Albany, Douglas) and some wrote calypsos or assisted the calypsonians who had little education in grammar and syntax (Wilkinson). They hired the bands and some had a hand in selecting calypsonians to make records.

Businessmen sometimes hired calypsonians to write and sing jingles advertising their shops or products:

When one Mr. Alphonso, a Portuguese rum dealer, sponsored a band advertising his rum, the leader of that band held a competition in the tent where the members met. As was customary, calypsonians from other tents were invited to take part in the competition. Lord Mentor was one such leader, and he won the prize with this song:

> Drink your rum, and tumble down
> But don't make basa [be foolish] around the town (repeat)
> For there is a man I know
> His name is Mr. Alphonso
> He is selling his rum so cheap and sweet
> It's bound to put you to sleep.[45]

Calypso and World War II

Carnival went through another major change as the depression shaded into World War II. Tiger expressed the sentiments of many poor Trinidadians about the European war:

> Times so hard you cannot deny
> That even saltfish and rice we can hardly buy (repeat)
> And now this war with England and Germany
> Going to mean more starvation and misery
> But I going plant provision and fix me affairs
> And the white people could fight for a thousand years.[46]

Early in the war, Trinidadian moviegoers cheered Adolf Hitler when he appeared in newsreels,[47] but as the war progressed, and truth and Allied propaganda took hold, opinions changed.

The war brought a boom as Trinidad became a center for Allied communication, intelligence, and transportation of troops and supplies between the Americas and the theaters of war on opposite edges of the Old World (fig. 13). In the Bases Agreement between the United States and Great Britain, the United States leased large parts of the northwest peninsula and north central Trinidad. On the peninsula, they built Chaguaramas naval base, and just south of the northern mountain range they built Waller Field, an air base (fig. 14).[48]

In the war years the British increased censorship of calypso, and political and union activities were repressed for the duration. Never-

13 ✳ American soldier Vernon Yeager, the "Dixie Guitarist," poses next to his commanding officer's Packard outside of Whitehall, Port of Spain, early 1940s. Courtesy of Charles Porter.

theless, employment was high and so were wages.[49] The cost of living rose too, and thousands of Trinidadians left the sugar and cocoa estates for jobs in the war industries. Prostitution and vice increased sharply, as did gang and mob violence. The myth of the superiority of whites was shattered, as Trinidadians saw white Americans perform physical labor, and the hard-drinking GIs were mimicked by masqueraders posing as bad behavior sailors. Soldiers of the American Navy Construction Brigade (the Sea Bees) were admired for their acumen. They built the north coast road to Maracas Bay and other public works as compensation for the occupation of the northwest peninsula in the lend-lease agreement. Although deference to whites became a thing of the past, American-style racism was cruder than the more subtle British version. All together, the American presence on the island helped pave the way for a new era of enfranchisement after the war.

Due to misguided notions of war preparedness, street Carnival was abolished between 1942 and 1945, yet the tents remained and flourished. British military personnel and especially American GIs

14 ✳ American and Canadian soldiers at Trinidad's Waller Field snack bar, early 1940s. Photo ref. no. 68022 from the Defense Audio Visual Agency, Washington, D.C.

packed the tents and fundamentally altered that forty-year-old Carnival institution (fig. 15). "The Americans had money, and as a result admission prices rose rapidly. The calypsonians would air their complaints against the Americans through calypsos sung in the presence of the soldiers. The good-natured songs defused any tensions that might have arisen from the presence of thousands of young men who were suddenly competing with the natives for the prettiest girls."[50] Lion refers to these as "good years," meaning that they were economically profitable for the calypsonians and their sponsors, the tent owners.[51] Classic calypso was modified, however, as singers catered to the tastes of the GIs and the tourists who came in great numbers after the war.

Before the war, the tents had been located around George, Henry, and Prince streets, near Laventille and Belmont.[52] Fear of hooliganism and desire to make the locations more appealing to the white soldiers drove tent promoters to move their locations west, to the vicinity of Park and St. Vincent streets, a better neighborhood and

15 ✳ Calypsonians at the Fort Read military base, February 1943. Left to right: Invader, Growler, Atilla, Lion. Courtesy of the U.S. Army.

one where transportation coming from Tragarete Road and the naval base and other points west intersected with routes coming from the east and south. These modern tents were more permanent than the bamboo and frond tents and, like Douglas's tent, contained chairs placed in rows. At the front was the stage, elevated a couple of feet from the ground. It was "decorated with flags, theatre posters, other advertisements like Coca Cola, the latest model truck or car—in short anything that would add a bit of colour to the rather drab surroundings."[53] In 1942 an American described a tent performance:

> The first time I went to hear the calypsonians was about the middle of January. The tickets were two shillings, and the tent was not really a tent, but a fairly large backyard, covered with sheets of corrugated tin and decorated with British flags, colored pictures of Hollywood movies and war posters saying, "Help Britain finish the job!" It was lit by a single bright electric bulb over the little stage that had been put up in the far end of the yard. There was an audience of about 150 people of various social standings. . . . Those who didn't have two shillings for a seat had standing room, which was six pence, and those who didn't

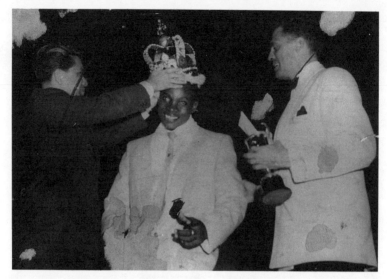

16 ✳ The Mighty Sparrow winning his first calypso crown, the Queen's Park Savannah, Port of Spain, early 1956. Courtesy of the *Trinidad Guardian*.

have six pence were standing outside, while some young boys had climbed on the surrounding fence. Everybody was in good humor and eager to hear and enjoy the new songs. Radio, the Lion, the Growler and the Destroyer were the calypsonians of the evening and they were accompanied by a little orchestra consisting of a trumpet, a saxophone, a guitar and a bass viol. They were well dressed, wearing coats and ties and green or brown felt hats tilted on one side of their heads.[54]

After the war, union halls, theaters, and other indoor facilities were rented as tents in the Carnival season. Tourists replaced GIs, as foreigners came to dominate the audiences. Pretender and Superior told Keith Warner that the clientele in the 1940s and early 1950s was mostly white,[55] and Iere told Chalkdust the same thing.[56] Chalkdust added that others in the audience were wealthy blacks, "the Maple Hill Crowd." Tents faded in importance for a while, and gossip in song about Trinidadians was nearly replaced by prattle that piqued peripatetics.

Yet this generation of calypso was becoming established abroad as part of world music, and this depiction of calypso as a risqué music for white tourists represents what some non-Trinidadian Caribbean people dislike about the music to this day. Fortunately, Trinidadians gained both the money and interest to outnumber the tourists in the "era of Sparrow" (whose road march "Jean and Dinah" reinvigorated calypso when he won his first calypso competition in 1956), and a revived tent, the "Original Young Brigade" led by the youthful Grenadian, the Mighty Sparrow, set the tone for tent performances for the few years before and after independence (fig. 16). With the political independence of Trinidad and Tobago, calypso—as kaiso and soca—once again reasserted itself as a significant medium of social commentary.

6 ✳ The Tent Singers

He was given this special brain.

source of comment not revealed

CHANTWELL was a generic name for singer in the Patois-speaking community of nineteenth-century Trinidad. When fancy masquerades grew in popularity, some chantwells led the masqueraders during Carnival and also sang in the calypso tents. As the tent singers gradually became professional, the term *calypsonian* came to refer to a person who sang in tents for money and was not associated with that tent's masquerade band, whereas a chantwell sang at the head of a masquerade band. This chapter will profile some of the legendary chantwells and important calypsonians.

Legendary Chantwells

Trinidad's first chantwells, those that may have sung on French estates in the late 1800s, are known today only through legend. Contemporary writers use the term *calypsonians* to refer to these chantwells, although strictly speaking they were not. By the middle of the nineteenth century, there is evidence from newspaper accounts that such singers existed and that they functioned like they were calypsonians—that is, sang topical songs. The best account of the legendary singers is that written by storyteller Mitto Sampson.[1]

The earliest of the mythological chantwells, Sampson recounts, was Gros Jean, slave griot or court minstrel for the feared and hated Begorrat, an immigrant planter from Martinique and aide to Colonel Thomas Picton (the first British governor of Trinidad and Tobago). Gros Jean was said to have been *Mait' Kaiso*—Master of Calypso—for Begorrat. As *Mait' Kaiso*, he had privileges that other slaves did not have. He wrote songs about his master, some of them painting the true Begorrat:

> Begorrat et Diab'la, c'est un
> Begorrat et Diab'la, c'est deux
> Begorrat forte, creul et mauvais
> Begorrat roi-la dans son pays.

> (Begorrat and the devil are one
> Begorrat and the devil are two
> Begorrat strong, cruel and bad
> Begorrat is the king in his country.)[2]

Begorrat and Gros Jean were lovers. Apparently Begorrat's wife suspected this relationship and became jealous of Gros Jean and poisoned him.[3] Sometime later, Begorrat heard an imprisoned slave, Soso, singing for his freedom as he waited in a cache to be executed:

> Begorrat entered his cell and inquired: "Jeune homme, pourquoi avez-vous arrete votre chanson?"—Young man, why are you singing that song?—to which Soso replied in Patois: "Met la, ba mwe pado, souple!"—Master, give me freedom please!—Smiling, Begorrat answered him: "Chantez, Soso, chantez!"—Sing, Soso, sing!—Apart from being reputed to have a taste for "wrinkled and decrepit women . . . making his house a cross between a hospital and a house of refuge," and thus supposedly bringing into the vocabulary of Patois the word "soso" for one whom seeks lovers amongst the aged, he [Soso] is spoken of as having been generous, humane, charitable, and in certain moods, extremely religious.[4]

There were other legendary singers: "Papa Cochon, who is remembered perhaps more as a notorious obeahman and finder of hidden treasures;" the free chantwell Danois, "a mediocre singer, a first rate rascal and an all round thief," who was caught stealing and was buried alive with all his limbs broken:

Danois Danois

Danois vole Begorrat laja (repeat)

Danois vole Begorrat laja

Danois vole tut mun-Dieg Martin.

(Danois steals Begorrat's money

Danois steals from everyone in Diego Martin.)[5]

Sampson's stories about the late-nineteenth-century chantwells, although exaggerated in detail, probably refer to real singers. There were Thunderstone and his wife, Cariso Jane, and Surisima the Carib, who gave fatigue to both. There were Zandoli, Hannibal the Mulatto, Dan the Mulatto, and the stick fighters, Rocou John and Tiny Satan, who enjoyed supernatural protection.

Then in 1870 a spate of calypsos emerged about the trial, held in Diego Martin, of a colored planter named Brunton for the murder of Abbé Jouin,[6] once canon of Roseau, Dominica, and also a former priest in the Mayaro District in the extreme south of Trinidad. At the request of Brunton's wife, the priest had spoken to Brunton about an extramarital affair he had flaunted, even bringing his mistress into their home. Brunton, in turn, thought that his wife was having an affair with the priest.

One evening, Abbé Jouin was lured out of his house by Brunton's workers and was killed by one of them—an East Indian—as Brunton watched. Brunton had promised the worker five hundred dollars for committing the murder.

Three lawyers conducted Brunton's defense, led by M. M. Philip, "a brilliant coloured lawyer," who, according to Anthony de Verteuil, won the case by selecting a jury that was "mainly coloured, Protestant and 'English'."[7] Some in the French party read the verdict as anti-Catholic. Popular opinion was that the notorious obeahman (magician) Djab Papa had influenced the trial by twisting the jury through magical means to let the English planter off.

Chantwells Hannibal, Zandoli, and Cedric le Blanc all sang about the verdict and the alleged influence of Djab Papa:

Hannibal:

Lalin cuwi ju bawe—i

Maldise su la tet Djab Papa—la

(The moon is running, but day catches it

Curses on Djab Papa's head)

Zandoli:

>Djab Papa se yo silira
>Djab Papa, ami de Lucifer
>Djab Papa se gaye libete
>De nom—la ki pchue lade [sic, "chue labe"]
>(Djab Papa is a criminal
>Djab Papa a friend of Lucifer
>Djab Papa won liberty
>For the man who killed the Priest)

Cedric le Blanc:

>The sun, the trees, all nature cried
>The day when Abbé Jouin died;
>Ah, what a brutal death!
>In a thousand years we'll never forget
>It was Djab Papa, the villain
>who saved the murderer![8]

Although acquitted, Brunton left Trinidad for Martinique only to return some years later.[9]

The Calypsonian's Image

The stereotype of the typical calypsonian has been repeated over and over by Trinidadians from all backgrounds, by foreign writers, and by the calypsonians themselves. In the first monograph written on calypso (in 1944), by Trinidadian scholar Charles S. Espinet and musician Harry Pitts, the authors imply that the calypsonians came from the lowest strata of society. A Trinidad-born and -bred orchestra leader expressed a similar view:

>You never mixed with . . . calypsonians. . . . The only way you speak to a calypsonian is—I have to speak with them 'cause I had a play with 'em, see? They were people from the street. . . . He wasn't a man who was any class at all. But he was given this special brain by God which God has given Trinidadians, a special brain different from any one else I know, to do things, a genius. . . .
>   They leave their homes and go on the street. They go and keep company with low people and they live on women. Woman took care of them, feed them, see. This is how it is. . . .

That is a calypsonian. He sat on the tree and wrote a song and . . . somebody . . . would carry a plate of food for him. . . .

Yes, it was a good life. They enjoyed themselves . . . because they didn't work. They had a suit to wear. And they have somewhere to sleep and food to eat. They didn't have to have money in their pocket. They didn't have pocket change or anything like that because they didn't need it. But they were happy.[10]

British author Aldous Huxley wrote, "The Calypsonians of Trinidad live in another 'Zeit'; so the 'Geist' they obey is not the same as ours. In that, it may be, they are fortunate."[11]

Wallace B. Alig, in perhaps the most wondrously excessive stereotype of the persona, states that "the typical Calypso Joe of Trinidad is a ne'er-do-well who often gets embroiled in fights and brawls. He uses obscene language which he frequently carries over into his songs. Sometimes he smokes opium or marijuana; sometimes he lands in jail. But on the nights when he appears at the Perseverance Club or at someone's party, he becomes the most popular citizen for miles around. Then he is in his element."[12] A *New Yorker* writer, Joseph Mitchell, claimed that calypsos were

written and sung by a band of haughty, amoral, hard-drinking men who call themselves Calypsonians. The majority are Negroes. With guitars slung under their arms, they hang out in rumshops and Chinese cafes on Marine Square and Frederick Street in Port-of-Spain, the principal city of Trinidad, hunting for gossip around which they can construct a calypso. Several brag truthfully that women fight to support them. Most of them are veterans of the island jails. To set themselves apart from lesser men, they do not use their legal names but live and sing under such adopted titles as the Growler, the Lord Executor, King Radio, Atilla the Hun, the Lion, the Gorilla, the Caresser, the Senior Inventor, and Lord Ziegfeld.[13] [fig. 17]

Trinidadian folklorist Andrew Carr wrote, "Calypsonians of the old days travelled all over the country, singing their calypsos. They used to stay overnight at some friend's. There was always some very hospitable young lady willing to put him up for the evening."[14]

The self-perceptions of calypsonians are also instructive. Lord Beginner commented that "Iere, me and Tiger got lodging [from young women] after walking for hours."[15] King Iere drew a distinc-

17 ✳ Calypso tent performers, 1948. Front row, left to right: Wonder, Spoiler, unknown tent manager, Invader, Pretender. Back row, left to right: Ziegfeld, Viking, Killer. Courtesy of the *Trinidad Guardian*.

tion between chantwells and calypsonians. "The calypsonians used to go to the tents and sing. On that stage you find chantwells mixed with calypsonians, the professionals. Tonight a man sing here. Tomorrow he will sing in St. James. Sunday night I hear a man singing good in Tunapuna. If its a real 'war,' I going to Tunapuna to meet him."[16] Iere told Chalkdust, "A chantwell in those days was more important than a calypsonian. A calypsonian was a dog."[17] Beginner stated, "The chantwells had privileges and opportunity. A chantwell is a man that you engage to sing for your . . . band. Everybody else have to buy their clothes for the band, but a chantwell's clothes is free. All members contribute and give [clothes to] the chantwell. And they give money when the day comes. They give somewhere to sleep, and he's alright. On the day when the band comes out, he sings in the streets with the band."[18] Lion expressed similar sentiments.[19] Calypsonians were sometimes supported year-round by female backers of the tent or masquerade band. Well-known singers visited the tents of their rivals, where they would engage in singing contests and then be feted. Lion noted that both the lower- and middle-class people did not like calypsonians; both groups tried to keep their children away from the singers. Some of the wealthy people, however, asked calypsonians into their homes, where the singers would encounter people they normally would not meet.

Profiles of Important Calypsonians

Little is known about the personal lives of the first calypsonians. Even less is known about a legion of singers who were semiprofessional, continued to mix French Creole and English Creole and sang throughout the island in the smaller tents. Thus, only the careers of the most well-known singers will be profiled.

Three chantwells—Julian Whiterose, Norman le Blanc, and Henry Forbes the Inventor—stand out at the turn of the century; each claimed or has received credit as the first calypsonian to sing primarily in English.

Julian Whiterose

Julian Whiterose took his name from his masquerade band. His given name may have been Henry Julian, J. Resigna, or even Henry Julian Resigna. Whiterose was the most important Trinidadian band leader from the mid-1890s until World War I. By trade he was a self-employed cleaner and dyer.[20] He led his band with the financial backing of a merchant, Bodu, and defended the rights of the social unions to upgrade Carnival by taking it away from the jamets and by anglicizing it through use of English words expressing British themes. As a result, he was also known as the Iron Duke, from a name he once took for a Carnival character. On the surface the appellation stood for the Duke of Wellington (Arthur Wellesley), who defeated Napoleon I at Waterloo in 1815, yet there is deeper symbolism in this name. An aspiring middle-class man, most likely of Afro-Portuguese descent, only a few decades earlier Whiterose would have been considered a member of the French party. Yet he sang calypsos mostly in English, and his masquerade symbolized an English defeat of the French. One reason for the rise of prestige of British symbols at the turn of the century was their success in the Boer War, a theme expressed in masquerades and songs. In addition, the general anglicization of the island's population also contributed to the increase in British prestige.

Jacob Elder called Norman le Blanc (Richard, Coeur de Leon) both an "upper-class singer"[21] and a "French aristocrat."[22] More likely, he started in the middle class and late in life fell into the lower class. He has been described as ethnically white and French. Elder claims that le Blanc established the first calypso tent in 1899 and then invited the "negro" singers to perform.[23] Although le Blanc appears from time to time in the contemporary press, he was not as publicized as Whiterose. Singing for Whiterose in St. Joseph in 1903, le Blanc played "a dashing, courtier of the Elizabethan Age" in a costume that cost forty-five dollars.[24]

Virtually all commentators, both contemporary and a full generation later, consider le Blanc to be the first calypsonian to sing consistently in English.[25] Executor sang his claim about Norman le Blanc's contribution:

> From abolition to ninety-eight
> Calypso was still sung in its true state
> From French to English it was then translated
> By Norman le Blanc who became celebrated
> Then it was rendered grammatically
> In oration, poetry and history.[26]

Among le Blanc's first English-language calypsos were "Jerningham the Governor" and "Not a Cent," although the latter may have originally been a Jamaican *mento* (folk song) that le Blanc adapted to calypso. As late as 1939, Lord Invader popularized one of le Blanc's songs including the interesting Patois line "*Mete limyè Inglich Kalipso!*" (Cast a light—a good spell—for English calypso!). For all this recognition, le Blanc is not on Atilla's list of the eleven greatest calypsonians of all time.[27]

Le Blanc also took the name of Richard, Coeur de Leon (Richard the Lion Hearted), possibly after a Carnival character he played. Whatever the origin of the sobriquet, again a French Creole was singing in English and symbolizing a semi-legendary English king.[28]

Few firsthand accounts of le Blanc have been found. Beginner once saw him on the streets, "singing songs with guitar, selling copies."[29] Tiger had a similar encounter as a boy:

This man was selling some copies on the busy corner shop, with a guitar. He had a straw hat on, sittin' on a bench. I got nearer listening to this curiosity. He was singing something about, "Goodbye, Iris; friends will support you." Iris was charged for murder, for killing some man in Port of Spain. He made a song out of that and he was selling it. The copies were six cents for one. In those days, six cents to me was a mountain of money. So I watched him for a good while and then turned away. Somebody said that was the man by the name of Norman le Blanc.

They were forced to take it to the street.[30]

Henry Forbes the Inventor

Henry Forbes, the self-titled "Inventor" of English calypso, was even more enigmatic than le Blanc. Forbes sang in both Patois and English, and his sobriquet lays his claim as the inventor of English calypso:

> If they ask you for me,
> Tell them I, Inventor, come.
> Tell them I come to teach them
> Some English calypso.[31]

Atilla knew Forbes well and provides most of the information about him.[32] In addition, Atilla included Forbes among the eleven great calypsonians. "I knew Henry Forbes as long as I can remember. Charlotte, Nelson, and upper Prince Street where I lived were his happy hunting grounds. Whenever he passed along this vicinity, he was always a cynosure of all eyes. From the knots of boys and young men gathered on the footpaths could be heard loud, excited whispers: 'That is 'im . . . that is Henry Inventor. He is champion, boy, Master Me minor.' "[33] Forbes was middle class like Whiterose and le Blanc, but unlike those two, he was an Afro-Trinidadian of dark complexion, a "handsome man."[34] He was slight[35] but well built,[36] with "the eyes of a poet, a dreamer."[37] Lion says that Forbes was originally a "barman in a well known downtown club,"[38] but Atilla described the Inventor as a small-time cocoa buyer, a middleman between peasant cocoa farmers and bigger buyers. The peasants called this occupation "coco-scorpion," but it was a profession "patronized by scions of middleclass society."[39]

Forbes "once enjoyed the questionable distinction of being kept by several women at one time,"[40] telling a friend, "You mean, Freddy, that you don't realize I have five women to contend with and business is not so good these days." Atilla says, "Yes, Henry Inventor was a man of parts." According to Executor, Forbes once sang with a devil band.[41] Later, he sang for the Artillery Social Union.

Atilla felt that the Inventor was one of the best singers of oratorical calypso, based on speech rhymes and the styles of great orators such as "Sir Henry Alcazar, M'Zumbo Lazare, Maresse Smith, and Bishop Hayes."[42] He was also a good extemporaneous singer, especially noted for competing against rivals who could not match his quick, biting *picongs* (insults). When a rival tried to criticize Papa Bodu, patron of mask makers and calypsonians, the Inventor devised:

> I intended to give you a castigation
> But instead you will get my compassion
> You have demonstrated your inability
> You can't sing on Papa Bodi [Bodu],
> Whom we all know,
> The friend and patron of caliso
> You can't give satisfaction
> You are a mock kaisonian.[43]

So many of Inventor's songs were extemporaneous and not written down that few have survived. He death is reported both in the late 1930s[44] and in the 1950s.[45]

Lord Executor

Philip Garcia—Lord Executor—was born in Trinidad around 1880. His parents were thought to be Venezuelans. Both Atilla and Lion state that he attended St. Mary's College, although Beginner says that it was Queen's Royal College.[46] As a young man Lord Executor was employed as a store clerk at Salvatori Scott & Co. in Port of Spain. In those days and still today, some occupational groups had their own Carnival bands. Store clerks joined the Crescent Boys band, which used to assemble in Tambran Yard on Duke Street, where Executor joined them in 1897.

Executor dated his first song to 1898, probably singing with the Crescent Band alongside the Duke of Malborough (Jamesie Adilla), the chantwell:[47]

> chorus:
> Hear me I do say!

Whenever I do play
The dice is not mine
So by that it cannot obey
I am not in the dice
To make it play as I like.
Moi pas un zo la
Pu feu zo la shuen par moi.[48]

Dice does not seem to be an appropriate occupation for a college boy, so it appears that by the time he reached his teens, Executor had become a jacket man, a middle-class Creole who chose to follow the grass-roots life-style. Atilla states that it was a wonder to see a "white-skinned man contributing to an art whose performances generally belonged to the lower stratum of society, and performing as well."[49]

Working at Salvatori by day and singing and liming (hanging out) by night were apparently incompatible. At work, he spent more time writing calypsos than tending customers, and he was fired.[50] After that, he occasionally worked as a sign painter. During Carnival season, Executor sang for a living, making him one of the first professional calypsonians, as distinguished from the chantwells.

Executor reached the height of his power as a singer in the 1910s, when he engaged Henry Forbes the Inventor and Chiney Patrick in war (extemporaneous calypso singing contests). In one contest against the Inventor in 1914, Executor seemed to be winning. Then Inventor sang:

Executor, if they should pass a law
Everyone must go back to their native shore
I of course will have to travel quite far
Right back to the west coast of Africa
The Chinese would have to make tracks for China
The Portuguese would sail back to Madeira
But Executor where would you go
You half-scald mulatto
Sans humanity.[51]

Executor hesitated in his reply to Forbes's rapier-like words and lost the day. The accusation of being mulatto is interesting, as Executor is usually described as white. Maybe singing calypso made the white

Executor mulatto, or perhaps Inventor accused Executor of being of mixed descent.

In the 1930s, the world's first *picong* by phonograph record occurred when Houdini, then based in New York, and Executor recorded songs making fun of each other.

During these years Executor was involved in tent management. Pretender noted that he engaged three singers as rivals in calypso war; as payment he "gave them three 'bob' and a bag of orange."[52] With the assistance of a financial backer, Executor built a calypso tent with Beginner and Radio on Henry Street (fig. 18).[53]

In 1937 Executor joined Atilla and sailed to New York to record for Decca. While in New York, he sang at a night club, Le Ruban Bleu. One night a patron asked Executor to define the word circle. Executor sang:

I'm just a simple kaisonian[54]
I am no geometrician
What is a circle? I for one don't care
But of one thing I'm sure it isn't a square.[55]

Later that year he returned to Trinidad. Probably around Christmas 1937 Executor suffered a "dreadful calamity," a freak accident that changed his life. As he told it in a recording:

A new experience that I had gain
In a hospital where I was retain (repeat)
By the blow that I received I went to get cured
And the doctor sent me to the eye ward
As in contemplation I lay
Among the afflicted on the Christmas Day.

Thinking I was doing an act of good
By helping a woman to chop some wood
When the wood rebound, I fell to the ground
I saw ten candles and the world went round
Immediately I went and made my report
And was sent to the eye ward by Doctor Stewart
As in contemplation I lay
Among the afflicted on the Christmas Day.[56]

Executor never completely recovered from the accident, yet he continued to record solid, vigorous calypsos for Decca in Trinidad for

18 ✳ Calypsonians in the Old Brigade tent, date unknown. Left to right: Radio, Beginner, Executor, Tiger. Courtesy of the *Trinidad Guardian*.

several years and also to perform in tents. His eyesight gradually failed, and he seemed also to slip into sporadic madness. Some say he "gave up his crown" as one of the greatest calypsonians in the late 1930s, others say around 1950. He lived with girlfriends, possibly including "Dorothy," a character in some of his songs.

By the late 1930s he lived hand to mouth much of the time, and foreign writers described him as a "beachcomber" or ne'er-do-well, eating irregularly.[57] In testimony given to an American lawyer, Louis Nizer, Trinidadian orchestra leader Gerald Clark described Executor around 1947: "Lord Executor, as I saw him, he is a bum, and he is incoherent—he is not consistent with a conversation. I can say a little more, he has a repulsive odor. I was glad to get rid of him. I gave him some money and got rid of him, because he begs alms, that is what he does for a living, he begs and I was glad to give him a dollar and get rid of him."[58]

Although Executor was perhaps in mental decline at the time Clark made his testimony, that testimony served Nizer's client, Lionel Belasco, more than Executor's dignity.[59] Even then, nine full years after the accident, Executor continued to perform in the tents, although calypso had changed and so had he. When he tried to sing, other, younger calypsonians rebuffed him. They did not honor the code of friendship that bonded the first and second generations of calypsonians. They sang in the newer styles that had more appeal to the crowds.

In 1954 Executor, now destitute, recorded an interview at the Government Broadcasting Unit in Port of Spain. Notes to the interview state that he was "blinded in a fall" and was "needing funds."[60] The radio station championed a fund to help support him.[61] He recorded a melancholy song, one of his best, at the close of his life:

The technical beauty of my elaborate praise
It must be mentioned by generations for many days
I, Executor, Calypso King
Now at the very moment that I was called to sing
What I have done to all mankind
Must be remember as I'm getting blind
So come and hear the story of my fatal misfortune
In this colony.[62]

Atilla, Executor's *apprentice de kaiso,* felt that he was the greatest calypsonian of all time, edging out Henry Forbes the Inventor at his apex.[63] Executor championed double-tone calypso and was also a master of extemporaneous calypso. When single-tone calypso came into vogue, Executor stuck with his long, ballad calypsos and thereby lost ground to the younger singers.

Simply listing the titles of the songs Executor recorded is an indication of his range:[64] "Three Friends' Advice," "I Don't Know How the Young Men Living," "Hold Up Blackbird Hold Up," "The Bells," "Shop Closing Ordinance," "Street Vendors" (not issued), "Xmas Accident," "Sweet Evelina," "My Reply to Houdini," "Arima Fete Santa Rosa," "Old Ginger," "Christmas Is a Joyful Day," "Reign of the Georges," "Lindbergh Baby," "Seven Skeletons Found in the Yard," "My Troubles with Dorothy," "The Orphan Children," "The Lajobeless Woman," "The Censoring of Calypso Makes Us Glad" (not issued), "The League of Nations," "Tobago's Scandal," "Poppy Day," "We Mourn the Loss of Sir Murchison Fletcher," "How I Spent My Time at the Hospital," "They Say I Reign Too Long," "Nellie Go out Mi Door," "They Talk about Nora's Badness," "Who Has Done the Best for Humanity," "My Life of Matrimony," "Alla Nom (Go Way Nan)," "The New Shop Law," "My Indian Girl Love," "Two Bad Men in the World," "Gambo Lai Lai before the Court," "Carnival Again," "Sambo Why You Are Go," and his last, "My Unconquered Will."

Atilla the Hun

Atilla the Hun was born Raymond Quevedo in Trinidad on March 24, 1882.[65] His father was a Venezuelan and his mother a Trinidadian. He grew up in Trinidad and was enrolled in Port of Spain's St. Mary's College, a Roman Catholic high school attended by middle-class and elite children. It is not clear if he finished, but Lion notes that Atilla worked for a time as a clerk for the Archer Coal Company, which was located on the wharfs of Port of Spain.[66] He was a fixture at the Port of Spain public library. Later, he sailed around South America, working in a ship's galley.

Atilla sang his first calypso in public in 1911.[67] By Carnival 1919, he was singing for the Red Dragon Band.[68] He apprenticed under the master of the ballad calypso, Executor, but soon developed his own style. One of his early leggos, the most popular of the season, was an advertisement for Toddy, a soft drink:[69]

> Mammy, dear Mammy buy some Toddy for me (repeat)
> I'm feeling weak, tired and broken down
> I know that Toddy will make me strong
> So drink Toddy everybody for pep and energy.[70]

After serving a stint with Chieftain Douglas, he joined the group that formed the Toddy Syndicate and the Victory Tent. Lion soon joined him, and the two sang together for four years,[71] creating the calypso duet style and the calypso drama.

In 1934 Atilla and Lion were sent by merchants in Trinidad to the United States to record for the American Record Company (see chapter 7). This was the first of Atilla's trips to the United States to record and to play in clubs (see chapter 8). On another early trip, he took part in a radio broadcast back home to Trinidad (see chapter 9).

Atilla toured the Caribbean as well. On one of his excursions to Grenada with Beginner and Tiger he got into an imbroglio with the colonial police there. According to Tiger:

> We got in Grenada and had a few drink and Atilla was buying some
> sapodillas by the bar. [It seems Atilla said something about
> Grenadians.] A policeman came up there and tell him he must be

careful, don't speak to people like that here. And Atilla called him an uncivilized policeman! So he arrested Atilla. [Meanwhile,] the ship outside waiting [for] us [before it sailed]! Though we asked to see Maryshow, a big man in Grenada, [the policeman] took us in front the court.

We said [to the magistrate] that we never come back to Grenada. [He] say, "No, Grenada's a nice place. Perhaps if the kaiso good [you] must come back again." [But we told him that we were on our way to America.] Well, he said, "The boys going to America, there's no use detaining them here." And he [then] said, "Go ahead and have a good time." But I never sang in Grenada. We just passing in transit.[72]

The incident was reported in Grenada[73] and in Trinidad:

Trinidad Calypsonian
Haled Before Magistrate
Yesterday Morning.

———

"Attila The Hun"
Released With Caution
For Obscene Language.

———

In Transit To New York To Make
New Phone Records.

Yesterday morning three Trinidad "calypsonians" en route to New York stepped ashore from the "Fort St. George" for a brief look at the city. They were "Attila the Hun," "Tiger" and "Lord Beginner."

They landed in the highest spirits and apparently found Grenada very much to their liking. But their uncontrolled exuberance brought "Attila" into conflict with the law and introduced him to a new experience.

As a result of a scene on the Wharf "Attila" found himself arrested by a police constable and hustled before the Magistrate Mr. C. H. Lucas, there to answer a charge of using obscene language in the public highway.

Mr. Lucas was good enough to expedite the hearing so that the passengers would be able to return to the ship.

"Attila" limped into the dock suffering, it is said, from an injury to his knee in an accident a few days ago.

He pleaded guilty and offered "extenuating circumstances."

The offence was committed, he said while he was under the influence of "First Best," a fine Grenadian liquor to which he was introduced on landing. He was very sorry for what had happened and offered his apologies. It was his first visit to Grenada and he promised to return but gave his word that there would not be a recurrence of that day's unpleasantness.

The Magistrate expressed satisfaction at the attitude he had adopted in court and dismissed him with a caution.

His partners, "Tiger" and "Lord Beginner" also thanked His Worship for treating their pal with such consideration. "Tiger" disclosing their mission to U.S.A. He said they liked Grenada and would one day pay the island a visit. The Magistrate humourously remarked that they would be welcomed, but he hoped they would be quite tame then.

The songsters left York House apparently pleased with the outcome of their Court visit and embarked immediately for the "Fort St. George" which sailed a few minutes later.[74]

Atilla was arrested at least one other time, in Trinidad during the oil field riots of 1937 (see chapter 10). He had composed and sung calypsos favorable to the strike leader, Tubal Uriah "Buzz" Butler, and unfavorable to the British governor, Sir Murchison Fletcher:

Our dear beloved governor
Is behaving like a beast from the wilds of Africa.[75]

Atilla was soon released without being charged.

Atilla was noted for his political songs. As a member of the Labour Party in Trinidad, his calypsos always came down on the side of the common man and against the colonial government. Yet during World War II, his pro-British songs bordered on the obsequious. He also sang obscene calypsos and took a strong stand against the censorship of calypso in the 1930s and 1940s.

Atilla once read an article in the *Trinidad Guardian* that originated in the British *Daily Mail*. The story said that Afro-Trinidadians were attacking white women in Port of Spain's Queen's Park Savannah. The article angered Atilla, who responded with his "Reply to the Daily Mail":

This vicious article and gross slander
Was reproduced from a big English newspaper

Who sent this rotten news out of the colony
Some say 'twas cabled by local authority
Just imagine how these people will twist the truth
To bring our little homeland into disrepute
With them vile denunciations
Condemning us with their lecherous imputations.
The white people who are sending out these false alarms
Came to our Island and we welcomed with open arms
They cause our children many sighs and sobs
For they live here like Princes with the cushy jobs
But like the dog that bites the hand that gives the food
They repay our kindness with ingratitude
Proving by their perversity
That they're devoid of every semblance of decency.[76]

One white American scholar who knew Atilla in the 1950s said that Atilla was one of the original Black Power advocates in Trinidad, even to the point of being antiwhite. His "reply" could be interpreted that way, as could this lyric from "Mixed Marriages":

Some people say when the colour man
Goes and marries a white woman (repeat)
He may get personal gratification
But has made an open confession
That the facts of life he cannot face
And is ashamed of his parents and of his race. . . .

In this world I know there are millions of whites
Who appreciated the coloured man's rights
And have a desire and willingness
To aid him in his pursuit of happiness
A white man would love a Negro to the core
As a brother but not a brother-in-law
So these mixed marriages in my opinion
Are the cause of all racial discrimination.[77]

But Atilla was not antiwhite; he was pro-black, pro-Trinidad, and against oppression in any form. The positive image he fought for was cultural, not racial. Although Executor was of Portuguese descent, Atilla saw in his music some of the best of Afro-Trinidadian culture. There was no racism in Atilla.

One time Tiger told this story about his travels in Barbados with Atilla and Beginner. "We went to get a haircut there in a hotel barber shop. [Now understand], Atilla is just a brown skinned man. You know they . . . would trim Atilla but they . . . wouldn't trim us for sake of our color! In Barbados!! Could you imagine that? They wouldn't trim meself and Beginner, [but] they trim up Atilla. And he giving us fatigue and saying, 'I'm a white man' and all this kind of 'ting."[78]

Atilla was Calypso King seven times, mostly in the 1940s.[79] His calypsos showed a very wide range in subject matter and form, even though, like his mentor Executor, he used only a handful of melodies to express his varied lyrics. Atilla sang on philosophical topics, on women, on social problems, and most especially on politics. "Graf Zeppelin," "Invasion of Britain," "Mixed Marriages," "An Ode to America," "Women Is Not the Weaker Sex," and "Commission's Report" are some of his calypsos. Between 1924 and 1941, sixty-four records were issued under his own name, another thirteen with Lion appeared, and he recorded many more backing other singers.[80]

Atilla was a leader of the calypsonians, and many looked up to him, although Lion once commented in an interview that the other singers were jealous of him.[81] In 1946, Atilla was elected to a seat on the city council and eventually became deputy mayor of Port of Spain.[82] He also served as president general of the Labour party. In 1950, he served as a member of the Legislative Council of the colonial government, where he was part of the opposition members delegation to the governor on constitutional reform in 1950 (fig. 19). He was active in civic affairs as well and served on the Carnival Improvement Committee.

In the 1940s, he and Lion published a songbook of calypsos and thereby helped formalize the earlier tradition of printing broadsides. Later, he published a series of historical sketches of Carnival, calypso, and calypsonians. For years after Atilla's death in Trinidad on February 22, 1962, this document was missing. At one point, a draft was lent to chief minister and historian, Dr. Eric Williams, for his perusal. It was not published until 1983, chiefly due to the efforts of John La Rose, whose editing of Atilla's original manuscript bordered on co-authorship, and Errol Hill.[83]

The Roaring Lion

The Roaring Lion was born Hubert Raphael Charles in Belmont, Port of Spain, in about 1910.[84] Atilla wrote that he was a "slim man of

THE HEMISPHERE

CANADA

Cold War

The theoretical shooting began last week in Exercise Sweetbriar, the joint Canadian-U.S. maneuvers to test North America's defenses against invasion from the Arctic. Across the mile-wide Donjek River, 170 miles south of Dawson, Allied troops fought off a mock invader driving into Canada from Alaska.

It was a brutal battleground. The temperature dipped as low as 52° below zero. Soldiers clad in nearly 25 lbs. of special Arctic clothing, carrying another 34 lbs. of special equipment, crawled through waist-deep snow, over hummocks of frozen muskeg. For hundreds of miles on every side stretched trackless pine forests and mountains. Said one corporal: "Anybody who'd invade this Godforsaken place is just plain damn wacky."

Candles Spiked. The corporal's opinion was shared by 5,000-odd army and air force personnel and 22 newspaper correspondents taking part in the Sweetbriar maneuver. In Arctic warfare, everything was different and difficult. Even breathing required a careful technique; a deep breath of the icy air could nip the lungs. Food was another problem; to maintain body warmth an Arctic fighting man had to eat almost twice as many calories as an ordinary soldier. The tallow candles issued to Canadian troops were spiked with food concentrates and could be eaten if rations failed to arrive.

The maneuver was centered around the Alaska Highway, the one road in the Northwest by which an aggressor force or a defending Allied army could travel. At night, troops had to leave the road to bivouac in the bush in their nylon tents and down-filled sleeping bags. But most of the transport was roadbound, an easy target for air attack.

Exercise Sweetbriar was a test to determine whether, in spite of all the known difficulties, men & machines could fight a war in the Arctic. A Canadian combat team was sent north from Whitehorse in the Yukon. An "aggressor force" of U.S. troops from the Alaska Command headed south. Later, a U.S. combat team, brought in from Colorado, went up the highway to reinforce the Canadian defenders. Referees ordered attacks, withdrawals and flanking movements and directed operations of U.S. and Canadian aircraft.

Warfare Feasible. By the end of the first week, Army experts were able to draw a few conclusions. The men were bearing up well under the North's rigors. Frostbite and colds took their expected toll. But enough soldiers remained in action to prove that warfare on a fairly large scale was feasible in the Arctic. Although the men could take it, some of the machines could not. The so-called all-weather fighter planes—U.S. F-80s and Canadian Vampires—functioned well

U.S. JET PLANES IN THE YUKON
Twice as many calories, and candles too.

enough mechanically but were frequently grounded by Arctic snow flurries and overcast. The U.S. Army's snow vehicle, the Weasel, was a dismaying failure; of 100 brand-new Weasels put into action, nearly half broke down in the first five days. The Canadian Army's counterpart, the Penguin, stood up better but was too bulky to maneuver among the pines off the road. Before Sweetbriar was half over, observers were recommending that the Allied armies study the use of Arctic-conditioned dogs, mules and horses for transport.

ATTILA THE HUN
Too much malnutrition.

Henry Wallace

TRINIDAD

Mastersinger

One of the most remarkable men in Trinidad is a thin, leathery mulatto known as Attila the Hun. Born in Port-of-Spain 58 years ago of a Venezuelan father and a West Indian mother, he claims to have been singing calypso songs for half a century—long before they took it out of the backyard slums and put it on Frederick Street." His Rover Calypso Tent, made of sheet iron and boards on Frederick Street, the town's main street, is the island's calypso center.

A master of satire and quick wit, Attila has made the calypso, often called Trinidad's "living newspaper," a potent force in local politics. Under his real name, Raymond Quevedo, he has been elected on the Labor Party ticket to Port-of-Spain's city council.

Last week, with the annual pre-Lenten carnival at hand, Attila the Hun journeyed to Port-of-Spain's Mucurapo Stadium to compete with other island troubadours for the unofficial title of Trinidad's 1950 calypso king. A crowd of 3,000 sweating Trinidadians—black, white and East Indian—sat jampacked under the glaring lights. A steel band, hammering biscuit tins, old oil cans and brake drums, made the place hotter with ear-splitting overtures. Then judges were picked from the audience, and the calypsonians started in. Besides Attila there were old mastersingers with such names as the Roaring Lion, Growling Tiger, Mighty Dictator, Small Island Pride and the Blind Sensation.

Politics and sex were the topical, tropical themes. The audience shrieked, howled,

TIME, FEBRUARY 27, 1950

35

19 * Port of Spain councilman Raymond Quevedo, also known as calypsonian Atilla the Hun, featured in *Time* magazine, February 27, 1950. Text copyright 1950 by *Time,* Inc., reprinted by permission; photo of "U.S. Jet Planes in the Yukon" reprinted by permission of AP/Wide World Photos.

African descent";[85] however, Lion told Patricia Gorman, an American writer, that his father was a French trader who settled in Trinidad with a woman who was of Afro–East Indian descent.[86] Lion said that his mother had been a maid for a wealthy Indian family but died shortly after he was born. He had no brothers or sisters and was raised by his mother's employers. Lion told Gorman that he entered school at age ten and attended for seven years, concentrating on music courses. He then quit and apprenticed himself to a pipe fitter, earning twelve dollars a week and singing calypsos he made up while he worked.

Around 1929, at age nineteen, Lion first sang in a small tent in Bedford Lane, Belmont. A pal mentioned to the master of ceremonies that Lion could sing, and so he was called on stage. He wanted to sing his song "Short Dresses," but he could not remember the lyrics. His improvised song proved very popular with the crowd, and he received a job for the season, earning from three to five dollars a night, a princely sum. He supplemented his calypso income by selling ices from a street cart.[87] He also sang in a gambling hall called the Grange.[88]

In the early 1930s, he joined Atilla.[89] The latter wrote that their relationship "was one of the most important in the history of kaiso and marked the erection of several milestones in the art."[90] Together, they created the calypso duet and the calypso drama. In 1934, they sailed to New York to record for the American Record Company and to perform in nightclubs and on the radio.

Lion seems to fit the mold of the calypso singer (fig. 20). An impeccable dresser, he was trailed by a "pack of lionesses" in his younger days and was considered a prima donna (Atilla's phrase) who had no doubts about his skills. In a field populated by characters full of braggadocio, Lion is the master of hyperbole, a veritable Jelly Roll Morton of calypso.

Yet in some ways, he differs from the image seen by his audiences. For example, he saved his money, telling Gorman

A man have a right to divide his money in three. For this reason: One part you should clothe yourself with, always look presentable, and that is because the first impression is the first impression. The second part, you eat what you want, drink what you want, enjoy yourself as you like. The third part is that which you save for the future.

Now the third part that you have saved—you should always consider that one-fourth of that will be thrown away to evil people. People who will ask you to lend them something and never pay it back. And another quarter of the remainder will go to worthy causes, people who are really in need. The remaining half takes care of you.[91]

20 ✳ The Roaring Lion, 1936. Courtesy of the Roaring Lion.

Lion feels that calypso has a French origin. Perhaps as a tribute to this belief, he changed his name from Hubert Raphael Charles to Raphael De Leon early in his career. He always seems to carry a wooden cane with a carved lion's head. He dresses in three-piece suits and has been described by Atilla as "the Beau Brummel of the kaiso ring."[92]

Lion was the first foreigner's calypsonian. He astutely curried the favor and adulation of whites (especially scholars), the rich, and the influential. In Trinidad, he was the first calypsonian to play for the country club set.[93] In the 1940s and 1950s, he played for soldiers, tourists, and expatriates. Yet, as much as any other calypsonian of his generation, he also infused his songs with Trinidad-styled African religious music, especially Shango ritual songs.

By 1945 Lion had reached the peak of his career.[94] He was probably the most widely known calypsonian of the late 1930s and early 1940s, both at home and abroad, with the possible exception of the Lord Invader (fig. 21). "Ugly Woman"—a song he claimed as his own, a claim supported by Atilla—was sung by Sir Lancelot in the American film *Happy Go Lucky* (which starred Mary Martin, Dick Powell, and Rudy Vallee). Lion had been to New York many times and had played for tourist boats in the Caribbean. At one time he owned a calypso club in San Fernando, Trinidad. On his 1945 trip to New York he "doubled" in two clubs, performing at the Village Vanguard in Greenwich Village from 10:00 to 11:00 P.M. and at a midtown club, the Blue Angel, from midnight until 12:30. On this trip to the United States, probably when his contract was up in October, he toured military bases. His place at the Village Vanguard was filled by Harry Belafonte.

Lion brought showmanship to calypso. He introduced new melodies to the basic kit of ten or twelve tunes that Executor once told Atilla were all the melodies used in calypso. Lion liked American popular entertainers, especially the Mills Brothers and Bing Crosby, whose vocal stylings he emulated. His voice has a rich, Afro-Creole vibrato and slight rasp, and "he used to lash people with it."[95] Unlike most calypsonians, he reads music, having once played the clarinet.

Because of these innovations and because he championed foreigners and their ways, Lion has remained controversial. Of his style, Tiger said, "I told him once that he was introducing a very dangerous trend to the calypso world, that sooner or later we're going to lose the value of the calypso or the outside world will take it away from us [by

21 * Lord Invader, circa 1953. Photo by David Jackson. Photo ref. FP904 (6914), The Folkways Collection, Smithsonian Institution.

our] interfering on the songs of America. [But] they [Lion's songs] were novelties and well received. It has gone that way now."[96]

Lion issued ninety-five record sides between 1934 and 1941, more than the sixty-nine of Atilla, his nearest rival in recorded vocal calypso before World War II. After the war, Lion sailed to England, where he joined Beginner and Kitchener for a few years.

Returning to Trinidad in the 1950s, Lion opened the "first true, true calypso institute."[97] Over the next decade his popularity continued as he performed and recorded in Trinidad, England, and in the United States.[98]

The Growling Tiger

The Growling Tiger (Neville Marcano) was born and grew up in Siparia, south Trinidad. He recalled,

> As a boy I used to go about singing from American records all the time. Gene Austin. Freddy Rose. Ross Columbo. Guy Lombardo. Chick Bullock. Rudy Vallee. "Blue Heaven." "Under the Texas Moon." "Tell Me Where Can You Be?" I never sang calypso. People liked to hear me sing. I'd go around to people's doors and sing, "I'm Like a Butterfly That's Caught in the Rain." But not the calypso.[99]

In fact, young Marcano did not like calypso at all and did not care to spend any money on an outing to a tent.

When he was fourteen years of age he took up boxing, calling himself Siparia Tiger and later San Fernando Tiger. In 1929 he defeated Kid Ram to become the flyweight champion of Trinidad.[100]

As a young man he worked in an aerated-water factory, where he became superintendent.[101] Later, he worked in a sugar factory as a pan boiler. These jobs were not steady, so "in 1934 myself and two pals went up from San Fernando to Carapichaima in search of employment. There was a bamboo calypso tent erected there with bamboo seats. Destroyer, a fellow named Puzzler, and another named Inventor were there. I listened to them."[102] Lion remembers this about one of Tiger's early tent performances at the Palace Cinema, in San Fernando: "We were waiting to go back stage when three very popular calypso fans—Pelham, tailor; a shoemaker whose nickname was 'Time' and Neville Marcano—approached us. The first two introduced Neville to us. Neville said he was interested in singing calypsos, and suggested he be allowed to sing one that evening on stage and we agreed. His performance was well received."[103]

Tiger says that in a 1935 performance, in the South, he sang one of Beginner's songs, "Dorothy, One Morning." The crowd was pleased, as was a merchant who had a dry goods and clothing store. He showed Tiger a newspaper that mentioned the trip to New York that Atilla and Lion were going to take to record calypsos. The merchant, a Mr. Mentor, asked why Tiger was not in Port of Spain, singing in a tent. He showed Tiger another headline in the paper, "Water Scheme Laborers Strike for More Pay."[104] He asked Tiger if he could make up a song about the strike, and Tiger replied that he would. Mentor, now his patron, saw to it that Tiger had food to eat and told him to go write the song. After only an hour and a half he had finished, much to Mentor's astonishment. He asked if Tiger could sing it in a tent that night, and Tiger said that he could. A few months later he made up another song on the tragic death of A. A. Cipriani's brother, Mikey, in an airplane accident. Tiger entered a contest for the best song on the event, singing against Lion, Atilla, Douglas, Executor, Black Prince, and Beginner. Because he had been a boxer, he was not afraid of the crowd, but he was not used to singing with an orchestra, and the crowd became restless as Tiger sang without a microphone. He needed a second chance to put his song over. Another calypsonian won the contest, but Tiger had made a strong showing. At a similar competition a month later, Tiger won against the same heavy talent, with the same song, "The Ingeniousness of Man."

In 1935 he sang with the Salada Millionaires on Nelson Street, near where he lives today. During that tent season he sang one of the all-time great Depression calypsos, "Money Is King." Said Atilla: "He came, he sang, and he conquered."[105]

Also in 1935, Eduardo Sa Gomes sent Tiger to New York to record (fig. 22). The trip was harrowing, as the *Fort St. George* ran into a storm.[106] Arriving finally in New York, Tiger says that the temperature was below zero. He, Atilla, and Beginner did not have the proper papers and had to go to Ellis Island for clearance. The American immigration officials thought that Tiger was trying to enter the country illegally as a boxer because his passport stated his occupation as pugilist, not calypsonian. So, Tiger, along with Atilla and Beginner, gave the officials a concert "on the spot," but it didn't help. Tiger and the others had to stay at Ellis Island for three weeks.

Meanwhile, the calypsonians' official sponsors, Decca Records, sorted things out. The singers eventually were released to Decca on a fifty thousand dollar bond. Gerald Clark, a Trinidadian-born orchestra leader who had lived in New York since 1928, was their guardian, so they stayed with him in Brooklyn.

In New York, Tiger recorded "Money Is King" and six other titles under his own name, nine with Beginner and Atilla as the Keskidee Trio, and several songs as vocal backup to the other two. These represent some of the finest classic calypsos ever put on record. They include a shango ("Shango"),[107] a calinda ("Congo Bara"), a parody of a Shouter's song ("Go Down in the Valley"),[108] and a leggo as the Keskidee Trio ("Marian Le' Go Me Man"). He recorded "Marabella Wedding," "Mannie Dookie" (a song about a barefooted, world-class Trinidadian runner), and "Sadu Man" (about an East Indian Hindu mystic).

The following year, Tiger recorded "The Gold in Africa" (a song about Italy's invasion of Ethiopia), "Yaraba Shango," "The Rats" (about political corruption), "Hell Yard and George Street Conflict," "Workers Appeal," "They Couldn't Stop the Masquerade," "The Whe Whe Banker Wedding,"[109] and "The Mysterious Tunapuna Woman."

In 1937 Tiger recorded in Trinidad for Bluebird, a subsidiary of RCA Victor. These songs include, "Civil War in Spain," "Down the

22 ✳ Touched-up photograph of calypsonians about to leave for performances in New York City. Left to right: Beginner, Atilla, Tiger. Courtesy of the *Trinidad Guardian*.

Road" (about wayward children), "Let Them Fight for Ten Thousand Years" (a neutralist position at the opening of World War II), and "In My Own Native Land" (a bongo).

Altogether between 1935 and 1945, Tiger recorded forty-six titles under his own name, far fewer than Atilla, Lion, Radio, or Houdini. Like Executor's songs, nearly every one is a gem, but unlike Executor, there is no emphasis on standard English, as Tiger moved among standard English, English Creole, and French Creole.

While in New York, Tiger sang in clubs and on the radio. He sang extensively in the Caribbean, going as far as Guyana. He had many memorable experiences, including a fire on board one vessel and a barroom brawl when some people tried to jump him and steal his money. In addition, there was Atilla's problem with obscenity in Grenada.

By 1939, Tiger was at the top of his form when he won the first generally recognized national calypso competition with "Try and Join a Labor Union."

In 1945, Tiger arrived by steamer in Florida on his way to New York to record, planning to take the train the rest of the way with only a sandwich to eat. On the second day, an African-American GI gave him an orange, the only favor he received on the segregated train. On this trip, Tiger recorded and played a club in Harlem, but he did not like the big city, so he returned to Trinidad, where his career has continued through the 1980s as a singer and as a composer of calypsos for other performers.

Perhaps Tiger's calypsos best signify human issues, as separate from strictly the colonial concerns. In a way, Tiger is an absolutely modern calypsonian. Tiger is a master of both English Creole and of French Creole. There are no high-flown anglicisms in Tiger as in the work of Executor, Atilla, and Lion. There is no playing up to the Crown in Tiger. Tiger is Trinidad and more: Tiger gives us English Creole at its highest level. Tiger's songs render the heartfelt consciousness of the people. Tiger uses his calypso more consistently than the others to bring home the open wounds of colonialism. It is Tiger, therefore, who is a harbinger of the re-afrocreolization that would dominate calypso in the second half of the twentieth century.

7 ✳ Calypso
on Record

'dis is di Growler!
Recording for di Decca!

Growler's tag on many of his recordings

WHEN calypso was recorded on phonograph rec-
ords, a fundamental change took place in the nature of this Carnival
music. Records are events, pieces of frozen history.[1] They take a
chunk out of an event and present it to another time and place. These
pieces may be stored and recalled in their original form ad infinitum.

Frozen History

Before recordings were made, calypso was a traditional music. Oral
tradition, in the folkloristic sense, can only be transmitted through
personal contact. Tradition is belief; it is a mental image of the past,
not an actual part of the past. As a remembrance of the past in the
present, tradition is always made to fit the times. In this way,
traditional Carnival music is functional and meaningful in the context
of live performance. Tradition lives; it also changes, although people
think that it is constant. But in that same folkloristic sense, once a
tradition is documented in some way, once it is recorded, it is no
longer tradition.

Contrast these ideas about tradition with mechanical recordings.

Unlike tradition, recordings endure just as recorded. Because they are absolutely true to the era in which they were made, phonograph records become dated, they go out of style, they need not fit a new era. Furthermore, a phonograph record of a calypso may be played and enjoyed by someone who knows nothing about the original context: The listener may know nothing about Trinidad, nothing about Carnival, nothing about calypso. Of course, that does not detract from the enjoyment a foreign listener may get from the recorded music; it simply means that the experience of listening to a record is not the same as being present at a live performance.

Until calypsos were put on phonograph records in 1912, each time a calypso was heard, it was sung by a calypsonian in front of an audience of peers within earshot and within view of the singer. Perhaps some of the singers wrote down their lyrics as a mnemonic device, but the primary way to remember the song was by singing it; hence, the early calypso tents were called rehearsals and were a time for the chantwell to teach both himself and his chorus of masqueraders the lyrics and the melody of the song.

Perhaps the greatest effect of recording on the development of calypso, then, was in the separation of the performer and his audience from the performance. Once a record was produced and thousands of copies made, the singer could hear the result as if he were an audience. The audience was no longer bounded by a culture of knowing peers: anyone, anywhere a record player could be found, could hear that record. For the first time, calypso spread beyond the constraints of live performance, beyond Trinidad and the southern Caribbean, to New York, to London, to West Africa, and to the rest of the world. The record-buying public in these places came to influence the course calypso would take, since by the 1940s the singers no longer catered exclusively to local interests but incorporated lyrical themes, melodies, and instrumentation from other peoples in other lands.

A live calypso performance was normally longer than a three-minute phonograph record. But length of performance is not a good indicator of a lavway sung in its natural state, because the songs could be continuously performed as the street bands masqueraded throughout the town, with one song blending into another. This phenomenon—that is, the lack of a "beginning" and an "end" to many outdoor calypsos—continues today and has never been studied. Emory Cook recorded swatches of road marches in the 1950s for his Cook label and in one instance most of a twenty-minute side is given over to one song. In Carriacou, Grenada, in 1970, I taped many road marches that seemed to go on forever; I would generally stop recording when I came to the end of a forty-five-minute tape.

The tent calypsos that developed as a result of the innovations of Walter "Railway" Douglas and others were meant to be heard and contemplated, not felt, as was the case with the lavways and calindas. Some tent calypsos were stories or ballads with a beginning, a middle, and an end. Unfortunately, we do not have an exact idea of how long tent calypsos lasted, except for a few intriguing suggestions. Once, Douglas was said to have sung a single ballad for more than an hour at a stretch, although five or six minutes is more likely the average length of a tent calypso.

When calypsos were recorded on 78-rpm records, their length had to be cut to conform to the medium. The result of this three-minute limit on calypso was profound: songs in tents, on printed texts (copies), in theater performances, and in club performances all came under the influence of the phonograph record. Ideas once expressed in a tent calypso, in a song of five or six minutes, now had to be expressed in three or three and a half minutes on the record.

This chapter, then, focuses on the history of recorded calypso until about 1950.

The First Calypso on Record

Sometime in early May 1910, Walter Stevens and his wife sailed up the South American coast and put in at Trinidad. He was the manager of the foreign department for Thomas Edison's National Phonograph Company. Edison cylinder records had been made by his department in Mexico, Puerto Rico, Cuba, and in several South American countries. Stevens was in Trinidad completing a three-month tour of Latin America with other officials from the company, mixing business with pleasure. Stevens wrote that "on our return trip we stopped at the island of Trinidad, a possession of Great Britain, with a population of about 350,000 inhabitants. The island is chiefly noted for its asphalt lake. . . . From a business point of view South America presents an unlimited field for the sale of American products."[2] But the National Phonograph Company did not make records in Trinidad, nor anywhere in the English-speaking Caribbean. The first records of Trin-

idadian music were made in New York.[3]

Modern immigration to the United States from the West Indies began in the 1910s, during World War I. In 1919, after the war ended, some West Indians who had fought with the Allies in the British West India Regiment settled in New York rather than return to the Caribbean. Other immigrants came directly from the islands. By 1930, at least one-quarter of Harlem's black population was West Indian.[4] At the beginning of this period, when a definable West Indian population in New York took shape, the first Trinidadians made records.

In 1912 Lovey's band, then the most respected string band in Trinidad, came to New York to make phonograph records (fig. 23). Lovey—George Bailey was his given name—recorded at least five sides for Columbia and eight for Victor.[5] All of Lovey's recordings were instrumentals, and most carried Spanish titles: "Mango Vert," "Manuelita," "Cavel Blanco," "666 Trinidad Paseo," and two especially interesting titles, "Mary Jane (Mari-Juana)" and "Oil Fields— Trinidad Paseo" (fig. 24).

The band Lovey brought to New York had twelve musicians. He was a schooled musician, as were most bandleaders in Trinidad. His group played for elite dances in Trinidad, with the governor sometimes in attendance. During Carnival, he played for fancy masquerade balls. There is no evidence that this band played in calypso tents or fronted a masquerade band on the streets during Carnival, although band members probably participated in Carnival in one fashion or another.

No doubt Lovey's band came to New York to record because merchants in Trinidad felt they could market his records (fig. 25). Trinidadians for some time had been exposed to the "gramophone," as it was known in the British world. Gramophones played disc records, not the cylinder records that Edison originally marketed (fig. 26). The first people who could afford the discs must have been middle-class or elite Trinidadians. As late as the 1930s, record players were a novel sight for many Trinidadians, and merchants sometimes set up a windup phonograph outside their shops to attract passersby.

Trinidad supported an occasional visiting opera and middling traveling shows. The first record-buying public probably consisted of the same elite and middle-class people who would attend these

DISCOS DOBLES PARA TRINIDAD

Discos Dobles Grabados para la Isla de Trinidad

(Double-faced Records made specially for Trinidad)

Número	Discos de 25 c/m.	
63790	666—*Pasillo* (Lovey)	Lovey's Mixed Band
	Campos Petrolíferos—*Pasillo* (Schneider)	Lovey's Mixed Band
63791	La Liebre—*Spanish Waltz* (Sucre)	Lovey's Mixed Band
	Y cómo le va—*Tango* (Valverde)	Lovey's Mixed Band
63792	Manuelita—*Spanish Waltz* (Gómez)	Lovey's Mixed Band
	Mari-Juana—*Pasillo* (Lovey)	Lovey's Mixed Band
63793	Trinidad Paseo (Lovey)	Lovey's Mixed Band
	Sara—*Pasillo* (Lovey)	Lovey's Mixed Band
67028	Slow Brakes—*Trinidad Paseo* (Jerry)	Belasco's Band
	Eugenio—*Venezuelan Waltz* (Gómez)	Belasco's Band
67029	Po'me One—*Trinidad Paseo* (J. Whiterose)	Belasco's Band
	Siempre invicto—*Venezuelan Waltz* (Gómez)	Belasco's Band

DISCOS DOBLES VENEZOLANOS

Discos Dobles Grabados para la República de Venezuela

Discos de 25 c/m.

63790	666—*Pasillo* (Lovey)	Banda Mixta Lovey
	Campos Petrolíferos—*Pasillo* (Schneider)	Banda Mixta Lovey
63791	La Liebre—*Vals español* (Sucre)	Banda Mixta Lovey
	Y cómo le va—*Tango* (Valverde)	Banda Mixta Lovey
63792	Manuelita—*Vals español* (Gómez)	Banda Mixta Lovey
	Mari-Juana—*Pasillo* (Lovey)	Banda Mixta Lovey
63793	Sara—*Pasillo* (Lovey)	Banda Mixta Lovey
	Paseo de Trinidad (Lovey)	Banda Mixta Lovey
67028	Eugenio—*Vals Venezolano* (Gómez)	Banda Belasco, Trinidad
	Slow Brakes—*Paseo de Trinidad* (Jerry)	Banda Belasco, Trinidad
67029	Siempre invicto—*Vals Venezolano* (Gómez)	Banda Belasco, Trinidad
	Po'me One—*Paseo de Trinidad* (J. Whiterose)	Banda Belasco, Trinidad

Above: 23 ✳ Lovey's String Band, circa 1912. Courtesy of Steven Smolian and Richard K. Spottswood. *Left:* 24 ✳ Victor advertising flyer for the Spanish-speaking record market, 1910s. Photo courtesy of Richard K. Spottswood.

Muir, Marshall & Co

Secure Your

MUSIC

For The

Victory Carnival.

Lovey's Records.

The Latest and Best
IN
The Waltz and The Paseo.

Double Sides—Price 75c.

Left: **25** ✳ Advertisement in the *Trinidad Guardian,* February 23, 1919.

Below: **26** ✳ Advertisement for gramophone records by Salvatori, Scott & Co.

THE TRINIDAD GUARDIAN, SUNDAY, MARCH 9, 1919.

Immense Reductions In Gramophones & Records.

RECORDS, from 12c. each.

Clear out the entire stock of Gramophones and Records, says the Chief!!

In order to carry out these instructions we have reduced every Gramophone and Record in the place to about half their worth and will be offering them at these greatly reduced prices from MONDAY, 10th instant, in our Centre Store. Come and see them. You will be sure to agree that they are REAL BARGAINS.

Salvatori, Scott & Co., CENTRE STORE.

UGENE BOISSIERE & CO.

Have just received and offer for sale—

1. Quality Milled Patna Rice.

ns Quality Pickled Salmon in tierces.

Singuineau Bros.
PROVISION MERCHANTS,
7 BROADWAY.

Trinidad & Tobago Discharged
Soldiers' Central Authority.

THE STANDARD

LIFE ASSURANCE COMPANY
1825.

THE STANDARD LIFE ASSURANCE COMPANY was established at Edinburgh, in 1825, was incorporated by special Act of Parliament in 1832. It is one of the largest of the Insurance Companies in Great Britain.

Revenue · · · £1,580,000

foreign performances. They bought a variety of records, including the same sort of classical and popular discs that the Americans and the British purchased.

The new records by Lovey's band were a welcome supplement to those already owned by Trinidadians. It is important to understand that it was—and still is—a rare Trinidadian whose record collection consisted exclusively of calypsos. Calypso, as a Carnival music, has always been seasonal. It was not the custom to listen to calypso year-round. Calypso never was the most popular music in Trinidad: It has always been an occasional music, not an incidental music. Records made it more likely for some Trinidadians to enjoy calypso the year round. In a sense, records turned a folk music into a popular music.

Two years after Lovey's band recorded in New York, Trinidad was poised for its first local recordings. "His Master's Voice: Victor Recorders in Our Midst" screamed the headline in the *Port of Spain Gazette,* as Victor's recording engineers set up shop in Trinidad to record local music.[6] At this Victor session in 1914, Julian Whiterose recorded the first vocal calypso. At the same date, Victor recorded calindas sung by Jules Sims and piano solos by Lionel Belasco. East Indian music was also recorded. Many of these discs were later advertised in the *Port of Spain Gazette* and in the *Trinidad Guardian:* "New Creole Victor Records, No Home in Trinidad should be without a Set," stated the *Gazette* during Carnival 1915.[7] The records could be purchased from Smith Brothers & Co., in the boot department. H. Strong's Piano Warehouse at 21 Frederick Street advertised "Exclusive Victor records of Carnival Music"[8] (fig. 27). Lionel Belasco's records were recommended in advertisements:

1–BELASCO'S RECORDS ARE BEST
2–EVERY INSTRUMENT CAN BE HEARD
3–NO BLURRED EFFECTS
4–ABSOLUTE ABSENCE OF SURFACE NOISE[9]

Among Whiterose's first discs was the calinda "Bayonet Charge by the Laws of the Iron Duke," a road march that dates from the Boer War; the Patois calypso "Belle Marie Coolie"; and "Iron Duke in the Land." In the *Guardian,* appeals to buy calypsos shared space with ads for gramophones and for recordings of classical music.

In 1914, the Columbia Graphaphone Company recorded Lovey in

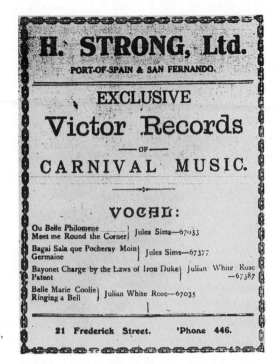

27 * Advertisement for Victor Records, H. Strong, Ltd., *Trinidad Guardian*, February 28, 1919.

Trinidad in what turned out to be his last recording session. He died sometime in the 1920s. Lovey's place in recording history was taken by Lionel Belasco, whose first forty-one issued sides were cut in Trinidad during Victor's 1915 field expedition. Belasco would go on to lead bands and orchestras that would record more than any other Trinidadian group of the era.[10]

In late August 1915, Belasco sailed for New York. At the time, he was manager and promoter for the London Electric Theatre, a British company that owned many theaters in the West Indies, where it staged shows and ran silent movies.[11] Belasco may have been looking for talent in New York, but while there he recorded his first piano solos. One of his unissued masters for Victor was "Maple Leaf Rag," composed by the great American ragtime composer Scott Joplin. Belasco also recorded tangos, waltzes, one-steps, and paseos. The latter term seems to have encompassed lavways and single-tone calypsos.

Over the next twenty-five years, Belasco recorded many times in New York. In 1916, he recorded with a string band, as he did again in 1918, 1919, 1920, and 1922. String-band music had been popular in

Trinidad since the 1890s, and Belasco was involved in the spread of this Venezuelan instrumentation. The first string bands to be recorded consisted of piano, violin, guitar, cuatro, and sometimes chac chac, bottle and spoon, flute, or clarinet.

In 1923 Belasco recorded with the Guyanese vaudevillian Phil Madison (fig. 28), who had been sent to New York to record by a Port of Spain piano dealer, H. Strong Ltd.[12] Most of the songs they recorded are best described as stage tunes and not calypsos, but Madison's first title was the calypso "Sly Mongoose."[13] The second, "Te-Le-Le," was a leggo. Belasco was now the most important entrepreneur of West Indian music in New York, a position he held for about a decade.

Belasco's friend Walter Merrick was also leader of a string band in this period. Merrick was born in St. Vincent and settled with his family in Trinidad while a small child. Merrick's first records, cut in late April 1921, were piano solos labeled as "Trinidad Carnival Paseos." These recordings were mostly lavways but also included one Dame Lorraine song, a "Valse Venezolano," a "Grenada Paseo," and a "Valse Creole." In 1921, Merrick recorded with the West Indian vaudevillian Johnny Walker[14] (fig. 29). Although none of these records survive, the ledger entries are interesting.[15] There is a "Trinidad Kalendar," a song we know as a lavway called "Argos Papers" ("latest telegram; Germany surrender under the British Commander"), a record described as a "Shouters Meeting" (an Afro-Christian sect in Trinidad), a "Trinidad Ragtime Song," a "Trinidad Carnival Calypso," and "Alexander's Jazz Band."

From 1925 through the end of 1926, Merrick recorded waltzes, paseos, and Mentor's "Who You Voting For? Cipriani." That song was a revision of the then well-known "Ambakaila," an obscene road march composed by Cat the Beginner.[16] Mentor's new lyrics were written as a campaign song to assist A. A. Cipriani in his successful attempt to win a Labour party seat in the island's first popularly elected Legislative Council in 1923. Mentor's song was sung by Charles Abdullah and credited to Merrick. After the 1926 recording session, although he avocationally remained interested in calypso, Merrick turned his career to medicine. He earned his medical degree, received postgraduate training in psychiatry, and became a neuropsychiatrist and director of the Department of Physical Medicine at Harlem Hospital in New York City.

28 * Vaudevillian Phil
Madison, 1930s.
Courtesy of the Roaring
Lion.

During this period, both Belasco and Merrick cut piano rolls for QRS, the largest piano-roll and player-piano company in the United States. Belasco's piano rolls were all calypsos—"Trinidad Carnival," "Tay-Lay-Lay," "Sly-Mon-Goose," "Bajan Girl," and "Buddy Abraham." Merrick cut "Sweet Elaine" (a calypso), "Harlem Baby," "Pas Mande" (a calypso), "Caribbean Honeymoon" (a "valse creole"), "Lignum Vitae" (an obscene stage song), and "Married to You" (a calypso). Jack Celestain, a band leader and pianist who backed Sam Manning on some records, also made a few piano rolls in this period. One of the most interesting piano rolls was the "Black Star Line," cut by Sid Laney in 1924. The song refers to a steamship company owned by the Jamaican-born Marcus Garvey, the first important black nationalist and a resident of New York in the early 1920s.

In 1924, Manning began his recording career with Cat the Beginner's lavway "Amba Cay La'" (Under the House), but with label credits going to Manning. Manning was a stage performer, actor, and writer. He recorded for Okeh, Columbia, Brunswick, and the American Record Company in the 1920s and early 1930s and appeared in musical reviews and plays. Manning's records, like those of Madison

29 ✳ Victor Records advertising supplement for calypsos, March 1922. Photo courtesy of Richard K. Spottswood; Victor trademark courtesy of BMG Music.

and Walker, ran from calypsos and vaudeville songs to spoken dialogues and blues. On his earliest records, he is accompanied by Palmer's Orchestra, a Trinidadian band similar to Lovey's, Belasco's, or Monrose's bands of the 1910s and 1920s. Manning's later records are accompanied by the Cole Mentor group, a small jazz band.

The competition between West Indians and black Americans was parodied by Manning in a set of comic records he made in the 1920s for Brunswick. "The American Woman and West Indian Man," for example, is full of outrageous stereotypes:

Man: "Say now look here American woman . . ."

Woman: "What is it now?"

Man: "Have you understand you flirting with the graveyard when you fool with a country man. I love you like I love no one. I give you all my dough."

Woman: "Got a right to!"

Man: "Fool with me you sure got cut. Then is 'Sing Sing' jail I'll go."

Woman: "Oh, oh, hold them dice brother, hold them dice. You going to 'Sing Sing' jail alright enough. That is if there is anything left of you when I get through with you. And you gonna shoot somebody—heh!"

Man: "That's what I said."

Woman: "Ha! Well, brother, if you just as much point a pistol at this pretty yellow woman you just as well give your heart to the Lord because your hips are gonna belong to me."

Man: "Me hips? Me hips? Woman, do you know you is talking under my clothes?"

Woman: "Yes, and that ain't all. I'll be standing over your cold carcass if you try to execute any of them cruel threats!"

Man: "Calm yourself American woman, I say be-calm yourself!"

Woman: "Calm myself nothing! I told you I was gonna quit and I had no right marrying you in the first place because you West Indian men are too treacherous."[17]

Except for the early discs cut by Whiterose and Sims in Trinidad in 1914, all calypsos on record to this point were made by vaudevillians, not tent-seasoned calypsonians. Most calypsos recorded between 1912 and 1927 were instrumentals in this first phase of recorded West Indian music.

Houdini's First Records

With the records made by Wilmoth Houdini on August 1, 1927, a second phase of recorded calypso began. On that date Houdini recorded for the Victor Company in New York. Frederick Wilmoth Hendricks[18]—Houdini—had played mas' with the African Million-aires masquerade band in Trinidad in 1919, and he had sung in calypso tents. A seaman by trade, he migrated to New York sometime in the late 1920s.

Houdini's first recordings were backed by Cyril Monrose on violin, Lionel Belasco on piano, Gerald Clark on guitar, and an unknown cuatro player. Today, calypso devotees consider this group to be among the best Creole string bands to make records. In this first set, Houdini cut three songs labeled paseo: "Caroline," "Good Night Ladies and Gents," and the Inventor's World War I lavway, "Run You Run." Houdini recorded again in July 1928; and in March 1929 he sang his first song making fun of Executor, "Executor Doomed to Die."

Houdini returned to Trinidad on at least one occasion during this time and visited the tents. He remembered or wrote down songs he had heard and added verses of his own. His recordings in 1931, for the American Record Company, are backed by a full New Orleans–style jazz band (Gerald Clark's Night Owls). In 1932, Houdini returned to the string band configuration to record songs labeled rumba, waltz, pasillo, and carol.

Houdini's songs covered the range of Trinidad music. Although he is credited on the record label as composing most of the songs he recorded and although he copyrighted many of them, he utilized traditional tunes and borrowed the lyrics of others, sometimes adding his own twist. This was resented by Trinidad-based singers, whose standard practice was to attribute any calypso to the person who sang it in the tents, regardless of whether that person composed the song:

> But since Houdini was not capable of producing (e.g., writing) songs suitable enough for such a venture . . . he decided to come to Trinidad every carnival season, and go around selecting what he thought was just the right songs for his business. When they came upon a good song, Mr. Smart[19] wrote the melody, and Houdini would get the words.
>
> In those days no one here [in Trinidad] knew anything about copyright. So [Smart] would pretend to like the song and kindly ask the owner for a copy. Some drinks would pass, and the song copy would be handed over in good faith. Once he got it, he went back and registered the songs on his name.[20]

Houdini, possibly through his connection with Belasco, was in the position to copyright songs, and the true composers were not. Houdini and Belasco's deceits followed the rule of the day in Tin Pan Alley, the name given to a section of Midtown Manhattan where songwriters gathered. For example, New Orleans jazz pianist, band leader, and composer Clarence Williams reputedly borrowed songs from jazz and blues composers (Williams and Houdini are listed as co-authors on many songs); the rural musician A. P. Carter copyrighted songs from country singers; and Ralph Peer, a record company artist and repertory pioneer, reputedly had taken from everyone. Whatever the circumstances of Houdini's copyrighting efforts, it was his ground-breaking recordings that paved the way for other, more traditional singers.

Gerald Clark, sometimes in concert with his friend Lionel Belasco, seems to have been partly responsible for establishing Houdini as the most prolific tent calypsonian to record. Clark, who returned home to Trinidad as often as he could, wanted to tap the talents of other active tent singers. Together with businessman Eduardo Sa Gomes, he planned to send two calypsonians to New York to make records.[21] Clark would handle projects in New York while Sa Gomes would arrange for the singers and their passage in Trinidad (fig. 30):

> Hubert R. Charles known as The Lion and Raymond Quevedo "Atilla The Hun" sailed on Wednesday in the Bermuda and West Indies Line Steamship Nerissa.
>
> The songs will be recorded as duets and solos. A certain number of each will be sung by the two singers who are under contract to Sa Gomes Ltd., the local gramophone and record dealers.
>
> Many of the calypsos to be recorded gained plaudits when they were sung in the tents before carnival.[22]

According to Atilla, "Thousands swarmed the wharves to wish the boys 'bon voyage' and hundreds accompanied them in launches to the 'Nerissa' which lay out in the stream to say last goodbyes. It was truly a national triumph."[23]

Atilla and Lion recorded for the American Record Company on March 7, 1934, and, according to Atilla, the American popular singers Bing Crosby and Rudy Vallee were in the studio during the recording of some of the takes.[24] It was on this trip that they made the first radio broadcast from the United States to Trinidad (see chapter 9). In the finest tradition of calypsodic hyperbole, Atilla wrote, "Preparations for their return were more lavish than the send-off. Tumultuous crowds assembled outside the old customs house to welcome the kaisonians back home. A stage was erected on the Railway lands nearby from which a ten-piece orchestra played kaiso. Lion and Atilla made speeches of thanks. . . .

"There could be no doubt that this first trip to the United States had brought the kaisonian to a realization of his worth."[25]

The following year, Atilla the Hun was joined by the Growling Tiger (Neville Mercano) and the Young Beginner (Egbert Moore). The three sailed on the Fort St. George. According to Tiger, they had "72

30 ✳ Trinidadian record dealer Eduardo Sa Gomes "advising" calypsonians on their upcoming trip to perform in New York City, 1937. Left to right: Caresser, Atilla, Lion, Executor, Sa Gomes. Courtesy of the Roaring Lion.

hours of bad weather" and then, near Cape Hatteras the weather improved.[26]

When they arrived in New York, the temperature was thirteen degrees below zero, and Tiger did not have a coat. Worst of all, they were held in Ellis Island for three weeks by immigration. Eventually the immigration problem was sorted out.

So we [went to New York City] under the protection of the [Decca] people. [Gerald Clark] had room [where] we can stay. I wouldn't be able to get away to go anywhere, you know, this kinda set up. Maybe [immigration] thought I wanted to stay in the States.

And we rehearse and get ready for the records. In rehearsing the songs, I singing "Money is King." Felix Pacheco—who write [down my] music—told me, "How do you find songs that so queer?" He said that I have broken all the laws in music [since I sing such strange songs]. He asked me if the people where I come from play this type of music, the way I sings it.

I told him, "yea."

He said, "Well, you have broken all the chords in music!" He said, "Anyway, you sing it to me. I'll write down the music and maybe we play it like that." So anyway, he take it on, [and] make a good job of it![27]

In 1936, Clark recorded some waltzes for the Latin market, Houdini recorded for the American Record Company, and Lion and Tiger returned to New York with King Radio (Norman Span) to record again for Decca.

Tiger was ill when it was time for him to record, so Lion and Radio recorded first. Tiger said that he was "just lost in a sea of nonimagination, seeing things and [people] I don't know."[28] When his turn came to cut his sides,

I had to do thirty two masters [at one time]. Sa Gomes, [wanted] the record for Easter, [just a few weeks off].

At that time they put the record face—one [side] Tiger and one Beginner. Then no one man was carrying a record, a two-faced thing. . . . They'd select which [of each singer's] is the best one and put them together.

And I was sick [but] in those days, you can't make a mistake. It was so important. The wax were imported from East Africa, this kinda 'ting I knew of. So if you miss a wax I mean you commit one of the greatest crime. I mean you mustn't make mistake! "Go on!" "You don't forget!" "Remember everything!"

So I did it. I stood up and made 16 masters . . . one after the other! Three minutes [for one recording]!! Two minutes and 48 seconds [for the next master]. That was the 78 [rpm] record that they were making at the time.[29]

Tiger recorded three other masters with Radio in 1936, for a total of nineteen.

Decca versus Bluebird

In 1937, recording resumed in Trinidad when portable recording equipment was set up in the St. James Theatre in Port of Spain. It had been over two decades since Victor was in Trinidad and now, as RCA Victor, the world's largest record company was there again recording for its Bluebird label:

> HUNT FOR OLD TRINIDAD FOLK SONGS GRAMOPHONE FIRM'S AGENT HERE
>
> Mr. Dan'el des Foldes, Recording Sales Manager of the International Division of the R.C.A. Manufacturing Company of Camden, New Jersey, . . . is here on a special mission, sent, all expenses paid, to Trinidad, to dig up the island's musical history. . . .
>
> He is here to make recordings of folk songs, calypsos, and specialised tunes belonging only to Trinidad, so that the records can be sold in America and all over the world, to give Trinidad greater publicity, and to preserve the music of the generations gone by—music which is now in danger of becoming extinct. . . .
>
> While in Trinidad, Mr. des Foldes is not only arranging to record the singing of local calypsos, but is also hoping to record the playing of the constabulary band and of local orchestras. . . .
>
> These recordings will be played back on the loudspeaker immediately and the fortunate ones will have an opportunity to listen to their talent on the spot.[30]

One of Daniel des Foldes's techniques was to offer prizes for the best singers by mimicking the established tent practice of holding competitions.[31] Fifteen, ten, and five dollars were the prizes given to the top singers as a fee for recording, with "the big possibilit[y] of drawing royalties" if the song were issued.

At about the same time des Foldes was recording in Trinidad for RCA Victor, Decca's man, Ralph Perez, sent out a call for several of the top singers to come to New York to record:

> CALYPSO SINGERS SAIL FOR NEW YORK
>
> With a smile on their faces and a tune on their lips, four of Trinidad's leading Calypsonians left last night for New York where they make recordings of all the popular Carnival tunes of 1937. They are Hubert Raphael Charles, "The Lion," Raymond Quevedo, "Atilla," Philip Garcia, "Lord Executor," and Rufus Callender, "Caresser" of San Fernando. . . . While they are in New York, the calypsonians are expected to broadcast over the General Electric Station in Schenectady. This is the third visit for "Lion" and "Atilla" while "Lord

Executor" who has been singing since 1896 and "Caresser," are making their first trip. They are expected to stay six weeks in New York where they will make a number of records.[32]

Nineteen-thirty-seven was a critical year in recording calypso and in the dissemination of the genre to wider audiences. RCA Victor issued an entire line of its comparatively inexpensive Bluebird records as a result of its foray into Trinidad featuring Beginner, Gorilla (his first recordings), Growler (his first recordings), Invader (first recordings), Lady Trinidad (the first and only female calypsonian to record for a decade), Edric Connor, Ralph Fitz-Scott, Bill Rogers, Fitz McLean (his only recordings), Destroyer (first recordings), Pretender (first recordings, fig. 31), Radio, Tiger, Ziegfeld (his first recordings), Audley Francis's Washboard Orchestra (first recordings), Vaughn Harry's Melody Makers Orchestra (first recordings), Bert McLean's Jazz Hounds (first recordings), and Roy Rollock and His Orchestra (first recordings). The Trinidad Constabulary band recorded for Bluebird, and even Captain A. A. Cipriani cut a private record. Decca issued calypsos by Atilla, Lion, Caresser, and Executor and instrumentals by Belasco, all recorded in New York in 1937. The American Record Company also got into the act and added to its releases with more instrumentals recorded by Belasco's band and vocals by Houdini. In 1938, there were more recordings by Decca (fig. 32).

Although the Bluebird and the American Record Company records did not sell well in the United States, the Deccas by the four tent singers did; this seems to have set off a boomlet of recorded calypso for a non–West Indian public in the United States, and in Britain, where Manning and Belasco had recorded in 1934 and Manning in 1935.

A similar development also occurred in the Caribbean:

Sa Gomes owns a network of stores throughout the Antilles and even in British Guiana where he sells the records of the men he controls. In Jamaica, for instance, more Calypso records are sold than in Trinidad; they are more popular than the native 'mentor,' more popular in British Guiana than the 'badji' of Demerara, in Barbados more popular than the Brumley melodies. Mr Sa Gomes has made a special point of seeing the idiom become a favourite. Commercialism is no respecter of tradition. Calypso is fast becoming a kind of international Caribbean swing, reaching from Jamaica to the southernmost tip of the Antilles, a hybrid novelty for Pan-American consumption.[33]

31 * Lord Pretender. Courtesy of Hollis Liverpool.

Other English-speaking West Indians also made records. Ralph Fitz-Scott, Phil Madison, and Bill Rogers were Guyanese and recorded vaudeville songs or Guyanese shantos. Furthermore, several of the best orchestras in Trinidad, such as the Mootoo Brothers Orchestra, contained many Guyanese musicians (fig. 33). Nevertheless, calypso was the primary form of music that spread by way of

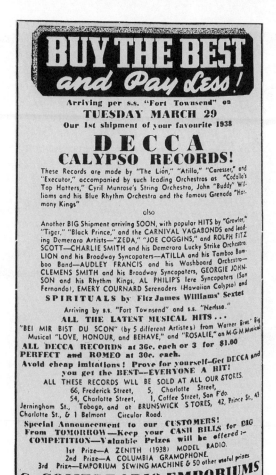

32 * Sa Gomes
advertisement
published in the
Trinidad Guardian,
March 27, 1938.

phonograph records through the English-speaking countries of the
Caribbean basin during the late 1930s.

About this time commercial calypso found its way to West Africa,
probably through British sources and through West Indian civil
servants stationed in British colonies there. By the late 1940s, calypso
melodies were recorded by Arthur S. Alberts in urban centers in the
Gold Coast (Ghana) where he had lived as a writer during World War
II[34] (fig. 34).

As the demand for more records increased, Perez decided to record
for Decca in Trinidad, as RCA Victor had done (fig. 35):

33 ✳ Calypsonians with members of the Mootoo Brothers Orchestra, 1949. Front row, left to right: Fitzie Bonie on the cuatro, and the Mootoo brothers on saxophone and clarinet. Back row, left to right: Small Island Pride, Dictator, Atilla, Terror, Lion. Courtesy of the Roaring Lion.

34 ✳ Label of a 78-rpm field recording made by Arthur S. Alberts of traveling Ibo musicians in Accra, Gold Coast, Africa, 1949.

NEWS! ·NEWS!

WE HAVE NOW INSTALLED

OUR

Recording Equipment

Comprising AMERICA'S Most Modern and up-to-date APPARATUS, at our

NEW STUDIO

58, Frederick Street,

For the purpose of Recording Our GRAMOPHONE RECORDS.

Recordings will be operated under the direct supervision of MR. RALPH PEREZ, Expert Recording Director, and MR. MONROE WAYNE, Expert Recording Technician of DECCA RECORDS INC., NEW YORK.

Our aim is to make history with LOCAL RECORDS by supplying the Trinidad Public with the BEST . . . REPRODUCTION—ARTISTES— MUSIC, etc. on the world's famous DECCA RECORDS.

Sa GOMES RADIO EMPORIUMS

" The Five Palaces of Good Music "

Port-of-Spain :: San Fernando ::: Tobago.

35 ∗ Eduardo Sa Gomes's call for calypsonians to record in his studio, published in the *Trinidad Guardian*, February 24, 1938.

Altho these disks have been made by Decca Records for the past few years, it has been only within the past year that the market for them has extended from the West Indies to this country. . . . The Decca library of Calypsos is extensive, since the waxworks has sent a recording unit down to Trinidad once every year, resulting in a yearly output of between 100 and 150 numbers. Ralph Perez, treasure of the company's export department, heads the yearly expedition. . . .

Decca does not plan any noticeable increase in production of Calypso disks, despite their growing popularity, feeling that its already large catalog plus the periodic excursions to Trinidad will take care of

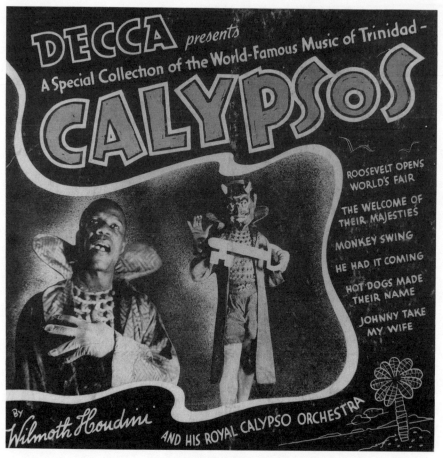

DECCA *presents*
A Special Collection of the World-Famous Music of Trinidad —
CALYPSOS

ROOSEVELT OPENS
WORLD'S FAIR

THE WELCOME OF
THEIR MAJESTIES

MONKEY SWING

HE HAD IT COMING

HOT DOGS MADE
THEIR NAME

JOHNNY TAKE
MY WIFE

by Wilmoth Houdini AND HIS ROYAL CALYPSO ORCHESTRA

36 ✳ Cover for Houdini's 78-rpm Decca record album no. 78. Courtesy of MCA Records.

any demand. Platter firm took cognisance, however, of the interest those records have here by releasing six sides in album form recently, waxed by Wilmoth Houdini, the only Calypsonian residing in the United States.[35] (figs. 36 and 37)

Actually, 1938 was the year of Decca's first trip to Trinidad, and it was prompted by competition from the other companies, especially RCA. Decca's agents returned in 1939 and in 1940; in 1941 Atilla, Growler, Invader, Lion, Destroyer, and Radio came to New York to record, and Sam Manning and several local West Indian bands also recorded for Decca in New York in 1941.

In 1939 the anthropologists Melville J. and Frances Herskovits made the earliest known noncommercial field recordings in Trinidad,

37 ✳ Inside cover for Houdini's Decca album no. 78, showing Carnival masquerades popular in the 1920s and 1930s. Clockwise from lower left: historical band, Scottish Highlanders, bad behavior sailors, beast, photographer with band, midnight robbers, historical band, midnight king, Arab sheiks, historical band, historical band, imps. Courtesy of MCA Records.

putting more than 350 songs on about 101 twelve-inch metal discs (figs. 38 and 39).[36] They recorded many different genres, including shangos, reels, belairs, paseos, bongos, and calindas in addition to calypsos.[37] Most of their recording took place in Toco, in the extreme northwest corner of the island, a community whose connection to the rest of the island was best made by sea. The Herskovitses were well aware of commercially recorded calypso: "Calypso is a name not often heard in Toco, except when commercial records are being discussed. 'Calipso, or caliso, as old people used to call it, is dancing in carnival,' an old man explained, and he added, 'Young people today go for creole dances with clarinet work.' . . . Even in the commercially recorded calypsos the same themes we have found in the Toco reel and bele [belair], 'bongo' and calenda, are to be constantly encountered."[38] Anthropologist Richard A. Waterman's

Above: **38** ✻ Yarriba (Yoruba) woman, probably Margaret Buckley, singing and being recorded by Melville and Frances Herskovits near Toco, Trinidad, 1939.
Left: **39** ✻ Yarriba drummer, probably Joe Alexander, being recorded by the Herskovitses. Both photos from Melville J. Herskovits and Frances Herskovits, *Trinidad Village* (New York: Alfred A. Knopf, Inc., 1947). Reprinted by permission of the publisher.

Ph.D. dissertation for Northwestern University provides an ethnomu-
sicological analysis of forty-five of these songs.[39]

Recorded Calypso through World War II: An Overview

Excluding the 101 discs recorded by the Herskovitses in 1939, more
than 650 records were issued by artists from Trinidad, Guyana, or
elsewhere in the English-speaking Caribbean between 1912 and
about 1945. Most of these records were waxed by orchestra leaders or
calypsonians from Trinidad. Because 78-rpm records had a song on
each side, a total of about thirteen hundred sides were issued. Table
7–1, based on Dick Spottswood's discography of West Indian records, 1912–45, categorizes these songs.[40] The table excludes certain
recordings that bear no relevance to Trinidad. For example, it is
possible that "Orquesta Tipica de Trinidad" and other Latin groups
recorded in Trinidad but for the South American market only. These
records have been excluded from this analysis as have a few West
Indianesque sides recorded in Europe. Other European recordings by
Manning or Belasco or others have been included.

Table 7–1 classifies the remaining 1,268 sides according to (1) how
the sides are labeled (either by vocalist or band/orchestra) and (2) by
the following categories: calypsonians (singers known to have performed in calypso tents), vaudevillians (stage performers), instrumentals recorded by West Indian orchestras (mostly Trinidadian,
Vincentian, or Guyanese), and miscellaneous (various orchestras and
singers, such as Harold Boyce, whose records seem aimed at an
American or West Indian–American audience). It should be noted
that vocals were sometimes issued under the orchestra leader's name,
not the calypsonian. For example, Houdini recorded many sides that
were issued under Gerald Clark's name. In this analysis, such sides
are treated as vocal calypsos under the name of the orchestra leader
("other"), not the calypsonian.

It is striking that the entire recorded calypso output is dominated
by a few calypsonians, vaudevillians, and orchestra leaders. Belasco
recorded 278 instrumental tunes under his own name, 63 percent of
the total records issued under the name of an orchestra leader.[41]
Houdini recorded 132 sides under his name, nearly 22 percent of the
total recorded by tent calypsonians. Sam Manning recorded eighty-
two sides, almost 44 percent of the total for vaudevillians. These three

Table 7-1. West Indian 78-rpm record sides by category, 1912–45

Calypsonians	sides	Vaudevillians	sides	
Houdini	132	Sam Manning	82	
Lion	95	Bill Rogers	38	
Atilla	69	Ralph Fitz-Scott	37	
Radio	59	Phil Madison	18	
Tiger	46	other	13	
Growler	36			
Caresser	34			
Executor	28			
Invader	24			
Beginner	23			
other	60			
Total	606		188	794

W. I. bands/orchestras	sides	Misc. orchestra/vocal	sides	
Belasco	278	Harold Boyce	10	
Gerald Clark	36	other	23	
Walter Merrick	18			
Lovey	16			
Cyril Monrose	15			
Bert McLean	12			
Codallo Top Hatters	10			
other	56			
Total	441		33	474
Grand total				1,268

New York–based performers recorded 492 sides, almost 39 percent of the total. The West Indian–based singers recorded 580 sides, almost 46 percent of the total. Of the vocalists, Trinidad-based calypsonians (that is, all except Houdini) recorded 474 sides, more than 37 percent of the total.

With an understanding of table 7–1 and some knowledge of West Indian immigration to the United States, a pattern of record buying emerges.[42] It appears that the calypso records made from the 1910s through the early 1920s were designed mostly for a West Indian market in Trinidad and in New York. Then, in the late 1920s the music becomes more assimilated in the recordings of Sam Manning. This music probably appealed to Caribbean people in New York more than those at home.

During the Great Depression—in the middle 1930s—the American Record Company, Decca, and RCA Victor offered discs at reduced prices.[43] These companies recorded calypsonians—both the now assimilated "Americans" such as Monrose, Belasco, Houdini, and Clark and Trinidad-based singers and orchestras. By the late 1930s, record companies sold discs to several distinct markets.[44] First, English-speaking people from the Caribbean, including West Indians in New York, bought calypso records. But so did Americans with no connection to the West Indies, as did the English and the Africans in British colonies (the Gold Coast, Nigeria, South Africa, and so forth).

At that time, the phonograph was a pleasure savored by middle-class Trinidadians, not grass-roots people, who could not afford one. Most Trinidadians enjoyed their calypso live or from the phonographs that merchants set up as advertising outside their shops. Buying a record or two or three was no big deal for the West Indians in New York or for other Americans, however.

Instrumental calypso had an even wider appeal. Indeed, many of the musicians in the small calypso bands in New York and some of the musicians in Trinidad were Latin Americans. Calypso was close enough in style to the *son* (rumba), *merengue,* and other dance styles to be popular with many different urban people in the Latin world. For West Indians, dancing to an instrumental calypso record in their own apartments was a metaphor for being home in the islands; it was the next best thing. It also got them in the mood for attending local dances in Harlem, of which there were many by the 1930s.

The vocal calypsos may be classified into three categories: songs recorded by Houdini (a phenomenon unto himself), the vaudeville numbers, and the later recordings by the tent singers. Houdini's era came first, and he had at least three distinct audiences: West Indians in New York, Trinidadians at home, and non–West Indian Americans, who by the late 1930s were mostly middle-class whites. Manning, as a vaudevillian more than a calypsonian, probably sold most of his records to emigrant West Indians and fewer of them to Americans. His singing in vernacular was a fond reminder of home for islanders in New York. He may have sold more records to African Americans than to white Americans; the former group would enjoy the stereotypes of islanders that his records invoked, stereotypes that most whites would not understand.

In all this, then, we see that records are a different beast from live performances. They are targeted to markets that may be far removed geographically or culturally from their sources. Records are mass mediated, a characteristic that can separate them from their source.

The ads and newspaper columns that mention records in Trinidad and in New York are instructive. In Trinidad, of course, Carnival was covered in depth. Record ads centered on Carnival season or, after 1934, on the arrival of a new supply of Deccas. In New York, there were some ads for calypsos in the 1920s in the *Amsterdam News,* an African-American newspaper. For example, some of Belasco's rare Gennett Records were advertised in that newspaper: "West Indians! Stop! Look and Listen!" the ad implored.[45] Other records were advertised in *Crisis,* the journal of the National Association for the Advancement of Colored People. The Pace Phonograph Corporation, a record company founded by Harry Pace and W. C. Handy, the father of the blues, pushed Belasco's records alongside classical, blues, and gospel releases (fig. 40).

Ads for calypsos also appeared in the white press, and most references to calypso by columnists were in the white press. For example, an ad for Gerald Clark's Varsity records seems aimed at whites when it states: "The Best Calypso Enunciation on the Market."[46] Mention of records or performances by calypsonians appears in Walter Winchell's column "On Broadway" in the *Daily Mirror,* in Danton Walker's column "Broadway" in the *Daily News,* in Malcolm Johnson's "Cafe Life in New York" column, and in other columns. Typical are Winchell's remarks: "The Calypso Entertainers' latest recording is 'G-Man Hoover,' a honey."[47] Then there is the notice of a new song, titled "Walter Winchell," in the *Telegram.* "Highly Recommended Pops . . . Walter Winchell (Varsity 3130). The Calypsos are at it again. George Clark and his Calypso Orchestra offer a pair of typical pieces—the other side contains Maria—that will give you many enjoyable moments. The line 'Flash! Walter Winchell peepin' at you,' ought to get a few laughs."[48]

40 ✳ Black Swan record flyer published in the NAACP journal *Crisis*, 1920s.

Recorded calypso had broken the boundaries of geography, culture, and tradition and had become just another mass-mediated vogue. But the calypsonians and their orchestras also moved into new venues, including nightclubs, theaters, and other stage shows. The next chapter will trace that development.

8 ✳ Calypso in Shows,
at Dances, at Clubs,
and on the Stage

The songsters will be appearing disguised.
Trinidad Guardian, February 8, 1929

ARNIVAL is at the center of Trinidadian perfor-
mance culture, and it is from this institution that calypso sprang. Yet
calypso hovered around other venues as it evolved in the Carnival
streets and tents. In Trinidad, the development of certain institutions—the Dame Lorraine show, vaudeville, and public dances—
paralleled the Carnival tent, feeding into and taking from the tent.
A few tent calypsonians traveled extensively and recorded in the
United States and elsewhere. Their songs were copied by other West
Indians or by foreigners not associated with masquerading or the
tents. The spread of calypso made it more diffuse and more difficult
to define.

When calypsos were performed in theaters or clubs, the focus was
on the professional calypsonian. A distinction was made between
performer and audience or between the nationality of the performer
(Trinidadian or Guyanese) and the nationality of the audience
(Trinidadian, West Indian, American, or English). These changes
make calypso on stage fundamentally different from—although related to—the calypso of Carnival season in Trinidad.

This examination of calypso in different venues will begin with live

performances in Trinidad—the Dame Lorraine show and dances—
and continue with calypso performance abroad.

Dame Lorraine

After the riots of the early 1880s and the laws suppressing jamet
Carnival, the urban canboulay went underground. Stick fighting
persisted mostly in out-of-the-way barrack yards and rural areas. One
of the most engaging elements of the Carnival, which took root in the
barrack yards of Port of Spain as a partial sop for the more raucous
stick fights, was the ludicrously obscene Dame Lorraine show.[1]

Dame Lorraine apparently was named after a prominent Port of
Spain madame, in whose brothel an early version of the show may
have taken place. The show consisted of a series of skits with
flamboyant and obscene masked characters—most with distorted
bodies. Speechmaking in Patois added to the rumpus. Physical
peculiarities, bodily functions, personality flaws, and class bearing
were all lampooned in the Dame Lorraine. After a Dame Lorraine
performance, pissenlit (a masquerade that consisted of a man dressed
in an obscene characterization of a menstruating woman) "polluted"
the streets of Port of Spain. Both lowlifes and respectable men would
attend these performances, as this was one venue in which jamets and
the middle class met. In the Dame Lorraine show, indoor abandonment replaced outdoor revelry in a curious reversal of the usual effect
of Carnival.

The dialogue in a Dame Lorraine performance was in French
Creole.[2] But even patrons who did not speak Patois could understand
because the plot was simple. Many gestures were used, the words
were direct, and some of the vocabulary had already entered into
English Creole. Furthermore, the actions were more interesting than
the dialogue. Performers in outlandish costumes danced as musicians
played tunes designed for specific characters and activities.

There were originally three acts to the show. The first act was set on
an eighteenth-century plantation. When announced by the butler,
appropriately dressed performers came onto the stage to the music of
their own special dance. Decorum was the rule, and each person had
to act in an exaggerated, formal way. As the years passed this opening
act was dropped.[3]

The second act was set in a schoolroom, and the action was a burlesque:

> The butler is replaced by a "mait" or schoolmaster. He calls roll as the pupils assemble, and marks down their presence in a big book. The mait wears a frock coat and carries a long whip, and his pupils wear ill-assorted clothes, mock crinolines, rags upon rags, and show the exaggerated physical characteristics suggested by such Rabelaisian names as Misié Koko, Ma Gwo Bunda, Misié Gwo Lolo, Ma Chén Mum, Gwo Patat, Koka, Bude, Toti, or Misié Mashwe Tune. These characteristics were represented by pads, coconuts, woodcarvings, masks, and the like, and there was much horse-play, with the schoolmaster finally licking them with his whip.[4]

"The schoolmaster shouted out comments to the children in his class: 'Marchez pointay mes enfants' (Walk daintily my children). 'M'sieu Gros Boudin, avancez' (Big belly, advance). 'Dancez, mes enfants, dancez. Jam A' jamb mais pas fair pollison. En nous! En nous! Ecoutez'! Faire con Frére e pis se mais par con nomme eh pis femme' (Dance, my children, dance. Leg to leg but no vulgarity. Let's get on, let's get on. Listen! Do like brother and sister, but not like man and woman)."[5]

After the second act the audience was served something to eat and drink. They could dance in the intermission if they so desired. On Carnival Sunday evening, the play and dancing might last all night and, at dawn, the entire throng moved into the streets for jouvay.

Dame Lorraine was hated by some proper Trinidadians and loved by others. Gradually, early in the twentieth century, a sense of propriety overcame the love of debauchery, and Dame Lorraine faded away.

Calypso Plays

In the 1920s, calypso skits developed. In 1929, for example, a group of calypsonians participated in a show held at the New Theatre in San Fernando.[6] Atilla, Munsee Daley, Lord Executor, and Lord Inventor appeared, dressed as classic West Indian characters. With the backing of A. A. Cipriani and other upper-class Trinidadians, this type of calypso show reached the ultimate acceptance in Trinidad:

EMPIRE GRAND VARIETY ENTERTAINMENT
by the concert party of H.M.S. DURBAN,
Under the distinguished patronage of
His Excellency the Governor and Lady Hyatt . . .
SATURDAY

. . . .

8:30 THE GRAND FINAL CALYPSO COMPETITION
With the Four Leading Songsters.
Douglas, Atilla, Lord Executor, and Inventor.
PROGRAMME:
1. One reel comedy.
2. Calypso Selections by String Band.
3. A Commercial competition
4. Orchestral Numbers (Hot Stuff).
5. Open Ballad Competition.
6. War—Picongs (Roaring items).
7. A Select Picture.
The songsters will be appearing disguised as follows:—
DOUGLAS representing A Railroad Millionaire.
EXECUTOR representing A Tea Planter.
MODERN INVENTOR representing A Labourite.
ATILLA representing Salada Singalese.
Apart from the big money prize offered by the management of the
Empire Theatre, prizes will also be given by Messrs. J. T. Johnson
(White House), Richardson & Selway Ltd., V. & J. Stable Bros. Patrons
are asked to secure their seats early as there will be no reserving of seats
for this show.[7]

This show was a precursor of the calypso drama.[8] True dramas—skits
approximately fifteen minutes long with most of the dialogue sung in
rhyme, accompanied by a band, and performed with little or no
rehearsal—did not begin until the performance of *The Divorce Case*
in 1933.[9]

In carnival season fierce tent competitions developed and the Silky
Millionaires had cut deeply into the attendance of the tent in which
Atilla was performing, the Salada Millionaires. Meanwhile, as the gate
receipts shrunk, he and Lion had . . . performed for a private party,
which was held in a restaurant. As Lion sang a song, "Doggie Doggie
Look Bone" Atilla extemporized. A customer mused that this might

make a good song for the Salada tent. They developed the song into a duet, which when performed in tent, became a success and an instant classic. They followed it with another duet in which Lion played local "hyperbolizer" and police hater, Gambolailai, a street person "with an immoderate penchant for unintelligible jawbreakers." Atilla played a "critic." These duets took their toll on the Silky Millionaires tent and Executor, Douglas and Radio joined Atilla and Lion at the Salada tent.

With everything going their way they decided to add a story line and "The Divorce Case," the first calypso drama, was born. The notion of divorce was in the air because it was illegal in largely Catholic Trinidad and a recent bill to make it legal lost in the Legislative Council, in spite of the backing of usually liberal Cipriani.[10]

These were the players:

JUDGE—Chieftain Douglas

COMPLAINANT—Atilla   DEFENDANT—Trafalgar
CO-RESPONDENT—Inveigler   WITNESS—Radio
DEFENCE COUNSEL—   COUNSEL FOR
   Executor   COMPLAINANT—Lion[11]

Each calypsonian dressed his part. The play did not resolve the issue of divorce but left that to the imagination of the audience.

Errol Hill has identified nineteen calypso dramas performed between 1933 and 1966.[12] Dramas were informal and were sometimes given with no rehearsal. The skits were gentrified versions of the Dame Lorraine show or the little dramatic routines that attended some of the street masquerades (midnight robber, sailors, devils, and so forth), with dialogue in English Creole (fig. 41).

Calypso dramas never constituted a major part of calypso performance. Today, they survive in two forms. The first consists of short skits, sometimes performed during the frequent intermissions in Carnival shows. The other modern vestige of calypso drama is the presentation of a tent calypso in costume. In this case, the calypsonian is sometimes aided by other actors.[13]

Dance Halls

Vernacular dance in the Americas is a physical embodiment of creolization. On the one hand, there is the European folk tradition of secular group dances for men and women (quadrille, cotillion, lanc-

41 ✳ Calypsonians dressed in drag to perform a calypso drama, 1949. Left to right: Killer, Radio, Atilla, Tiger. From *Holiday* magazine (January 1949); photograph by George Burns.

ers, polka, mazurka) and couples dances (waltz). On the other hand, there is the West African tradition of single-sex dancing in contexts that mix entertainment with religion (Shango, the Big Drum, Voodoo, Rada, calinda). Between these extremes exists a range of creolizations: belairs within Afro-Creole rites, the "African quadrille," as it is known in Carriacou (including propitiations to the ancestors), and many couples dances, accompanied by syncopated string bands (tango, danzón, urban rumba, castillian, paseo, and so on).

Generally, the outdoor Carnival dances of Trinidad (the calinda and the breakaway, for example) seem to be more Afro-Creole than Euro-Creole. The indoor ballroom dances, held by elite groups during Carnival season, were more Euro-Creole than Afro-Creole (waltz, European lancers, and quadrilles, and so on). In between were a range of Creole dances in dance halls and social clubs.

Trinidad's dance halls may have evolved from the bouquet dances of the rural Antilles (such as the lancers and quadrilles of Carriacou and rural Trinidad and the reels of Tobago), and from the public couples dances held in cities during the second half of the nineteenth century.

Nothing could illustrate the duplicitous effects of colonial law in Trinidad during the 1930s better than the legal and social rules that applied to dancehalls attended by the poor as opposed to the country-club dances for the elite.

In such a profoundly class-based yet cosmopolitan society as in Trinidad, it comes as no shock that there were so many local characters: badjohns, jamets, stick fighters, jacket men, calypsonians. There was Gumbolailai, son of badjohn and drummer Johnny Zee Zee, who almost single-handedly ruined the English language with his malaprops. There was Myler the Dentist, stick fighter, who could extract an opponent's tooth with a single blow. There was Lady Mataloney, the brawling, quarrelsome jamet who was one of the few female calypsonians of the era.

Then there were Cutouter and Gooter. Cutouter was one of the fiercest stick fighters of his time. The line of Small Island Pride's calinda—"Cutouter, meet me down by Green Corner"—is pure braggadocio as Cutouter rarely lost a battle. That is, until Gooter's terrible vendetta was played out in the Wang, a notorious dance hall on the second floor of a Charlotte Street building in Port of Spain.[14]

Gooter was a small-time badjohn from la Cour Harpe, a yard noted for highly rated badjohns. Gooter was the kind of person, Lion relates, who would strategically lose his first fight. In subsequent fights, however, he would not hesitate to use any weapon at hand: knives, chairs, broken glass. One Saturday night at the Wang, Jerry, the clarinetist, was leading his band in lancers, paseos, and bram dances. Over in a corner badjohns were playing dice. Cutouter was betting heavily against Gooter, who was throwing dice. As Cutouter continued to lose, he smelled a rat. He grabbed the dice and tossed them away, but Gooter demanded that the dice be returned or that Cutouter pay for them. Cutouter was forced to challenge Gooter, "since badjohns were usually 'sweetmen,' that is financially supported by women," and if Cutouter appeared to be a coward, he could "lose about half-a-dozen of his women."[15] Amazingly, after Cutouter landed a few blows, a defeated Gooter said, "Partner, you win, no hard feeling."[16] Those who knew Gooter knew that this was the beginning of the fight, not the end.

Some days later, again in the Wang, Gooter offered Cutouter a drink from his bottle of rum, in an apparent gesture of friendship. Cutouter became drunk and began to get sleepy. Gooter shouted at

Cutouter, claiming he had broken the badjohn's etiquette by getting drunk and falling asleep in a dance hall. He slammed a full bottle into Cutouter's face, knocking him to the ground. Gooter hit the other man again, this time breaking the bottle. Then, Gooter left the Wang as Cutouter lay bleeding on the floor.

The middle class despised these sorts of dance halls. The antics of the badjohns and jamets were the antithesis of middle-class morality. Reverend C. G. Errey lead an attack against this debauchery:

> To the Editor of the Port of Spain Gazette.
>
> Sir.—Dance Halls are becoming something of a pest in this town. And it appears that they are very nearly outside the law, so far as any control of them is concerned. Within recent times two or three such Halls have been established in the very centre of San Fernando. No one desires to interfere with the rightful liberties of the people, although there can be little doubt that the average Dance Hall is a veritable breeding place for vice. Certainly no self-respecting young woman would be seen in one, if she valued her reputation. I beg respectfully to submit the following suggestions with reference to Dance Halls:—
>
> (1) They should be licensed.
>
> (2) It should not be necessary to go to the Supreme Court to obtain an injunction against the issue of such license. A petition signed by three-fourths of the adult population resident within 300 yards of such a proposed Hall should be sufficient to secure the refusal of such license.
>
> (3) Only soft stringed music or piano with soft pedal down, should be allowed. Clarinettes, flutes and kindred instruments of torture should be prohibited after 11 p.m.
>
> (4) The uproar that almost invariably takes place between the dances should be suppressed. Failure to suppress it should bring about the cancellation of the license.
>
> (5) The crowd that assembles outside a Dance Hall, and that remains as long as the Dance lasts, should either be orderly or be dispersed.
>
> Most people who are unfortunate enough to live near to a Dance Hall will recognise the necessity of some such regulations.
>
> I am, Faithfully yours,
>
> C. G. Errey
>
> San Fernando
>
> February 7th. 1918[17]

Some middle-class Creoles were not as concerned about dance halls as Errey was. To Errey's open letter, none other than the dean of Trinidadian orchestra leaders, Lovey, replied:

To the Editor of the Port of Spain Gazette

Dear Sir.—In to-day's issue of your paper there appears an article above the name C. G. Errey. I am in complete accord with the rev gentleman when he states that Dance Halls are a nuisance. This is not only true in San Fernando, but doubly so in Port-of-Spain. I also agree with him that those places should be licensed as is done in New York and other big continental cities. The holders of these dances should be made to pay for the services of the police for maintenance of the public peace on the premises. But I cannot locate the intelligence in the suggestion that "only soft stringed music or piano with soft pedal down should be allowed," as in this case, the area of the Dance Hall would have to conform with the idea of Robinson Crusoe when he demonstrated of necessity, his architectural ability to Friday (not on Saturday night) in Tobago area "fo-be-fo." The rev gentleman must be possessed of a depth of soul the Kaiser would envy when he deliberately characterises such instruments as clarinets, flutes, etc. "instruments of torture." I admit that in the hands of soulless beings and novices all musical instruments are apt to produce sounds the reverse of inspiring, but I fail to see how the blame can rightly be attached to the instrument itself.

I cannot help thinking that the Rev Mr. Errey must either be a disciple of a certain one-time judge or Attorney-General of Trinidad, who tried, by legislation, to stop dogs from barking after nine at nights, cocks from crowing etc. or that, indeed, he is a very brave man, having regard to the fact that he resides in the same locality as Trinidad's premier musician, the Rev. Canon Doorly.

Thanking you. etc.

Lovey

20 George Street.
Port-of-Spain.
Feb. 9 1918[18]

Lovey, in his defense of sedate dance halls, pointed out that places like the Wang did not represent all dance halls. Nor did the rough-and-ready dances of the Wang represent all dances.

While a wealthy man might "slum" at the Wang on occasion in

much the same spirit as the jacketmen of an earlier era, elite women would not. For them there were other venues: large Carnival balls, ethnic associations and private clubs, and for the select, the country club. For example, during World War I there was a

DANCE OF THE ALLIES
A HUGE SUCCESS

As announced the Allies Dance, promoted by Miss Inez Scott, came off at the Princes Building on Monday evening (the first day of Carnival) and as had been anticipated was in every sense of the word, a ripping success. The dancing hall was tastily decorated, the flags and emblems of the Allies predominating in the elaborate scheme so excellently carried out. The attendance was all that could be expected, there being certainly no less than five hundred present. Lovey's String Band supplied the music with the result that enjoyment was writ on the faces of all even those who did not trip the light fantastic toe. There was an excellent "souper a la carte" to which the fullest attention was paid and with delightful results. We beg to congratulate Miss Scott and the others associated with her on what was undoubtedly a most enjoyable evening's entertainment.[19]

Lovey's band played these society venues. He also played for ethnic associations such as the Portuguese Club, an association of Madeirans in Trinidad.[20] These friendly societies were a way that immigrants could get together, give mutual help, and, in the elite associations, participate in good works. On one occasion, the Portuguese Club raised two thousand dollars for the poor; it also sponsored a children's Carnival, a society event for the children of middle-class and elite Creoles. Lovey's band played for that occasion also.

The most important dances at which calypsos were played were held at the country club. Scandal sometimes lurked at the country club, as the small group of elite Trinidadians and British colonials worked out their social relations under the eyes of the hired help and the band. One such scandal began one evening in 1933.[21] While the band played at a party inside the club, a man and a woman inconspicuously departed and had a nude swim together in the sea nearby. Their empty seats in the dining section of the club silently spoke of the affair. The female swimmer's husband remained inside, where he asked other patrons if they knew where she was, but no one did. The man, who was well known for his jealous rages, drank a whiskey and then headed outside to look around, where in a clump of bushes he found what he suspected, his wife with the other man. He watched the lovers for a moment and then returned to the clubhouse. He downed another straight whiskey, returned to his table, and waited for the couple to return. When they returned, he danced with his wife and with other women as if nothing had happened. But he began to gossip about some "unknown" couple dancing nude in the moonlight. The next day, the people of the colony were abuzz about the "white people" scandal at the country club.

On his way home from work that day, the jilted husband stopped by Sa Gomes Emporium, where a certain calypsonian was known to hang out.[22] He met the calypsonian and they talked together in a back room; as they left, the cuckold was seen to give the calypsonian some money. Several days later the calypsonian sang a new song, which broadcasted the incident throughout the island. The calypso did not identify the couple by name, but everyone knew who they were.

The song was all the rage. Its composer sang it at parties and in the tent. Albert Hicks claims that the lovers were shamed and eventually had to leave the island and that the story is "true in outline if not in detail."[23]

The story probably refers to an incident that occurred in 1933. As Atilla tells it, one night during Carnival season, Radio was busy handing out advertisements for his new song on the "Country Club Scandal."[24] He intended to sing the song at the Silky Millionaires tent on Henry Street that night. A rumor circulated that the song was about an important officer in the police force. As usual, when whites were involved in gossip, the tent was packed with an audience hungry to hear the latest rumors. Also present were plenty of uniformed police, one of whom brought a message to the stage that this particular calypso should not be sung. Captain A. A. Cipriani, then a Labour member of both the Legislative and the Executive councils, said, "Put a chair for me on the stage and sing your song. Let the police do their damnedest [to stop you]. I am by your side."[25] And so Radio sang:

> From the swimming pool
> To the servant's room
> That is where
> Mrs. X met her doom

The Country Club scandal

Was a hideous bacchanal.[26]

The song shamed the unfaithful wife and her rejected husband and embarrassed the inspector general, her lover: "It was alleged that a certain highly placed lady, the wife of distinguished officialdom, made the unforgivable mistake of allowing herself to be caught 'in flagrante delicto.' The co-respondent was the then Inspector General of Constabulary, a highly placed government officer."[27]

During Carnival season 1934, the *Guardian,* perhaps referring to lingering renditions of Radio's 1933 monster hit, implored:

> Some of these abuses the Trinidad Guardian has already pointed out. The most important was the blackmail method employed by some calypso singers. Despite our previous comments, some calypso singers were heard during the Carnival singing malicious songs about prominent persons, probably because they had not been paid to refrain from singing them. These songs were sung openly on City Streets—sometimes even within hearing of the persons who they were intended to slander. The abuse of privilege is, as we have already pointed out, a serious menace to the future development of our Carnival and is one which drastic steps should be taken to curb.[28]

In 1934, the inspector general introduced a bill, the notorious Theatre and Dance Hall Ordinance, in the Legislative Council. On December 13, 1934, the new ordinance became law. It established a licensing authority, appointed by the governor, with complete authority in licensing or closing dance halls, theaters, and tents. The inspector general had his revenge.[29]

Vaudeville and Theater

Variety shows in Trinidad have a history that intertwines with that of the calypso tents. One source of these shows was minstrel shows in the United States, where they were associated with blackface entertainment. The first blackface minstrels were whites who developed a series of characters in the middle of the nineteenth century that supposedly mimicked southern rural and urban African Americans. These characterizations, however, did not reflect the behavior of real people. Furthermore, minstrel shows originally played to audiences in the North, where few African Americans lived. Thus, northern whites received outrageous and inaccurate images of African Americans.

Later, African-American entertainers took up the same racist form of entertainment, adding a layer of pathos and humanity to the depictions. The most famous African-American blackface minstrel was an Antiguan-born immigrant named Bert Williams. He and his American partner, George Walker, put on stage reviews and plays. After Walker died, Williams went out on his own. He recorded a few records for Victor and many for Columbia and became the lead performer for the Ziegfeld Follies in New York City in the 1910s. Williams's routines were culturally American, not West Indian. Nevertheless, he influenced many Caribbean vaudevillians including Sam Manning, Bill Rogers, Phil Madison, Johnny Walker, and Ralph Fitz-Scott.

The classic white minstrel show of the late nineteenth century had three acts. The first consisted of a grand opening, in which all the minstrels were on stage, seated in a semicircle. At the center of the semicircle was the interlocutor, who engaged the minstrels in dialogue. The second part of the show was called the olio and was a variety show. While stagehands prepared for the finale, in front of the curtain individuals or small groups of minstrels performed skits, sang "coon songs,"[30] and made mayhem. The finale was set on a levee or a plantation, with all the minstrels present, some dressed in drag to play women. A simple skit and a rousing song closed their performance.

Minstrel shows toured the United States, and some traveled to South America and the Caribbean, where they were very popular. Although there had been blackface routines throughout the Americas before, the arrival of blackface minstrels from the United States in the late nineteenth century gave the stereotypes renewed popularity and focus. Vaudeville troupes, in which the blackface characters were only a part of a larger cast of entertainers, also toured the Caribbean.

In Trinidad, American-style blackface routines were added to Carnival and were called minstrels or the Yankee band (fig. 42). Their mask was part black, part white. This Carnival masquerade was accompanied by a band consisting of guitar, vera, bones, and banjo[31] that played American folk or popular tunes.

The vaudeville team of (Johnny) Walker and Berkeley also mim-

42 * Yankee minstrels at Carnival in Trinidad, circa 1940s. Courtesy of Sydney C. Hill.

icked American minstrels. Walker and Berkeley were called comedians and played theaters and other venues beginning about 1910. One such show, the "Grand Annual Children's Carnival Matinee," took place at Trinidad's London Theatre on Sunday, February 25, 1925.[32] At about the same time, the soon-to-be calypsonian King Radio began his career as a comedian.

Vaudeville in Trinidad seems also to have been influenced by the British music hall, especially in the performances of Phil Madison and Bill Rogers of Guyana. Madison was a one-man band; he wired a harmonica around his neck and strapped a guitar on his back. He played theaters and shows of all kinds, including a "poor people" concert for people with infirmities and for the indigent in 1921. He was "loudly applauded" for his rendition of "Too Much Bigger Than Me" and was asked to sing an encore.[33] Rogers was responsible for developing the "shanto" in Guyana, a popular song genre similar to calypso but with a dash of the British music hall.

Sometimes vaudeville routines, musical hall songs, and calypsos were sandwiched between films (see chapter 9). The R.A.F. Syndicate (named after the British Royal Air Force and consisting of calypsonians Invader, Caresser, Pretender, Destroyer, and Ziegfeld) played three theaters in one night in 1941. Shticks and songs alternated with films—*Secret Valley* at the Roxy, *Broken Melody* at the Ritz, and *Son of the Sheik* (with Rudolph Valentino) at the Royal. Prices in the latter theater were eight cents for "pit" seats, twelve cents for "circle," eighteen cents for "house," twenty-four cents for balcony, and thirty-six cents for box seats[34] (figs. 43 and 44).

West Indian Vaudeville and Theater in New York

After World War I, West Indian culture added to the African-American cultural kit in New York City. For example, use of obeah (Afro–West Indian magic) was reported at an international Elks' convention held in New York in 1927.[35] Carnival also took root in New York when Rufus Gorin, newly arrived from Trinidad, "played mas" in a bat costume in his apartment in Harlem during New York's cold February of 1928.[36] West Indian Carnival in New York would eventually become one of the largest Caribbean festivals in the United States.[37]

An interesting report in the *Amsterdam News,* dated February 6, 1929, refers to the sixteenth annual "Dance Reunion" held by the Sons and Daughters of Barbados to be held Thursday, February 14, at Rockland Palace. Such voluntary associations were an important way islanders maintained links with each other in New York.[38] On February 13, 1929, the *Amsterdam News* reported on the "Young Peoples Social Set's" sponsorship in Brooklyn's Howland Studio of a "unique pre-Lenten dance."[39] It is not known whether these young people were West Indians, but it may be that this was a Carnival ball.

Except for the highly visible activities of Marcus Garvey early in the decade, the West Indian contribution seems submerged in the wider African-American culture of the city. Nevertheless, West Indian vaudeville was well established in New York by the early 1920s, with the records of Phil Madison and Johnny Walker and the slightly later work of Sam Manning (see chapter 7).

The next important figure in the growth of Trinidadian culture in New York was Gerald Clark. He was born in Trinidad in about 1899.[40] As a boy, he regularly visited Lionel Belasco's home, where he, Walter Merrick, and other musicians gathered. Clark may have recorded in 1914 as the guitar player for Belasco and for the band that accompanied Julian Whiterose.[41]

43 ✳ Globe Theatre, Port of Spain, early 1940s. Courtesy of Charles Porter.

Clark came to New York in 1927. His recording career began soon thereafter and lasted until some time after World War II. Although Clark's was the top West Indian band in New York in this period, he did not neglect another side to his life. In 1936 he completed a four-year evening course at Harlem Evening High School, earning a diploma. A few years later he harbored thoughts of following in Dr. Walter Merrick's footsteps by earning both a bachelor's degree and a medical degree from Howard University in Washington, D.C., but he chose to stay in show business.

44 * Wartime movie advertisements published in the *Trinidad Guardian*.

Clark's impact on Trinidadian cultural affairs in New York was broadly based. As an agent for Decca, he assisted calypsonians in making records. Many of these same calypsonians sang with his band in club engagements in the city. He was at the center of the calypso fad that hit white New York in the late 1930s.

Clark, other orchestra leaders, and calypsonians found themselves entertaining two distinct audiences in New York—West Indians and a few African Americans in Harlem (and later in Brooklyn), on the one hand, and a mostly white audience in nightclubs in lower and midtown Manhattan, on the other. Clark's band accompanied a new generation of Trinidad-born but New York–oriented performers. The Duke of Iron, Sir Lancelot, and MacBeth the Great began their careers as calypso singers in the Big Apple, not in Trinidad.

The biggest catalyst in setting off a calypso boom in the United States was the engagement of Clark and his orchestra at Max Gordon's Village Vanguard in 1939:

Mr. Gordon, the proprietor of the Vanguard, knows exactly when the calypso entertainers first came to his attention. . . .

"It was at 4 A.M. on August 28, last year," he said. "The last patron had left. The hat-check girl brought over a record to me and said that evidently some customer had forgotten to pick it up on leaving.

"I waited for two weeks and when no one called for the record in that time I decided—well, at least I could play it. The recording was by the Calypso Singers. . . . The music was unusual and the ballads, based on the romance of King Edward VIII and Mrs. Simpson was delightfully satirical, I thought. It would be something new in night club entertainment. With this in mind I got in touch with these players and immediately signed them for the Vanguard. They worked here for ten weeks, during which time my business more than doubled. Enthusiasts who had heard their records flocked to hear them in person. Only previous commitments forced them to leave. They returned to the Vanguard about a month ago. And they can stand as long as they like.[42]

Gordon had opened the Village Vanguard in Greenwich Village in the late 1930s. It soon became a hangout for Bohemian intellectuals and assorted left-wing whites and African Americans, a place where an integrated audience could sample a range of music and entertainment centering on jazz and, later, folk music. By 1940, Clark and his Caribbean Serenaders were a fixture at the Vanguard. Clark not only headed the band, but he arranged for the singers and other entertainers to perform elsewhere in New York. For a few years they regaled patrons with a New York version of vaudeville and calypso.

Several tent singers gained fame for the first time outside Trinidad by singing with Clark at the Vanguard, including Caresser and Invader. Others, although born in Trinidad, had no extensive background in singing calypso there. These singers, including the Duke of Iron, MacBeth the Great, and Sir Lancelot, took advantage of the circumstances at the beginning of the boom. They became identified with calypso in the view of the American public in the next decade and a half.

The large metropolitan dailies fully reported the doings at the Vanguard as the calypsonians, especially the New York–based singers, created songs for American audiences. Chief among these songs was "Roosevelt in Trinidad," recorded for Decca by Atilla with Gerald Clark and his Caribbean Serenaders on February 16, 1937. This song describes the president's recent visit to Trinidad. Another popular song in America was "Edward VIII," recorded by Caresser at the same session. This song gossips about the abdication of the King of England and his intent to marry an American divorcée. It was Caresser's first recording and, next to "Roosevelt in Trinidad," was probably the biggest seller of the period outside Trinidad. Its sales brought whites to the Vanguard to hear calypso in person:

> Catering to the younger set of Greenwich Village, those who seek "atmosphere" in that section and, all in all, a politically well-informed group, Max Gordon, after successfully bringing to the fore the Vanguard (Calypso) Players, is again featuring a unique floor show.
>
> Starring the Calypso Kid, Dancers and Gerald Clark and his Caribbean Serenaders, the show is entertaining and different. It is exactly what the Vanguards patrons want. While the show seeks to depict the change in the Village, this Calypso group reflects the time when the club was the Bohemian hangout for poets and writers. The show runs 40 minutes.
>
> Knowing that his audience understands the political situations Bill Matons, "the Calypso Kid," who also stages the revue, has brought prominent political issues and events to the front in each act. The first, "King Edward and Wally," shows in pantomime and dance Edward's problem of choosing between the crown and "the woman he loves," Ailes Gilmur.
>
> "President Roosevelt in Trinidad," with Matons as FDR, shows the great admiration these people hold for the Chief Executive. . . . The "Duke of Iron" (Cecil Anderson) handles the narration.[43]

New York's calypso boom was on. Houdini and Manning both cut 78-rpm albums. Houdini's albums included many songs of interest to Americans. Calypso's new downtown audience—in Clark's own phrase, a "sophisticated clientele"[44]—enjoyed "U.S.A.," "Walter Winchell," "G-Man Hoover," "Roosevelt Opens the World's Fair," and "I Love to Read Magazines," all recorded for Decca by Houdini, the Duke of Iron, or Sir Lancelot. Most of these songs were featured at the Vanguard. Gossip columnist Walter Winchell, himself a subject of one of the new songs, frequently covered the Vanguard in his column, including this mention of a sophisticate enjoying one of Lion's calypsos, "Ugly Woman": "Peggy Hopkins Joyce in Village Vanguard, highly amused at Clark's calypso-and-sos singing."[45]

In the late 1930s, Clark headed a drive to formalize the Carnival begun by Rufus Gorin in 1928. So by 1942, Clark was able to move his Harlem dance to downtown Manhattan:

> The first large-scale presentation of its kind ever to be offered in this country is the task that Gerald Clark has set for himself—the staging of the colorful . . . "Dame Lorraine" Festival[46] and Carnival Dance of Trinidad Sunday Evening, February 15, at the Royal Windsor on W. 66th St.
>
> This annual ceremonial affair, heretofore confined more or less to the local populace of Harlem . . . [has] attract[ed] more and more Trinidad-enthused audiences from outside that sector who have been regaled by the native calypso music and dances which identify this event. . . . [The dance includes] masks, costumes, painted bodies and all: and, as such, will be an authentic duplication of what goes on just at that time in the native land. Never before attempted on a big-time scale, the carnival will have, among its many features, Gerald Clark's Caribbean Serenaders, of radio and recording popularity; Calypso Singers of Trinidad; other native entertainers performing Rumbas, Congos, Spanish Valses and Paseos and calypso contests.[47]

Tickets were priced at one dollar at the door. The show featured MacBeth the Great and Houdini "in a battle of calypsos." As in Trinidad, prizes were awarded for best fancy costume (one hundred dollars for first place) and for "comically dressed" masqueraders (fifteen dollars for first place).

The boom expanded after the war. Invader's unrecorded road march hit of 1944, "Rum and Coca Cola," was covered by the Andrews Sisters, the most popular American female vocal group of the time. There were popular versions of Houdini's songs "Run Joe" (by Louis Jordan) and "Stone Cold Dead in the Market" (by Ella Fitzgerald). There were more performances at the Vanguard, and Carnival grew into a street parade in Harlem in the late 1940s, with Jessie Wardle as its principal organizer, assisted by Gerald Clark.

Calypso gained even more favor for some Americans with a show at Carnegie Hall, the New York venue that signifies recognition:

CARNEGIE "POP" CONCERTS
presents
CALYPSO!
THURSDAY, MAY 8TH, 8 P.M.
FEATURING WORLD'S GREATEST CALYPSONIANS
WILMOTH (Stone Cold Dead) HOUDINI
LORD (Rum & Coca Cola) INVADER
THE GREAT (Uncrowned King) MACBETH
-Plus-
Princess Orelia and Her Native Dancers
Babu Belasco and His Orchestra
Stick Fights ! ! !
TICKETS NOW ON SALE AT BOX OFFICE
CARNEGIE HALL
7TH AVE. AT 57TH ST.[48]

Invader introduced Pretender's "God Made Us All" in this concert, although Pretender did not get much reward from the then most popular calypsonian in New York: "Invader won first prize and he brought a kinda gold wire tie pin marked 'Pretender' [for me], with the usual promise [of money later]."[49]

Then, on November 28, 1947,

> Broadway will see its first All-Calypso musical revue when "Caribbean Carnival," a big singing and dancing show opens Friday, November 28, at the International Theatre.
>
> With such headliners as Pearl Primus and Josephine Premice, the revue has a score written by Adolph Thenstead and Samuel Manning who also serve as producer and director, respectively. Thenstead and Manning have previously written a number of song hits that have served to further the popularity of Calypso music in this country and are the owners of the Cyclone Record Company which leads the field in Calypso recordings.[50]
>
> Other featured players include Claude Marchant, remembered from "Cabin in the Sky" and "Show Boat"; The Duke of Iron, foremost Calypso singer; the Smith Kids, Peggy Watson, the Trio Cubana, and Gregory Felix and the Caribbean Calypso Band. The supporting cast includes a chorus of fifty singers and dancers.[51]

With shows like this one, a new pan-Caribbean artistic culture was being formed. Primus was Haitian, and Thenstead from Jamaica. Gerald

Clark and Gregory Felix led orchestras that included Latin musicians and played Latin venues. Calypso was folding into a broader, newly developing Caribbean culture, one that included West Indians, African Americans, and white Americans. It was also during this period that Katherine Dunham, an American, established her pioneering dance company, which included many Caribbean elements.[52]

West Indians in the United Kingdom

In the early 1900s, there were few West Indian immigrants in Britain.[53] They made up a small middle and working class of seamen and other laborers.[54] During World War I, West Indians volunteered to serve in the British West Indies Regiment. Captain A. A. Cipriani, a Trinidadian of Corsican descent, served in the regiment, as did Sam Manning, Charles Jones (the Duke of Albany), and Walter Douglas (Railway Douglas). Most of the volunteers served in Europe or in North Africa. The West Indian community in Britain remained small until World War II.

One of the first Trinidadian musicians to settle in England was Al Jennings, who recalled that "in World War I, I was stationed at La Palace and while there we got together a little band for our own amusement. After the war we gave a few concerts for wounded coloured soldiers in London before their repatriation."[55] Jennings later played at the Canadian Skating Rink, Tottenham, and at the Regent Dance Hall at Brighton, where he experienced racism from some patrons. He was denied the opportunity to play in some British dance halls but played in others. "From Cardiff, Liverpool, Manchester and the West Indies I am responsible for bringing nearly 50 per cent of the coloured musicians to London. I brought the All-Star Coloured Caribbean Orchestra to London."[56]

Another of the early West Indian musicians in England was Cyril Blake, a guitarist and orchestra leader.[57] From the early 1920s through the late 1930s he played popular music and jazz, not calypso. He was a member of the Southern Syncopated Orchestra in England and played for the American torch singer, Josephine Baker, at the Follies Bergère in France. It was not until the Second World War, in an engagement for the British Broadcasting Corporation, that Blake concentrated on calypso. In 1950, his Calypso Serenaders backed Lord Beginner and Lord Kitchener on their first London recordings. Until the era of Kitch and Beginner, records made or issued in England seem meant for a general audience, not specifically for West Indians.[58]

The Trinidadian entertainers Sam Manning and Lionel Belasco came to England together by boat and arrived in Southampton on July 27, 1934.[59] On August 9, they made their first London recordings. This began a decades-long association each had with Britain.

In 1935, as the first rumblings of World War II were heard with the Italian attack on Ethiopia, a Trinidadian intellectual, C. L. R. James, founded the International Friends of Abyssinia in England. Amy Ashwood Garvey (Marcus Garvey's former wife), Manning, Kenyan nationalist Jomo Kenyatta, and Trinidad-born Pan-Africanist George Padmore—all in England—joined the new group. They formed a welcoming committee for Haile Selassie when he arrived at Waterloo Station in 1936 in the midst of the Italian-Ethiopian war.[60]

In 1936 Manning, together with Rudolph Dunbar, opened the New London Club.[61] In 1938, Manning appeared in the play *The Sun Never Sets*. The music for this play was not calypso but was by the Tin Pan Alley composer Cole Porter.[62]

Ken "Snakehips" Johnson was "*the* most important black West Indian musical personality in Britain in the 1930s."[63] He brought several members of the Trinidad Police Band to England in 1937: clarinetist Carl Barriteau, reed man George Roberts, trumpet player Dave Wilkins,[64] and sax player Dave Williams, brother of Trinidad bassist and orchestra leader John "Buddy" Williams.[65] During World War II Manning, Blake, Johnson, and British jazz fans all frequented the Jigs Club. On March 8, 1941, as he was leading his orchestra at the Cafe de Paris in London, Johnson and band member Williams were killed by a bomb dropped by a German aircraft.[66]

Wilkins was born in Barbados but had played in Trinidad with the Jazz Hounds, the Blue Rhythm Orchestra, and the Police Band. While in Trinidad, he played a variety of styles: marches, popular tunes, jazz, and a music new to him, calypso. Soon after arriving in London, Wilkins recorded with the American jazz pianist Fats Waller, then at the top of his career. Later, Wilkins recorded popular songs with Johnson's West Indian Orchestra and even made a television broadcast with that group in 1939. He did not perform calypso in England until 1950, when, as a member of Cyril Blake's orchestra, he recorded behind Lord Kitchener and Lord Beginner (figs. 45 and 46).

Above: **45** ✳ Lord
Beginner, probably
performing with an
English band in
London, 1949. From
the *Trinidad Guardian*.
Left: **46** ✳ Lord
Kitchener, date
unknown. Courtesy of
Herman Hall.

After World War II, immigration to Britain increased as West Indians became a small but permanent minority in greater London, Huddersfield, and several other industrial areas in England. Belasco returned to London in 1948 and recorded two sessions.[67] Beginner arrived on the *Windrush* with the young Lord Kitchener at Tilbury on June 21, 1948.[68] Kitchener would soon become the most important writer of road marches both in England and, later, back in Trinidad.

About fifteen years after a similar process had unfolded in New York, an intensive period of calypso recording began in London, lasting well into the 1950s, when Trinidad was turning away from the older forms of calypso and when America was modifying Trinidadian calypso with recordings by middle-class West Indians (such as Sir Lancelot and Lord Flea) and American popular or folk singers (such as Harry Belafonte and Stan Wilson).

In England, Kitchener and Beginner focused on lavways. Kitchener especially was responsible for carrying the lavway to its greatest heights. Now called "road marches," the short, bouncy forms of calypso composed by Kitch during these years were full of double entendres. Lion also recorded extensively in England during this period.

By the 1940s, then, Trinidadian calypso had established itself for many audiences: Trinidadians, Jamaicans, and Guyanese in their home countries; West Indians in New York; Americans in New York; the British; and the increasing number of West Indians in England. It was also influencing indigenous music in other Caribbean countries and in West Africa.

9 ✳ Selling Calypso in the United States: The Hucksters and the Media

They began selling their copies in Mayaro, Sangre Grande, even at San Fernando in High Street by Black Cat Rum Shop. They were selling their copies in the [Woodford] Square in Port of Spain. Then from there, these people have come to the tent to satisfy the more elite of the calypso crowd. From there to the American radio, and then to Radio City in New York City. It's great, and I think these people really should be taken care of and given special consideration. God have prepared them to take it up to the top.

Tiger

WHEN calypso left Trinidad, its character changed, both at home and abroad. Calypso was on phonograph records; calypso was broadcast over the radio in the United States, including a few broadcasts beamed to Trinidad. Calypsonians appeared in film. A few individuals—Lionel Belasco, Wilmoth Houdini, Sam Manning, Gerald Clark, Lancelot Pinard—were responsible for calypso's foothold in the United States. This chapter will review the professional careers of the calypso hucksters and sketch their impact on radio and in films.

Lionel Belasco and Wilmoth Houdini: Mr. Smartman and the Magician

At home, no two Trinidadian performers were more hated, feared, mistrusted, and yet admired than Lionel Belasco and Wilmoth Houdini. One calypsonian sarcastically called Belasco a real "smartman." Belasco and Houdini, he said, were "two man rat in the same hole." It was said that Belasco was a slick calypso entrepreneur who merchandised Trinidadian folklore to his own advantage. He went to Trinidad many times to hear songs in the tents and to ask the performers to

mid
sic Department
ner Av
VI 53211

Description	Format	Our Price	Total
Hill, Donald R.	Hardcover	$49.95	$49.95

Subtotal		$49.95
Shipping & Handling		3.99
Order Total		53.94
Paid via Visa		53.94
Balance Due		0.00

es your order.

the "Your Account" link on our homepage.

m, and please come again!

Additional Comments:

2/00

New Castle, DE 19720-4172
USA

Problems, Questions, Suggestions?

If you have any questions regarding this order, please e-mail us at: orders@amazon.com

You may also contact us via:
Telephone: 1-800-201-7575 or 1-206-266-2992
Fax: 1-206-266-2950

Thanks for shopping at Amazon.com!
http://www.amazon.com

amazon.com ®

Our Return Policy

Our return policy is simple. **Within 30 days** of receipt of this shipment, you may return:

- any book in its original condition, or any book we recommended (and you didn't enjoy) in any condition

- any unopened CD, DVD, vinyl record, cassette tape, VHS tape, video game, or software

- toys, electronics, tools, home-improvement items, and any other merchandise in new condition, with its original packaging and accessories

We will issue a full refund for the price of any item you return that meets these conditions. We can only refund shipping costs if the return is a result of our error.

Reason for Return

☐ Customer Choice

☐ Incorrect Item Received

☐ Arrived Damaged

Return Instructions

How to Return Home-Improvement, Tools, and Electronics Items (except Software)

To return tools, home-improvement, or electronics items, simply call us at 1-800-201-7575 or e-mail us at electronics-returns@amazon.com for electronics and home-returns@amazon.com for tools and home-improvement items. An Amazon.com customer service representative will issue a return approval and assist you with return shipping. Please keep the original packaging and accessories to return with the item.

NOTE: These items will not be accepted at the return address below without prior approval from a customer service representative.

How to Return All Other Items

Simply indicate the reason for your return, include this packing slip with your return, wrap the package securely, and send the package to the address below. For your protection, we recommend that you use UPS or Insured Parcel Post for shipment.

http://www.amazon.com
orders@amazon.com

W
UW–Milwau
3223
Milwa

Amazon.com
1 Centerpoint Blvd
P.O. Box 15550
New Castle, DE 19720–5550
USA

Toll–Free: (800) 201–7575
Voice: +1 (206) 266–2992
FAX: +1 (206) 266–2950

Your order of March 30, 2000 (Order ID 002–6956850–3716266)

Qty	Item
	In This Shipment
1	Calypso Calaloo : Early Carnival Music of Trinidad (76–5–722)

This shipment

You can always check the status of your or

Thanks for shopping at A

sing their best calypsos for him. Then he returned to New York and made their calypsos his own.

Yet some of the songs copyrighted by Belasco and Houdini and performed by them refer to experiences in New York, not Trinidad. When they used the songs others probably composed, they were conforming to established practices in the sleazy environment of Manhattan's Tin Pan Alley. In addition, a case could be made that Belasco, Houdini, Manning, jazz pianist Clarence Williams, and others modified traditional songs or the compositions of others sufficiently to qualify for copyright. Such a practice may have been immoral in that the true originator of the song was not rewarded for his efforts, but it was not illegal. Furthermore, Belasco, Houdini, and the other New York–based West Indians were partly responsible for putting Trinidadian culture on the map in the United States. They initiated a process that ultimately benefited the calypsonians whose songs they took, although not to the degree they should have been rewarded.

Lionel Belasco

Lionel Belasco was the most important calypso entrepreneur in the first half of the twentieth century. Despite his visible presence and the lengthy interviews he gave to Leonard de Paur and others, little is known about his personal life. Belasco was a secretive man; he told conflicting stories about his life to different people. For example, some people believe he was born in Hastings, Barbados; most who knew him say he was born in Caracas, Venezuela, in about 1882.

His preteen years were spent in both Venezuela and Trinidad. His father, Butin Belasco, was a Sephardic Jew. Butin was a tallyman, a small-time merchant. He played piano and violin and sang baritone. Belasco's mother was a Barbadian Creole who played the organ for St. Patrick's Church in Newtown, Port of Spain.[1] "My mother was one of the best known pianists [in the southern Caribbean]. She studied in Europe. She was the accompanist for Madame [Black] Patti.[2] She went with [her troupe] to B.G. [Guyana] and Barbados. There [were few other] professional[s] in the southern Caribbean at that time."[3]

Belasco's family was prominent in colored Creole circles. For example, his sister married the surgeon dentist of Port of Spain at his mother's church.[4]

Young Lionel studied piano with his mother and with other

instructors, both in Trinidad and in Caracas. The piano was a parlor instrument in those days; it took a great deal of effort to keep it in tune in the tropics, and the presence of a piano in one's home signified a certain social standing. Nevertheless, although Belasco studied European classical music that was composed for the piano, he preferred local, folk, and popular music:

> I use to do all the heavy things [but] I like the "bush" music, as I use to call it, "jungle" music. [My parents] used to think I was crazy. My mother would say to me very often, "Don't bring that thing in here. Please don't play that music, I don't want to hear it here."
>
> I would go out to these jungles. They use to have cock fighting and stick fighting. Those things were prohibited by law but they get in these places. You are a privileged character to be invited to come into these ceremonies. [At that time] I was still playing the classics. I [also] like[d] to go and hear [bands] play [for dances]. The only instruments they [had] were the guitar, violin, flute, clarinet, cuatro. There was no pianist there [in those bands]. I was about the best pianist for that type of music, dance music.
>
> [Eventually, with some] boys that I knew at school—we formed this little band and we started to play Venezuelan waltzes, joropos, Trinidad pasillos, danzas, and that type of thing.

One of his musician friends was a St. Vincent–born Creole named Walter Merrick. Merrick learned to play piano at about age six by copying Belasco.

> I grew up with young men who were all in love with calypso music. . . . [Carnival] bands rehearsed in a bamboo tent adjoining my mother's and father's land in Belmont. There was not a song composed that I did not go there and hear them sing, and join them, and the fellows would come with me and go around with the band.
>
> [I had] copied [Belasco's] style of playing—imitation is the sincerest form of flattery—and even today [1948] in playing of a Spanish waltz or a calypso you can scarcely tell the difference of my playing from Belasco's.[5]

Gerald Clark added to Merrick's comments. Referring to 1906, he said:

> We idealized Lionel Belasco as a great composer of Trinidad who had brought the calypso to a higher state. I played the guitar, and I

learned Belasco's tunes and played them on my guitar. He lived in
Duke Street and I lived in Woodbrook.

Belasco taught [us] to play numbers that he composed, and I used to
go around there and he would show me some and I would catch—we
all never read music—and I would run home and pick up my guitar
and practice it what I had learned from him. I went there myself, but I
met others there, Cyril Monrose, a fellow by the name of James
Minerve, there was Lovey, Donowa. There were quite a few boys.[6]

By the early 1900s, Belasco's band ranked second only to Lovey's as
the most sought after organization for dances and other affairs in
Trinidad. Newspaper notices advertising his band were common.
They played elite dances and parties, including some at the governor's house.

Belasco traveled throughout the Caribbean and the Atlantic coast
of South America in search of talent and accompanying singers and
musicians. One time he "went with the circus company to Brazil and
Argentina. I went around playing the piano and assisting a magician.
When I was 16 or 17 years old I went up the Orinoco [River] in the
jungle, all the way to the Amazon."[7]

A few years later, Belasco got involved in the first commercial
motion pictures shown in Trinidad:

An Englishman came out [to Trinidad] who was interested in oil and
asphalt. I think [his partner's] mother owned a street car system [in
England] or something of this kind. He had an interest in films, silent
pictures. And he says, "There's no picture house around here."

So there was a boy that I had gone to school with who was secretary
of the organization that handled the business of these people, the
asphalt and oil deal. He said he'd put [up] a picture house if he could
get somebody to run it. He called me and explained that this man
wanted to put up a picture house and would I look after it. So I said,
"Yes."

[He said], "You are the only fellow that knows anything about show
business."

Belasco became manager and talent finder for this organization. He
managed the London Electric Theatre in Woodbrook and the Olym-
pic Theatre in Belmont (both districts of Port of Spain).[8] Soon he
visited nearby islands to set up theaters. "So I am really the pioneer of

the motion picture business in Trinidad, B.G. [British Guiana, later Guyana], Barbados, Grenada, St. Vincent because there was no picture houses in those places. The first one that was ever built [in the area] was the one in Trinidad which I had [1914]. I put one up in Port of Spain and one in San Fernando. Then I went to Barbados and I built one. Then I went to Demarara [Guyana] and put up one there."9

In the middle 1910s, Belasco moved to New York. It was rumored that he was forced to leave Trinidad because he had an affair with the governor's daughter, who was one of his piano students. He left the island and she was returned home to England.10

After settling in the United States, Belasco recorded often, including his first recording sessions for Victor in 1915, 1916, and 1917. Belasco described his contributions: "America never knew anything about calypso, pasillos, Venezuelan waltzes, joropos and all that type of music. I was the first one that ever brought that music here. [The Victor Company] left everything to me. At one time I made so many records that I was sick of seeing my name. . . . It was only in the 20s that the West Indians came here and they started buying West Indian records that I had made."

In the late 1920s or early 1930s, Belasco opened a piano store in Harlem. His son, Bert Belasco, recalls that Fats Waller, the American jazz pianist, organist, and entertainer, would drop by the elder Belasco's store to practice a few songs before a night's engagement.11 In 1927, Belasco began to winter in Trinidad where he could learn the latest Carnival songs.12

During one of his trips to Trinidad in late 1932 and early 1933, Belasco found himself in a calaloo.13 Apparently, an arrangement was made for Belasco to help establish and then manage a new movie theater in Port of Spain. The principal financial backers were the Gokools, Trinidadian merchants. The plan was devised by Mikey Cipriani, the Gokools' lawyer, and his brother, A. A. Cipriani, Belasco's longtime friend.14 Belasco was to go to New York with Noor Gokool to buy equipment for the theater. But there were problems almost immediately. Noor Gokool alleged that Belasco had to bribe an immigration official at Ellis Island to get Gokool into the United States (Gokool was a Trinidadian of East Indian descent, and U.S. immigration legislation at that time restricted "Asiatics").

Once in New York, the two set about buying the theater equipment. Very soon, however, Gokool accused Belasco of retaining a "secret commission" when he used the Gokools' money to make purchases for the theater. Belasco said that Gokool "did not understand New York business methods." The Gokools, having paid Belasco's round-trip passage between Trinidad and New York, dropped him from their theater plans. Back in Trinidad, Belasco sued the Gokools and Mikey Cipriani for alleged breach of contract. Belasco lost his case.

After this fiasco, Belasco returned to New York. He recorded for the American Record Company in May 1933, for Bluebird in June, and again for American in July 1934; he then sailed to London with Sam Manning (see chapter 8).

In the late 1930s, Belasco toured the United States with soprano Massie Patterson. Their songs mixed operatic arias and song cycles with formal renditions of African-American and West Indian folk songs, often using their own arrangements. Patterson and Belasco collaborated on a booklet of West Indian songs that included "L'Année Passée," the song on which "Rum and Coca Cola" was based.[15]

After World War II, Belasco continued to travel and to record. "I've recorded all over the world: America, Canada, England, France, Belgium.[16] A lot of these records were folk tunes, a lot of them were my own compositions. I use to do sessions and make 30 or 40 records at a time—20, 25 records. They were made for Venezuela, Trinidad, for Colombia, for Panama and those places."

In the late 1940s, a celebrated American trial lawyer, Louis Nizer, won a historic case for Belasco and his co-plaintiffs in the precedent-setting "Rum and Coca Cola" plagiarism trial (see appendix 1).[17] After this settlement, Belasco made a few records and toured the United States.

In the 1950s, Belasco continued to record. He again toured the United States, this time with Gracitia Faulkner, a concert singer (fig. 47). Lionel Belasco died in New York City on June 24, 1967, at age eighty-five.[18]

Whatever the calypsonians thought of him and however shadowy his persona may seem, the list of Lionel Belasco's public achievements is impressive. As a classically trained pianist who loved the folklore of the islands and coastal South America, he transcribed hundreds of folk songs that might otherwise have been lost. He wrote many songs based on folk material and he wrote popular songs. He performed as a piano accompanist and as an orchestra leader for approximately sixty years in the West Indies, in South America, in Europe, in the United States, and even in Soviet Georgia.[19] He copyrighted hundreds of songs, including many West Indian tunes, that have become world standards. His recording career stretched from 1914 until the mid-1960s, when he recorded a test pressing of a popular song he wrote entitled "Ecstasy." He was the first person to open and manage silent movie theaters in the southern Caribbean. He published two books of stories based on folk tales or personal experiences in tropical South America. He wrote music and lyrics for a movie script (*The Rajah of the Islands*) during the last year of his life. He co-authored music folios of his songs with classically trained singers (Leighla Whipper, Massie Patterson, and Gracitia Faulkner). Clarence Williams (a New Orleans pianist, bandleader, composer, and music publisher) co-authored one of Belasco's song folios.

Belasco's achievements are singular, yet they illustrate social process. As a musically educated man, he represents the imposition of middle-class interests into the grass-roots folk domain in Trinidad. He interpreted grass-roots life because he knew it: It was almost as if he was part of the West Indian masses. Yet he was the son of a petty bourgeois tallyman and a concert pianist. At best he was calypso's greatest entrepreneur and at worst a hustler out for personal gain. As an orchestra leader, his world was writing (or overseeing the writing of) musical scores, managing and leading performances and recording dates, and making tour schedules. This world contrasts with that of the calypso singer with whom he shared the spotlight. Usually calypsonians did not read music and lived a different life-style. Although Belasco mixed with calypsonians, he also lived the life of a middle-class West Indian and that of a sophisticated New Yorker. What he tells us in his interviews with de Paur is colored by his class perspective. Nevertheless, as a West Indian and a participant in all phases of Carnival life, his is also the view of an insider. He represents the type of person who, as the nineteenth century faded away, took control of Carnival in Trinidad, making it the centerpiece of Creole culture.

Wilmoth Houdini

Wilmoth Houdini was the "Calypso King of New York" from the late 1920s through about 1948 (fig. 48). Sam Manning, Phil Madison,

47 * Concert singer Gracitia Faulkner looks on as folk-song popularizer Lionel Belasco directs his orchestra during a tour of the United States, late 1950s. Courtesy of Gracitia Faulkner.

and Johnny Walker—his competitors in New York in the 1920s— were vaudevillians who sang calypso and other popular song forms. MacBeth the Great, Sir Lancelot, and the Duke of Iron, New York– based Trinidadians who sang in the 1940s, appealed primarily to the downtown nightclub audiences. Unlike those singers, Houdini had legitimate Trinidad credentials, having competed in tents before coming to New York, where he continued to borrow heavily from tent singers and kept his calypso close to its Trinidadian roots. He recorded a series of calypso wars against the great Trinidad-based singers, especially Executor and, later, Lion. He established Trini- dadian customs in New York, together with Lionel Belasco, Walter Merrick, Gerald Clark, and Rufus Gorin.

Facts on Houdini's life are quite contradictory, down to his Chris- tian name and where he was born. He sometimes gave different stories to different people.[20] One version of his vital statistics seems to have been created for New York publicists: He was born in Brooklyn, he returned to Trinidad as a young child, he had to leave school because his father lacked money to keep him there, he organized a masquerade band, he triumphed against Executor in the

48 ✳ Houdini, calypso king of New York City. Cover for the 78-rpm Apollo record album no. A-8, late 1940s. Courtesy of Malaco Records.

calypso wars. This mixture of vital statistics and panegyrics is how he wanted his public to see him. Only Errol Hill and John Cowley have seen beyond the magician's illusion.

Houdini told Errol Hill that he was born Frederick Wilmoth Hendricks into a Catholic family in Port of Spain on November 25, 1895.[21] His father was a marine engineer or a steward.[22] As a boy, he was wild and liked to stick fight, a skill he learned from the Tumblin brothers of Chaguanas; he claims that he played *a la trois* in La Cour Harpe against the fabled Fitzie Banray (Gonday) and Jacketman Picou, but his family did not want him to associate with the likes of batonniers in this jamet environment. He said that he attended St. Mary's College in Port of Spain but had to quit because his father could not afford it. Sometime in the late 1910s, he began his participation in Carnival:

> In the year 1916 a band were organized in Port-of-Spain by a distinguished girl named Maggie Otis. She was Queen of the band. I was King. It was called the African Millionaires. It had twenty-four men and girls. The men wore striped green silk shirts, flannel pants, and white shoes, and each had strung to him a camera, a stuffed crocodile, or a pair of field glasses. That was to ape the rich tourists who come to Trinidad. The girls dressed in a manner likewise. At Mardi Gras, which falls on the two days before Lent, the big stores and companies in Port-of-Spain give prizes of rum and money to the Calypsonian who improvises the best song about their merchandise. In 1916 I had the African Millionaires behind me, and I was inspired to become a Calypsonian. So I entered the advertising competitions and won seven in one day, singing extemporaneously against men like the Senior Inventor and the Lord Executor. I collected the big prize from the Angostura Bitters people and the big prize from the Royal Extra Stout brewery people, and all like that. In those competitions you have to improvise a song on the spur of the moment, and it has to be in perfect time with the band. You must be inspired to do so.[23]

Years later, in the interview given to Hill, Houdini said that he sang calypso at his own tent in the Chinese Junk Yard on Prince Street, the practice yard for his band, the African Millionaires. He also sang for this band as chantwell during Carnival. Houdini took his name from the great magician, whose film, *Houdini—The Master Mystery,* played theaters in Trinidad in 1916.

Houdini told Hill that his father wanted him to leave Trinidad because of his wild nature and see some of the world. Houdini's regular job had been to work on the docks of Port of Spain as a stevedore.[24] Occasionally he would sail out on interisland schooners, working as a seaman or as a longshoreman when in port. Soon, just as Atilla had at about the same time, he shipped out of the Caribbean for more distant ports. He served as a seaman, steward, and cook, taking jobs on boats that sailed the Atlantic and put into ports in the Americas.

In 1928, Houdini settled in New York, where he made his first records, with Lionel Belasco and Gerald Clark. He recorded "Uncle Joe Gimme Mo," which, he told Hill, became road march of the year for two years back home in Trinidad. Houdini recorded prolifically after that. In 1934 he claims to have helped Lion and Atilla in their first recording venture in New York. He waged song battles with Executor and others, both on record and in theaters in Trinidad.

Houdini continued to record in the late 1930s and 1940s. The titles of his songs suggest that the major market for his records was in New York and was split between immigrants from the islands and the cafe society set. In Trinidad, the tent singers sold more records than Houdini.

In the late 1930s, Houdini was well established in New York. He sang at the New York World's Fair and recorded several 78-rpm album sets of New York–oriented songs. He actively participated in West Indian bashes centering on the annual Carnival fetes. In spite of this popularity, he lived in a furnished room on West 114th Street in Manhattan's Harlem.[25]

After World War II, several of his songs were covered by Ella Fitzgerald, Louis Jordan, and others and were published as sheet music. For a few years he seems to have been at the top of his career as he gave frequent concerts in Harlem and in midtown Manhattan. He performed at the Caribbean Club on upper Seventh Avenue under the sobriquet King Houdini along with the Duke of Iron, Lord Invader, MacBeth the Great, and others.[26] Then he was accompanied by Gerald Clark's "famous calypso band" for a "Moonlight Caribbean Cruise" up the Hudson River on Friday evening, August 23, 1946.[27]

In 1947, he sang at the Golden Gate Ballroom at 142nd Street and Lenox Avenue in an "Afro–West Indian Shango Carnival and Dance"; also on that bill were Sir Lancelot, Lord Kitchener (before he departed for England with Lord Beginner), the "Hindu Pass Fire King," the "Human Thunderbolt," the Duke of Iron, Lord Invader, Lady Trinidad (the only woman calypsonian to record for Decca in the late 1930s), and "Queen Calypso."[28] Trophies were to be given to Ella Fitzgerald and Louis Jordan, who had recorded Houdini's "Stone Cold Dead in the Market" and "Run Joe," but it is not known whether they attended to pick up their honors. Houdini then played the fabled Apollo Theater in Harlem for one week, beginning on March 28, on a bill with saxophonist Tab Smith's band, slick blues singer Lil Green, and "Pigmeat" (possibly the comic Pigmeat Markham).[29]

In midtown Manhattan, for a mostly white audience, Houdini was on the bill for a major variety show at Carnegie Hall. This concert was held on Thursday, May 8, 1946, and Houdini performed along with Invader, MacBeth, "Princess Orelia and Her Native Dancers," and "Babu" Belasco and His Orchestra.[30] Other concerts followed, including one at Town Hall in October.[31] In 1948, Houdini participated in a show at the Renaissance Casino, a ballroom that would continue to host Trinidadian dances well into the 1980s.[32]

Houdini almost disappears after 1948. His old style of calypso faded in popularity among West Indians in New York in favor of Kitchener, Melody, Beginner, and others. White Americans were turning to America's own singers for their West Indian songs (Belafonte, Stan Wilson, Jordan). Houdini's ebb was in part self-induced. Once described by a fellow calypsonian as "a very pushy little fellow," he reverted for a time to the wild behavior of his youth, and he became embroiled in several serious brawls and in a lawsuit involving accusations of fraud. He made his last records for the Apollo label in New York in 1947.

Houdini visited his home for the last time in 1972. He died in New York on August 6, 1973.[33]

Houdini will be remembered as the first true calypsonian to record extensively and popularize the genre outside Trinidad. Those of us who have not had the good fortune of growing up in Trinidad are in his debt.

Sam Manning

As with Houdini, vital statistics on Sam Manning (fig. 49) are conflicting. He may have been born in Trinidad and attended St. Mary's College, but then again, he may have been born in Barbados and raised in Trinidad. As a young adult in the 1910s, Manning worked as a jockey in British Guiana and in the southern Caribbean.[34] Next he was a motor mechanic. During World War I, he served in the Middlesex and British regiments and in Egypt. After the war, he migrated to New York, cut his first phonograph records, and became a stage performer.

His first appearance on Broadway was as Rastus in the *Processional,* in 1924. He then appeared in *Hey Hey,* a musical said to have been written and produced by Marcus Garvey's former wife, Amy Ashwood Garvey,[35] Manning's traveling companion. Another musical, *Brown Sugar,* opened on August 17, 1927, and was a hit.[36] The

49 ∗ Sam Manning, circa 1935. Courtesy of Max Jones and Musical Traditions.

show featured the title song, written by Manning and Porter Grainger. Manning performed in the *Pepper Sauce Review* and in *Crazy Blues Review,* both staged at the Alhambra Theatre.[37] In August, the papers reported that he was to give his last performance before going into his new career of journalism. No evidence of Manning's writing has turned up, but on February 20, 1929, the *Amsterdam News* reported that Manning, "a former newspaperman and now a musical comedy producer," was suing George W. Harris of the *New York News* for libel.[38] Harris allegedly said that Charles Foley, the publisher of the *Amsterdam News* and the *West Indian Times,* was suing Manning for forgery and larceny. Manning claimed that no warrant for his arrest was issued. He told the reporter that he had eight hundred dollars in receipts from Foley, proving that he had been paying Foley all along what was due him as Manning's publisher. Amy Garvey was also involved in this dispute.

Manning had a short run at the Lafayette Theatre before heading to

Jamaica, where he had theatrical contracts.[39] On the last day of April 1929, he arrived in Jamaica:

SAM MANNING AND SYD PERRIN ARE NOW WITH US
Will Appear At The Palace And Other Theatres
Of Palace-Wilcox Saenger Co.
GREAT FUN MAKERS
First Artist Produced "Lignum Vitae," Second Character Actor
Both Win Fame
Sam Manning the celebrated West Indian comedian is with us and
so is his partner Syd Perrin. They both arrived on the S.S. Celba from
New York yesterday morning and will appear at the Palace and other
theatres which are operated by the Palace-Wilcox Saenger Company.

. . . In a few days we will hear his living voice at the Saenger theatres,
and we will probably learn to appreciate the talent of a man who has
held the coloured as well as a large section of the white population in
New York spell bound.[40]

Their show, *Fine Comedy,* was followed by a "big farewell party,"
and then they were off to Panama "where they will fulfill certain
engagements" and then to Trinidad, Barbados, and England "where
they have a four months' contract." "Mrs. Amy Garvey, who is in
partnership with Mr. Manning in the musical business also left on the
Metapan for Panama. She will be away from the island for a couple of
weeks."[41] The following year, Manning was back at the Alhambra in
New York in a routine entitled *Mr. Squash Meets a Girl.* George
Tichenor described Manning's appearance: "Sam Manning comes on
the stage wearing a pinkish vest and white top hat. His suit is checkered
gray, the trousers fitting close to his stout legs and not quite long
enough. It is Sam's favorite costume and is never out-moded, whatever
the act in which he appears this evening. Sam is ingeniously beguiling,
in the hunching way he walks and his Jamaica accent."[42] In December
1930, Manning made another appearance at the Lafayette Theatre.[43]

In the mid-1930s, Manning lived in London, where he continued
his vaudeville career. He returned to New York in 1941 and briefly
drove a taxicab for a company owned by a Jamaican musician and
entrepreneur, Adolph Thenstead. Manning also had an informal
booking agency for musicians. His career stretched into the 1950s,
when at least one 45-rpm recording was issued, a re-release of
recordings made in the late 1940s.

Calypso over the Radio

In the 1930s and 1940s, radio influenced calypso in two separate ways. First, broadcasts from the United States to Trinidad, although of little artistic success, gave prestige to the singers and their vernacular song style. Second, local and national broadcasts by calypsonians from New York helped to spread calypso to Americans outside New York.

Just like traditional performance, radio was live. As a medium, a radio broadcast is not like newspapers or phonograph records in that the other two media capture time, while radio does not. But radio, like newspapers and records, captures space, while a live performance does not.

In 1934, Atilla and Lion were in New York to cut their pioneering recordings for the American Record Company and Decca. During their recording session for Jack Kapp at Decca, American singer Rudy Vallee was present and liked what he heard. He

> was so struck by this form of music that he arranged an audition for the next day. . . . He selected "Ugly Woman" for inclusion in a programme which he was then doing over the National Broadcasting Company. This broadcast was on coast-to-coast hookup which meant that, weather permitting, it could be heard all over South America and the Caribbean. Elaborate preparations were made in Trinidad. Specially powerful receiving sets were provided in Port-of-Spain by the local distributor of the records and loudspeakers were set up on the roof of adjoining buildings for the purpose of accommodating the large crowds that were expected to gather to hear the broadcast.[44]

The event was advertised heavily by Eduardo Sa Gomes, the sponsor:

SA GOMES RADIO
EMPORIUM
Have Pleasure In Announc-
ing To Radio Fans That On
THURSDAY NIGHT
(NEW YORK TIME—8 P.M.)
FROM
STATION W2XAF
our popular calypso singers
at present in New York

making records of last carnival calypso hits
LION AND ATILLA THE HUN
WILL BROADCAST
Two Peppy Calypso Hits
accompanied by the Carib-
bean Orchestra (Gerald Clark)

———

Don't fail to listen and
hear two of our best
calypso hits come over
the ether

———

SA GOMES RADIO
EMPORIUM
Distributors
Brunswick Record
Corporation[45]

Although the broadcast was not entirely successful—in San Fernando, islanders could tune it in, but at Sa Gomes Emporium in Port
of Spain it could not be heard—it was an important symbolic gesture
in legitimizing calypso outside Trinidad in the eyes of Trinidadians
themselves.[46] Atilla and Lion recorded a song detailing their experience on that Rudy Vallee show:

We were making records for the Decca Company
When we were heard by Rudy Vallee
Well he was so charmed with our rhythmic harmony
He took us in hand immediately
"You boys are wonderful," by Rudy Vallee we were told
"You must throw your voice through the radio
   to the whole wide world."
And so you should a see the Lion and me
With Mae West and Rudy Vallee.[47]

In the following year, Beginner, Atilla, and Tiger, on a recording
trip for Decca, again broadcasted to Trinidad.[48] For a while, they may
have broadcasted every year to Trinidad after Carnival season, for

there is another notice of a broadcast of calypsonians accompanied by Gerald Clark's orchestra over a Schenectady, New York, radio station. As intriguing as these first broadcasts of calypso were, they were one-shot deals. More significant were the regular local and, later, network broadcasts from New York for the American audience. Only after World War II was calypso regularly broadcast in Trinidad itself.

The postwar broadcasts had varied audiences. Some radio performances seem to have been arranged by Clark, whose orchestra backed many different calypsonians. He broadcasted over WHN in New York City on Sunday evenings from 5:00 to 5:30. His group participated in the *Daily Mirror*'s comedy show, "Goldmine in the Sky," broadcast over New York's NBC affiliate, WINS, on March 25, 1940.[49]

By 1941, the Duke of Iron, who gained fame in New York singing with Clark's group at the Vanguard, had his own radio program (fig. 50). He broadcasted on WOV on Sundays and Tuesdays. According to a *New York Amsterdam News* article published the day before the U.S. entry into World War II, Clark and his orchestra were popular in Latin America, "where the musical aggregation was acclaimed as one of the most outstanding exponents of South American swing."[50]

During the war, calypsonians were regularly featured on Orson Welles's "Mercury Theater," one of the most popular radio shows in the United States. After the war, calypso over the airwaves intensified as both African Americans and white Americans with no special West Indian connections recorded calypsos. For example, Fred Robbins featured calypso on his radio program, the "1280 Club," on WOV in New York.

In 1947, Sir Lancelot, another alumnus of Gerald Clark's stand at the Vanguard, broadcasted nationwide on folk singer Burl Ives's radio show, "Philco's Friendly Troubadour."[51]

Meanwhile, the Lord Caresser, still another graduate of the seminal stage review at the Vanguard, was in Canada, broadcasting "to listeners through the Dominion of Canada."[52] Calypso, in a form that was no longer Trinidadian, was on its way to becoming a branch of North American popular music.

Sir Lancelot and Calypso on Film

To this point, all of the calypsonians and entertainers who have been examined in detail performed first for a Trinidadian audience, then

50 ✳ The Duke of Iron with unidentified musicians, publicity photograph, late 1950s. From Allied Artists.

for a generalized West Indian audience, and then for an African-American and white American audience. Sir Lancelot represents the first entertainer whose primary audience was the last group.

The white American interest in calypso in clubs in New York and on records spread throughout the country in the early 1940s. Some calypsonians, such as Caresser, the Duke of Iron, Lord Invader, and Lion, modified their performances to appeal to this new audience. One of this new breed of calypso singers, Lancelot Pinard, brought calypso to the motion pictures.[53]

Lancelot Victor Edward Pinard was born in Trinidad to wealthy parents[54] (fig. 51). His father was a bureaucrat who loved European—especially English—culture. Young Pinard's education included tutors, parochial schools, German lieder, Italian operatic arias, and, when he completed secondary school, New York City, where his father wanted him to study medicine. In New York, he ran into Gerald Clark, who was in need of a singer for a recording date on the Varsity label. Clark had heard Pinard give a concert of lieder and arias. Lancelot had never sung calypso, and his family came from an upper-middle-class back-

51 ∗ Publicity photograph of Sir Lancelot, 1950s. Courtesy of Lancelot Pinard and Ray Funk.

ground in which calypso was pleasantly amusing—as long as it was sung by someone else and as long as the women of the family were kept away from the calypso tents. But this was New York, not Trinidad, and so Pinard accepted Clark's offer. Pinard recorded with the Caribbean Serenaders and then worked with Clark and MacBeth the Great at the Village Vanguard. When he returned home he found that he was not the success with his family and friends that he expected to be. "Gentlemen didn't sing calypsos at that time. I was the first, and when I went back to Trinidad, my friends did not receive me, and my brothers told my dad, 'You can't let Lancelot sing those calypsos down here. It'll ruin us.' "[55] Back in New York, Sir Lancelot, as he was now known, was booked to sing with Lionel Belasco on a tour of Oregon and California. The California appearance resulted in a small role singing in *Two Yanks in Trinidad,* a film starring Pat O'Brien and Janet Blair.

Lancelot liked California and decided to stay, and his film career was launched. Over the years, he appeared in many films, some of them classics. He sang in *Happy Go Lucky,* a 1943 film staring Mary Martin and Dick Powell.[56] He sang his monster hit, "Shame and Scandal on the Family" (fig. 52), in *I Walked with a Zombie,* a 1943 film that later became a cult classic in the United States. He had a brief nonsinging appearance as Horatio in *To Have and Have Not* (1944) with Humphrey Bogart and Lauren Bacall. He played the pirate, Scipio, in *The Buccaneer* (1958) with Anthony Quinn and Yul Brynner. His résumé following that film read:

SIR LANCELOT——CALYPSO BALLADEER
(Lyric Tenor)
ACTOR, SINGER-GUITARIST, COMPOSER
LINGUIST, WORLD TRAVELER

Age range: 45–50	Hair: Black
Height: 5' 7"	Eyes: Brown
Weight: 168 lbs.	Born: Trinidad W.I.

Twenty-five years experience in Radio, Stage, Screen and Night Clubs. Speaks with typical British Colonial Accent. Sings in—and speaks some . . . FRENCH, MALAY, HINDI AND RUSSIAN! IS AN AUTHORITY ON CARIBBEAN DIALECTS INCLUDING FRENCH PATIOS (MARTINIQUE), AND TAKI-TAKI (SURINAM).

CARLOS ALVARADO AGENCY	DALE GARRICK
652–0272 & 655–6840	INTERNATIONAL
	HOLLYWOOD

OL. 7–2661   (For T.V. only)[57]

Altogether, Sir Lancelot sang or acted in fifteen films and wrote songs for several additional films or cartoons.

In his years in Hollywood, Lancelot appeared often on the radio

52 * Label for a 78-
rpm Sir Lancelot
record. 1940s.

and on television (fig. 53). He wrote calypsos, calypsos, and more calypsos. Many of his songs written in the 1940s have an idealistic, left-wing, or patriotic flavor ("Century of the Common Man," "Defenders of Stalingrad," and the most famous of these, "Walk in Peace"). He may have been the first English-speaking West Indian to maintain a strong presence in North American commercials, which he wrote himself and read or performed. He usually sang in them with a calypso-esque touch:

> The Plymouth car is the best by far
> So comfy with no sway, no jar
> Look at the features, the luxury line
> The beautiful Plymouth is new a long time.

Pinard was popular on the dinner circuit, composing calypsos to fit specific occasions as in this example:

> I would like to sing a little calypso
> About a distinguished gentleman whom we all know
> The newly appointed District Attorney
> Of Los Angeles County.
> William B. McKessen is his name
> His name is secure in the hall of fame
> A friend to the youth of our country
> And a fighter in the cause of humanity.

53 ✳ Sir Lancelot with Gerald Clark and His Orchestra, New York or Hollywood, 1940s. Left to right: Gerald Clark, guitar; Rogelio Garcia, bass; Gregory Felix, clarinet; Jack Celestain, piano; MacBeth the Great, maracas; Sir Lancelot; Felix Pacheco, violin. Courtesy of Lancelot Pinard and Ray Funk.

Lancelot exuded a warm, laughing confidence that was not threatening to the white male Americans upon whom his career depended. He was assertive without being aggressive, and he could play stereotyped roles, as the best of the tragic African-American performers were forced to do, with humor and grace. In the film *I Walked with a Zombie*, Lancelot's lead song, "Shame and Scandal on the Family," set the stage for sweating and shirtless Haitians who beat voodoo drums amid bloodsucking zombies.

Sir Lancelot certainly was not a calypsonian by a Trinidadian's definition of the term. Had he remained in Trinidad, he would never have become a calypsonian; his family would have not allowed it. Furthermore, his smooth, cultivated tenor voice seems more at home with "I'll Take You Home Again Kathleen" than with "Out the Fire!" Nevertheless, he surely would have become a fine ghostwriter of calypso lyrics in Trinidad, if not a calypsonian.

Lancelot Pinard knew many languages and several cultures. He was at home with the people in Hollywood who, in large measure, shaped North American popular culture. Pinard translated calypso for American tastes, and they learned his calypso and mimicked it. No Trinidadian had more influence on the form of the 1950s calypso boom in the United States than Sir Lancelot. One can see this in the style of his songs, especially his cute couplets with lockstep rhymes. Although some of the songs in the American calypso boom were legitimate calypsos, American compositions in a calypso vein followed Lancelot's pattern. One of the best examples of this type was written by Louis Gottlieb and Malvina Reynolds:

> There is a girl called Grace Kelly
> She's as pretty as she can be
> And when she weds she does it good
> According to the rules of Hollywood.
> Monaco, Monaco
> A delightful place I know
> If you want to make a show
> Marry the Prince of Monaco.

10 ✳ Censorship
and the Steel Band

Well, the last train to San Fernando
Well, the last train to San Fernando
And you miss this train, you never get
  another one

"Last Train to San Fernando"

"Last Train to San Fernando" was the most popular road march (lavway) of 1950. It was played through the streets of Port of Spain by steel bands, the brash new orchestras that had gained musical hegemony over Carnival. The words refer to the closing of the passenger railroad, once the most important north-south link between Port of Spain and San Fernando. The train had been opened in 1882, ironically, the year after the first canboulay riot. A paved highway for buses, autos, and carts would take its place. Trinidad was on a new route, and so was calypso.

At the beginning of this metamorphosis, three developments contributed to change in Carnival and even to change in Trinidadian society. First, calypsonians in some of the established tents introduced more political and sexual themes into their songs. The government turned to draconian measures to stop these new calypsos. Next, this censorship in the tents paralleled labor unrest among Creole and East Indian workers on the sugar estates and in the oil fields. Third, unrest grew among the working class and the jamet in Port of Spain, especially after World War II, when unemployment was high. From this urban unrest, particularly in Laventille, one of the most important acoustic musical instruments of the twentieth century—the pan—was developed.

Restriction of Carnival and the Censorship of Music: An Overview

Music censorship has a long, sordid history in the British Caribbean. It was a part of wider restrictions applied to both slaves and free people of color before emancipation and to nonwhites after emancipation.

In many British colonies, drumming was restricted for fear that slaves would drum as a means to incite rebellion.[1] In Trinidad, only one month after the 1797 Capitulation of the Spanish, the British passed a law requiring free coloreds to get police permission to hold dances after eight o'clock at night. Slaves could dance only in "appropriate places" and only before that hour.[2] This law was amended in 1808. The terror of Governor Thomas Picton's rule resulted in the Slave Ordinance of 1800, which put slaves almost completely at the mercy of their owners.[3] In 1802, slaves were overheard singing a rebellious song, as part of a secret society complete with kings, mock courts, and ominous plans to murder hated planters. This plan was brutally suppressed.[4]

After emancipation, an ordinance was passed (Ordinance Number 6, 1849), restricting Carnival to two days and making it illegal for blacks to appear masked.[5] In 1868, a law prohibited singing obscene songs.[6] To enforce that law, the police needed proof; that is, someone had to sing the song before he could be prosecuted. In 1869, restrictions on Carnival were tightened as carrying lighted torches was regulated.[7] After the Carnival riots of the early 1880s, regulations were imposed in 1884 on Carnival and its music (see chapter 3). More rules were applied to jamet Carnival in 1891, 1893, and 1895. The censorship of the 1930s and 1940s follows this tradition.

In 1930 Atilla sang a calypso about Kenneth Vincent Brown, a city magistrate who had been made a judge:

> Kenneth Vincent Brown
> You always doing something that's wrong (repeat)
> West Indian papers all freely state
> That you are no good as a magistrate
> For you always cause dissatisfaction
> With your rotten jurisdiction.[8]

Atilla thought that his song resulted in Brown's ruling to close tents exactly at 10:00 P.M. Previously, some leeway was allowed in interpreting the regulations for closing the tents.

The Theatre and Dance Hall Ordinance, which passed the Legislative Council on December 13, 1934, in time for Christmastide and Carnival (see chapter 8), must be viewed in the light of the earlier ordinances. While the 1868 law censored topical songs after they had been sung, the 1934 ordinance called for calypsonians to submit lyrics to the police before singing them in the tent. "Imagine going daily to apply for a permit and waiting from 8.30 a.m. until 3.30 p.m. to obtain it, when the show was due to commence at 8 p.m."[9] In effect, the police could ban any song they wanted to ban, based on requests from senior government officials: "Use your influence to stop the calypsonian from singing the song, cause it is very embarrassing."[10]

The Roaring Lion recalled, "Sometimes the police would come to the shows . . . and try to stop the song." He tricked censors by submitting Biblical verses written out as calypso lyrics. Along with the supposedly obscene songs that he wanted to take to New York to record, songs that censors routinely banned without a reading, the police censored the biblical passages.[11] On another occasion, Eduardo Sa Gomes tipped police that certain Bluebird calypso records in customs, imported by his rival Akow, contained "smut."[12] The British customs agents took control of the records, listened to a few, and ordered the shipment dumped in the ocean. To get back at Sa Gomes, Akow made the same claim against the next shipment of Decca records imported by Sa Gomes. Those records also were dumped in the sea.

There are many other examples of restrictions on free speech in Trinidad under this ordinance. Just as the police turned up the heat, however, so did the calypsonians. In 1937, Executor wrote a calypso against the Shop Closing Ordinance (see appendix 1). In 1944, he penned another against the government food distribution plan.[13] In the same year, Atilla, a newly elected member of the Port of Spain City Council, continued to attack the government with his calypsos. In 1948, the police attempted to censor Pharaoh's "The Governor Tall Tall Tall." In 1949, Atilla needed legal assistance to get permission to sing "That Questionable Canon." Tiger got by the censors with one of his rare obscene calypsos, "Leggo the Dog Jemma."[14]

In 1940, while Decca was recording calypsos and East Indian songs in Trinidad, the police entered the recording studio and "enquire[d] whether a record was being made having to do with His Excellency the Governor. The reply was no. The police rejoined that they would permit no such record to be made."[15] The police were worried that Lion would sing his song on a mysterious murder of a military officer just outside Government House, in the savannah. Lion did not record this song, but he apparently sang it in the tents:

> A man was found dead around the savannah
> Some say it's suicide, others say it's murder
> You may draw your own conclusion
> I reserve my opinion.[16]

Other songs were not censored in 1940. Atilla's songs that year were innocuous. Beginner's calypsos were about Hitler or were the usual Carnival road marches. It was the same with Caresser, Executor, Gorilla, Growler, Invader, Lion, Destroyer, Ziegfeld.

However, Pretender's song "Policemen" seemed to be a candidate for censorship. Tiger sang "In My Own Native Land," a song about the restriction of bongo music at wakes. He also sang "Let Them Fight for Ten Thousand Years," in which he took a neutral position on World War II.

The most interesting of the censorable songs recorded by Decca in 1940 is Radio's "Sedition Law":

> Believe, I warning the rich and poor
> Be careful, friends today, from this seditious
>   law . . .

> If you talk without defense, you have no evidence
> They mean to license we mouth
> They don't want we talk . . .

> I agree with any man who speaking for their rights
> But you cannot say everything what you like
> There's certain things would affect the authority
> Who was the strength and the force in this colony
> And when you get the blow, in the jail you'll walk.

> You wants to be versed in politics
> I mean, you got to be cocky with a lots of tricks

First you got to use a little diplomacy
Mix up with common sense and psychology
And when you get the blow, not only talk
They mean to license we foot,
They don't want we walk . . .

Politics improving our native land
We lectured and preached by women and men
But you gotta know, friends, what you talking about
As you're sure to pay darn dear for your mouth
So, if you know you can't use the knife and fork
They mean to license we mouth,
They don't want we talk.[17]

In the tent version, this song concerns Buzz Butler and the labor unrest. Radio probably adapted it to fit broader censorship issues; after all, Radio's 1934 song got the government enraged on this issue in the first place. In the recorded version of "Sedition Law," Radio may have left out the Butler verses in an attempt to get it by the censors. This and the other critical calypsos were probably recorded when the police were not present. The masters were then taken to New York, where the records were pressed. Most were not allowed back into Trinidad or were destroyed when found by the police.

Tubal Uriah "Buzz" Butler, the Oil Workers Strike, and Calypso

Between 1934 and 1936 the calypsos that were censored were considered obscene or involved peccadillos by important people. But the labor problems that the colony experienced at the beginning of Britain's involvement in World War II added a new category of calypsos to be censored—those concerning labor.

The most militant labor supporter was an enigmatic worker named Tubal Uriah "Buzz" Butler (fig. 54). Butler was born in Grenada in 1897 and immigrated to south Trinidad in 1921 to work in the oil fields in Fyzabad.[18] He was active in the Trinidad Labour Party until 1935, when he and Adrian Cola Rienzi broke with party leader A. A. Cipriani, believing that Cipriani was out of touch with south Trinidad and the more militant methods its labor leaders used against the oil interests.

Butler and Rienzi were reacting to a ruling by the Wages Advisory

54 ✳ Labor activist
Tubal Uriah "Buzz"
Butler, date unknown.
In 1937 Butler led
Trinidadian oil workers
out on strike,
precipitating rioting
and government
censorship of calypsos
written in support of
the workers. Courtesy
of the Roaring Lion.

Board that had lowered the minimum wage from 1920 levels to an astonishing forty-six cents a day in the countryside and sixty-nine cents a day in Port of Spain.[19] This action occurred in the face of two commissions that had heard testimony that housing and sanitation conditions around the oil fields "lack[ed] of elementary needs of decency."[20] Furthermore, workers could be fired without cause.

Cipriani had agreed to the terms of the Wages Advisory Board, with their disastrous consequences, even as the oil companies gave their stockholders dividends of 30 percent in 1935 and 1936.[21]

Butler mixed his unionism with his own version of the Moravian Baptist Church, which was called Butlerism. Rienzi was a socialist. Together, they founded the Trinidad Citizens League in 1935.[22] In 1937, Butler, with his charismatic appeal and Christian imagery, pulled out of the Trinidad Labour Party entirely. In June 1937, he led a strike of the workers in the south. When the authorities tried to arrest Butler on June 19, wildcat strikes broke out in Fyzabad, followed by rioting. The unrest spread throughout Trinidad.[23] Atilla reported on the discontent:

> I wanted material for a calypso
> So I took a bus to San Fernando
> But I wouldn't tell you friends all I saw
> For I'm afraid of the sedition law.
> Fyzabad was like a battlefield
> Police surrounded by a ring of steel
> With blood and carnage litterin' the scene
> And pandemonium reigning supreme.[24]

In several violent confrontations, twelve civilians and two policemen were killed, while nineteen people were wounded.[25] Tiger sang about a supposed participant in the riot:

> (I mean to say) your advice was fine
> Miss Marie, but I change my mind
> (Thank you so much) your advice was fine
> Miss Marie, but I change my mind
> Is you that say that four dollars a week for me pay
> Can't support no woman today
> I joined the strikers and what happened finally
> They gave me three months in custody . . .

> (You could believe, I mean to say) my business was low
> So I joined the longshoremen and stevedore
> And I strike, going along the town
> Closing down business right around
> I persevere, I saw a police in the rear
> He discharged a shot in the air
> I had no fear but they shot me partner St. Clair
> I greased me heel and disappear.[26]

Like the fictitious striker in "Miss Marie's Advice," Butler went into hiding:

> The police, the police, they search here and there
> Sergeants and majors, they tore out their hair
> In kitchens, in attics, in country and town
> But still, elusive Butler, he couldn't be found.[27]

Cipriani and the Trinidad Labour Party denounced the strike and the rioting as the one-time champion of labor railed against "Communistic tendencies."[28] Labour was crushed. Butler reappeared and was placed under arrest, to be put on trial for sedition. He was found guilty and was jailed.

Governor Sir Murchison Fletcher and the acting colonial secretary, Howard Nankiwell, were not prepared to blame Butler or the strikers for the riots. Both spoke out against the sugar and oil interests and their maintenance of low wages and poverty of their workers.[29] Atilla sang about Nankiwell's speech to the Legislative Council:

> Hand me the Port of Spain [*Gazette*]
> To read Mr. Nankiwell's speech again
> Hand me the Port of Spain [*Gazette*]
> To read Mr. Nankiwell's speech again
> Replete with tact and sympathy
> Fair play and Christian charity
> We promise that, whatever they do
> Trinidad will remember you . . .
> He spoke feelingly and strikingly
> Logically and conscientiously
> His diction was perfect, elocution great
> To describe his speech, words are inadequate
> He said: "We who plant the cane and dig the oil
> And develop the estates with sweat and toil
> While employers are living luxuriously
> Why should we die in misery?"[30]

Fletcher gradually returned order to the colony by meeting with groups of strikers. He helped to pass an ordinance that established an eight-hour workday and a minimum wage.

But the business interests in Trinidad moved against Fletcher and Nankiwell and were able to get the governor to change course and request British troops. Because he once had sympathy for the strikers and then changed his mind, the Colonial Office considered Governor Fletcher to be indecisive. They removed him from office and recalled him to London:[31]

> In my opinion, Sir Murchison Fletcher
> Was our ablest governor (repeat first two lines)

We only wish the Downing Street authorities
Would send more men like him to the West Indies
His resignation was a shock to me
Regretted throughout this colony.[32]

In February 1938, as the Petroleum Association and the Sugar
Manufacturers Association were reasserting their power, the Forester
Commission released its report. Although it noted the poor working
and living conditions of labor, it backed the suppression of the rioters
and of the government's quest to control Butler's union. Atilla lam-
basted the report:

The report of the Commission of Inquiry
Has arrived in this colony
The report of the Commission of Inquiry
Has arrived in this colony
It touches health and sanitation
Housing, wages and education
It stated the riots were terrible
And declares Butler was responsible.

Through the unrest that we had recently
A Commission was sent from the Mother Country
To investigate and probe carefully
The cause of the riots in this colony
They accumulated a bulk of evidence
I cannot speak of their competence
But I can say independently
The report was a revelation to me.

They criticize our ex-governor
The beloved Sir Murchison Fletcher
And Howard Nankiwell, they said that he
Had uttered speeches wrong to a marked degree
They castigated him severely
Our ex-Colonial Secretary
But all these things just appear to me
An example of English "diplomacy."

They said through the evidence they had
That the riot started at Fyzabad

By the hooligan element under their leader
A fanatic Negro called Butler
Who uttered speeches inflammatory
And caused disorders in this colony
The only time they found the police was wrong
Was when they stayed too long to shoot people down.

A peculiar thing of this Commission
In their ninety-two lines of dissertation
Is there is no talk of exploitation
Of the worker or his tragic condition
Read through the pages there is no mention
Of capitalistic oppression
Which leads one to entertain a thought
And wonder if it's a one-sided report.[33]

This song, "Commissioner's Report," although recorded in Trinidad, was banned on the island.[34]

Later commissions called for a guided labor movement, but even this was too much for the business interests.[35] With Butler in jail, Rienzi and others expanded labor's role in economic affairs. A decade and a half later, the labor movement in Trinidad would become the dominant force in the political life of the colony on the eve of independence.

In addition to the anticolonial calypsos and the labor trouble in the South, there were other Creole voices speaking out against colonialism, both at home in Trinidad and abroad. There was the Negro Welfare, Cultural and Social Association, led by middle-class blacks. This group also attacked Cipriani's labor leadership.[36] Other developments included concern over Italy's invasion of Ethiopia, the rise of the Pan-African movement in London led by Trinidadian George Padmore, and the development of an intellectual movement in Port of Spain that was partly modeled after the Harlem Renaissance of the 1920s.

Yet the most concrete development in the north, paralleling Butler's religio-labor movement in the south, was not so much the labor and upper-class cultural developments in Port of Spain but the grass-roots involvement in Carnival. Their interests eventually pushed some middle-class Creoles to become an effective voice for the disenfranchised Creoles. The new Carnival spawned by the grass roots was the steel-band movement.

The Steel Band

The steel-band movement fell right in place along other overtly festive but symbolically political developments in Carnival. Fancy masquerade social unions had ushered in modern Creole Carnival and had set in motion a series of changes in Trinidad's folk culture. These changes led to the tents and to the development of calypso as a form of popular music. If fancy mas was a harbinger of colored Creole power for the middle class, the steel band was a forerunner of a re-afrocreolization of the entire Creole complex, a development that eventually led to political independence. Carnival was once again being pushed by the grass roots, as in the 1880s. These groups tended to retain Afro-Creole culture to a greater degree than the middle and upper classes. The fusion of the new steel-band Carnival to the structure of the middle-class fancy mas' Carnival that had been evolving for fifty years resulted in a modern, truly Creole-Trinidadian popular culture, a re-afrocreolized culture.[37]

The deepest roots of the steel band go back through calinda to West Africa.[38] A ban on drumming, on which calinda depend, was passed in 1883 in the wake of the 1881 Carnival riot. This led to the increased use of bamboo orchestras to accompany stick fights in the urban areas where the ban could be enforced.

Bamboo accompaniment to calindas was recorded in the 1910s. Among others, Jules Sims recorded "Meet Me Round the Corner" in Trinidad in 1914 with a bamboo band. In 1935, Houdini recorded in New York with the tamboo bamboo, even as that configuration was phased out back home.[39]

The depression of the 1930s forced a creative idleness on some urban young men in and around Port of Spain. Depression-era Carnival, for the poor, began with bamboo bands exploding from Hell Yard—the same Hell Yard where the likes of Cutouter used to play stick. Other bands came from yards in East Dry River, John John, Newtown, and elsewhere. Then, in the middle of the decade, bamboo instruments were gradually augmented with instruments made from assorted metal containers, especially biscuit tins.[40] Over a period of years, the sound of bamboo tubes being struck with sticks was drowned out by the "terrific din set up by the clanking pieces of tin," as one newspaper story put it in 1937.[41] The deeper sound of a brake drum hit with a piece of steel was added to the sound of the bottle and stone, bottle and spoon, or gin bottle that had been a constant feature of the bamboo bands.

By the end of the decade, the biscuit, lard, pitch oil (kerosene), or dust tins had become the backbone of some pan bands, which might contain some twenty pieces of metal containers, one bottle and spoon, and one brake drum per band (fig. 55). These instruments survive today in small configurations, accompanying "job molassie" (which tends to use pitch oil tins) and other rude devil bands in Carriacou, Grenada, at Brooklyn's Labor Day Carnival, and, of course, in Trinidad. Raphael De Leon notes that in the late 1930s, biscuit tins were beaten as part of the "Judas parody" in which schoolchildren burn an effigy of Judas on Good Friday.[42] Yet the degree to which the Judas parody influenced the development of the pan band is not known. By 1938 there were several bands that had more or less converted from bamboo to metal instruments, and by 1940 pan bands were undergoing constant evolution in several yards.

One such band, not necessarily the most important one, was the Newtown band out of Big Yard, a barracks yard in Newtown near Woodbrook.[43] In the early 1930s it was a bamboo band whose members were poor young men from the area. By late in the decade the Newtown band had converted mostly to pans. At the time its leader was Carleton Forde of Woodbrook. For Carnival 1940[44] its name was changed to "Alexander's Ragtime Band," the title of a popular American film musical released in 1938 and probably shown in Trinidad in 1939 after Carnival. For Carnival, the band was supported by its own group of masqueraders whose theme was based on the film. Lion wrote a song about the group in 1940:

> Here the kind of song they sang in Town
> Christmas night when the bands were going around (repeat)
> They had the bottle and the spoon and biscuit-pan
> Better known as Alexander Ragtime Band
> And the leggo was,
> > "Zhuway, zhuway talalee levay"
> > We know it as job molassie band

55 ✳ Biscuit-tin band, probably in Port of Spain, before 1945. Photograph by Y. DeLima.

> Bad behaviour and boboley band
> But New Town boys changed the name
> And decided to invade Port-of-Spain
> So they marched down Town banner in hand
> Signed "Alexander Ragtime Band."
> They were singing, etc., etc.[45]

Sometime after 1939, several individuals and groups experimented with their new pan instruments by shaping notes on the top of the tins and playing simple melodies. One of the first was Winston Spree Simon of John John, whose mythic account of this development was recited at his eulogy in Brooklyn by Father Albert Clarke in 1976:

> In the year 1939, between the months of May or June—I cannot remember exactly which month—it happened one evening when the John John band was parading the streets of the village in full force. I lent my kettle drum, which had a special sound because it was made of a light, soft metal, to a strong friend of mine called "Wilson." I wanted to get a "jump up" and I wanted to rest from the drumming. Upon my return, I found that the face of the pan was beaten in very badly and the particular tonal sound that I had was gone. I also recognized the concave appearance. I then started pounding the inside surface of the drum to restore it to its original shape. I was using a stone. While

pounding at different points with varying strength I was surprised and shocked! I was able to get varying sounds or pitches. I then tried a piece of wood; the sounds or pitches were a little mellower. I was fascinated. I was able to get distinctly separated musical notes.

Thereupon I was able to knock four notes out. I turned my knowledge over to the other members of the band and steel band was born.[46]

Actually, Simon's story could stand as well for others who were experimenting with the pans in many yards in Port of Spain.

In 1940, Decca Records returned to Trinidad for their last field recording session before the war closed in. And record they did: calypsonians Ziegfeld, Tiger, Atilla, Beginner, Caresser, Executor, Growler, Invader, Lion, Destroyer, Pretender, and Radio all cut sides, and the Sa Gomes Rhythm Boys sang a tune called "Cambulay" with a bamboo band. Louis L. Sebok, a vice president of Decca, in Trinidad for the recordings, described "the real native music that is so characteristic of the Trinidad Carnival. No longer does the bamboo band hold sway, it having given place to the steel drums with bottle and spoon. This 'Steel Music' as it is called, has also been recorded."[47] As far as is known, no record masters of the steel band survive from these Decca sessions.

In 1942, outdoor Carnival was banned by the British authorities. Nevertheless, some of the pan men attempted to take to the streets and the first of a series of disturbances began.[48] One American wrote of the incident:

> On Carnival Monday, [I went out] . . . to see whether there would be any celebrations in spite of the law against it, but all I saw was more people than usual standing around in the streets and on the sidewalks looking sort of angry. A man told me they were having music and dancing up on Laventille Hill and if the cops tried to stop that, they would beat them up.
>
> The following morning there was a notice in the newspaper: "Four carnival players jailed. Except for a few miscreants, four of whom were sent peremptorily to prison for twenty-one days, Port of Spain yesterday observed the government's order prohibiting the celebrations of carnival this year. The men were members of a band estimated at 150 and the policemen who intervened were stoned. Major Knights, who prosecuted, told the magistrate that a band of about 150 strong was parading Duke Street about 6:30 o'clock in the

morning, jumping and shouting to music provided by biscuit drums, bottles and spoons. The police intervened and arrested four of them. . . . The magistrate, in convicting the men, said, 'This is a serious offense. These are not ordinary times: you must know there is a war going on and for that reason people cannot go about as at other times. You must do twenty-one days.' "[49]

This police crackdown was probably popular with the general public.[50] For the average middle-class Trinidadian, this rump Carnival was just another rude celebration coming from bacchanalia, Laventille.

While some pan men fought with the police, others took their creations to the tents. In one such tent, on Dimanche Gras night, "the band accompanying the singers consisted only of percussion instruments: drums, biscuit pans of different sizes, bottles and spoons, which produced strange sounds and piercing rhythm."[51]

The next year, still under wartime restrictions, Trinidadian folklorist Edric Connor lectured on the steel band's development at the Princes Building in Port of Spain, with the Gonzales steel band demonstrating its sound.[52] This was the first step in a long march toward respectability for the steel band.

For the next few years a debate was joined within middle-class circles about whether the incipient steel orchestras represented a corrupting influence or an art. Canon Max Farquhar, chair of a newly constituted government committee set up to investigate the issue, wrote this of the steel-band musicians:

Educationally they have been denied everything beyond a smattering of the 3 R's. Vocationally they stand in No Man's Land. Socially they are condemned to conditions in which home life, as understood by their critics, does not exist. In the matter of religion they have been literally abandoned to their own resources. They are normally shunned as the unwanted and undesirable and subjected to taunts and reproaches. Thus ostracised and estranged from the circumstances and the people who alone could help them, they are driven out like lepers of old into the wilderness and waste places of society. . . . Instead of surrendering to sullen despair or violent retribution, they turn to the escapism of music and roam our streets, the gay troubadours of a race who traditionally in the face of adversity have found relief in dancing and song.[53]

In 1941 the United States, as a part of its lend-lease arrangement with Great Britain, constructed a naval base and airfield in Trinidad. After the war, when they scaled down their operation, empty fifty-five-gallon oil drums were plentiful. These gradually replaced the flimsy metal containers that had been used to make steel drums.

One person who used these discarded drums was pan tuner Ellie Mannette, a youth from Woodbrook. He was among the first steel-band players to tune the oil drums, which he did by annealing the drum's bottom and pounding out a series of concave notes in it. Mannette then cut the cylinder to about five or six inches high, and the oil drum's base became the pan's melody-making top. The tuned pan was fitted with straps, which allowed the musician to play the pan at his waist with the strap passing behind his neck. Later, special rod-iron carts were invented to carry entire pan orchestras through the streets during Carnival.

The key pan in the early steel band was the "ping pong," a tenor instrument that could play more than one octave. There were several different schemes for arranging the notes on the top of the pan, none of them standard, although Mannette's and several others were widely copied. In addition to the tenor pan, cello and a set of four bass pans were used.

In 1950, Spree Simon gave a concert that included calypso and European classical music, a genre much savored by the pan men. On July 6, 1951, the government-sponsored Trinidad All Stars Percussion Orchestra sailed for London (fig. 56). By this time, outdoor Carnival music had become dominated by the steel band. For an exhibition on Carnival, Trinidadian folklorist Andrew Carr and others labeled the era beginning in 1942 as the "Huge modern (fancy masquerade) bands and Steelband Period."[54]

The steel band quickly spread throughout the Caribbean to the United States, to Venezuela, to Panama, and to other parts of the world. Antigua became a major center for steel-band activity. The American navy sported its own steel band, as did several American colleges. And the steel band became a fixture of the Trinidadian-style Carnival in the remote Venezuelan mining town of El Callao, where West Indians had settled for a century.[55]

The Carnival of 1946, the first street affair since the early years of the war, was as significant as the Victory Carnival of 1919. It was the first Carnival to be dominated by the dialectic established between

56 ✳ TASPO steel band in London, 1951. From the British Broadcasting Corporation.

the large fancy masquerade bands and the tough new steel bands. Now, outdoor calypso was no longer the lavway or the more distant calindas of the chantwells. The medium became the message, as the very nature of the steel band required a new kind of calypso, the road marches that replaced the older lavways. The level of sound sent out from the steel instruments, together with the infectiousness of the music, gradually extinguished nearly all other forms of outdoor calypso. The quieter string bands, even with the reed augmentation that existed after World War I, were drowned out by the heightened experiences of the pans and the very large fancy masquerade bands. The best calypso songwriters, such as Kitchener, now wrote for the steel band. The focus was on the rhythm of the pans and the rhythms of the streets, not the contemplation of the tents.

Meanwhile, the tent changed just as the Carnival street changed. After the war, tourists replaced soldiers in the major tents, and the calypsonians played to this new crowd.

11 ✳ Conclusion

Tuesday this Carnival glorious day celebration
I am giving you a recapitulation
Of my glorious long reign
But now, I cannot sing again
My resignation has come to me
And this is my history
So come and hear this story of my fatal
misfortune
In this colony.

Executor laments his blindness in the last
verse of his final recording, "My Unconquered
Will," mid-1950s.

THIS study of calypso began with a look at nineteenth-century Trinidadian society and the development of Carnival after emancipation. Next, this work focused on Carnival of the early 1900s, when the calypso tent brought English-language Carnival songs into vogue, centering on the development of this classic calypso in Trinidad and abroad. The focus has been on media—the way calypso has been presented in live performances, on phonograph records, on the radio, in film, and in clubs. The public lives of a few chantwells and calypsonians have been profiled. This study ends about 1950, when the steel band took hold, when postwar political conditions prepared Trinidad for independence, and when calypso at home and abroad seemed dominated for a time by mass media and foreign interests as opposed to local interests.

The calypsonians profiled here were extraordinary people. With a twist of a word or phrase they made everyday events mythic. When one realizes that this process unfolded in a setting similar to that of many other modern societies, then the significance of the calypsonian becomes clear. With Trinidad's many ethnic groups and its important role in the economic and political development of the Caribbean, the country represented many Caribbean and colonial possibilities. Trini-

dadian society was West Indian society and West Indian society was
colonial society.

Among the first peoples to undergo mass forced migration for
incipient industrialization on plantations were the foreparents of
most West Indians. This population disruption resulted in the formation of a modern society whose central purpose was to grow the raw
product to help feed (sugar), clothe (cotton), and soothe (coffee,
rum) industrialization in Western Europe.[1] After slavery ended,
indentured servitude furthered the same purposes.

These economic motives resulted in the formation of a cosmopolitan colonial society in Trinidad. By the 1890s, Trinidad's population
consisted of disparate cultural strains, a patchwork of West African,
Western European, and East Indian cultures fused to shreds of
American Indian culture and later imports from the United States and
Venezuela. This neoteric society groped its way toward becoming a
single social system even as it retained distinctive cultural compo-
nents.

One can see the process unfold in the development of calypso. The
calypsonian's view of these epic events was abstract expressionism
with a sense of humor. It came to include rural and urban scenes and
essays on colonialism, Hollywood movies, sex, and British education.

West Indians out of necessity adjusted to or fought colonialism,
both real and metaphorical. They encountered suppression of culture
and oppression of spirit. They lived in a society with great distance
between the elite and the poor. They were among the first modern
people to experience an estrangement between men and women, an
estrangement derived from the slave condition and exacerbated by
wage-labor migration. The calypsonian was there to note it all.

Historical Overview

After the Decree of Population (the Spanish decree that opened the
way for the rapid growth of French- and British-owned estates) and
the Capitulation (the British assumption of political power from the
Spanish), French influence in Trinidad became considerable. Within
the slave population, creolized African culture was also important.
The resultant Afro-French culture found on the French estates was
almost medieval. Carnival, secret societies, and drumming all acted

as informal social controls in the tightly closed social systems that existed on different estates. Slave law was Roman law, implemented with great latitude by each estate owner. The slaves' daily lives were almost completely in the hands of the masters, and the masters were primarily concerned with laws covering commerce and laws that kept slaves' rights in check. In that atmosphere, Carnival and its music may have functioned as a safety valve for the expression of the slaves' sentiments.

Caribbean Carnival was once an annual rite of solidarity, with ecological, social, and quasi-political functions. The Carnival of Trinidad's estates took place in the dry season, that break between harvest and clearing the land for planting or ratooning. Although many British estate owners and the British colonial government frowned upon Carnival, the French did not—it was their fete. The French elite and the slaves were caught in symbiosis in Carnival, each contributing and each receiving. For once, slaves could enjoy themselves over the several days of the festival in extraordinary ways. By disrupting the usual routine through intensive preparations for feting and excessive eating and drinking, that routine could be examined. Under the pretext of making fun of a specific individual, society as a whole was called into question. In this process, a chantwell may have been a "privileged arbiter of morals."[2] Master would mimic slave (as in the original canboulay) and slave, master (as in some belair dances). Each would pick apart the other in jest. Individuals would attack their enemies in song or in actual fights. As long as the brouhaha was contained and ended on Tuesday night before Ash Wednesday and slaves returned to their bitter tasks, the Carnival was a success from the point of view of the overlords. The Creole French understood this process, but the British did not, and they feared Carnival.

In times of normalcy (if that word fits a slave colony), Carnival was a conservative force. No doubt this was the Carnival that pleased the French. Carnival was a way of understanding the absurdities of the economic, social, and cultural distance between people in Trinidad's highly stratified society. It was a means of blowing off steam so that everything could return to normal once the celebration was over. But in times of crisis, Carnival diversions could spill over into incipient revolt. This Carnival confirmed the worst fears of the British.

Toward the end of the slavery era and through the first five or six decades following emancipation, four major forms of topical music in Trinidad contributed to calypso: belairs (several types of topical songs), bongos (topical songs for wakes), calindas (stick fighter's songs), and lavways (outdoor festival songs). These song types are best thought of as incipient calypso and indeed, when looking back on the nineteenth century, twentieth-century writers sometimes call these genres calypso or kaiso (especially the belairs).

In the last twenty years of the nineteenth century, belairs and calindas were used, in whole or in part, as the basis of French or English Creole Carnival songs. These new songs, together with the traditional lavways, were the first calypsos in the modern sense of the word.

The change in Carnival songs in the late nineteenth century reflected basic changes in Carnival itself. A large lower class became entrenched in Port of Spain, consisting of rural migrants, once-indentured laborers from Africa, and Creoles from nearby islands. Their grass-roots Carnival was boisterous. It incorporated African-like social bands and their music, bongos from the wakes of rural migrants, Creole belairs, and calindas brought from the estates of Trinidad, Grenada, Carriacou, and Barbados. Carnival, as an instrument of expression for this polygenetic class, was forced to the back streets and small towns and was nearly crushed in a series of riots, police suppressions, and legal maneuvers in the early 1880s.

A new, middle-class Creole Carnival followed the demise of the jamet carnival. Several factors led to this fancy masquerade Carnival, including the restriction of the jamet Carnival, the increasing British cultural hegemony over all segments of the island's population, and the rise of the colored middle class. Fancy Carnival incorporated all levels of Creole society. English became the main language of Carnival, and membership in a particular fancy masquerade band indicated one's class status or occupational group. Calypso was the musical expression of this Carnival.

The late 1800s may be viewed as a watershed in Trinidad's history. In the manner of Fernando Ortiz's classic description of the contrast between the cultivation of coffee and sugar in nineteenth-century Cuba,[3] a division may be created between two Trinidads, a metaphorical old Trinidad of the plantations and a twentieth-century Trinidad of commerce and industry. Fancy ballroom Carnival and canboulay belong to the old ways. Fancy masquerade Carnival and calypso tents belong to a commercial, industrializing Trinidad. Belair and calinda go with the former; calypso with the latter. French Creole goes with the former; English Creole with the latter. Afro-French Creole culture in Trinidad goes with the former; Trinidad Creole culture—that is, Yoruba-Congo-Franco-Anglo Creole culture—goes with the latter.

As the influence of the sugar estate weakened, Trinidad's polycephalic elite blended. There had been a rivalry in elite circles, most simply expressed as the distinction between the English (actually British and especially Protestant) party and the French (actually Catholic) party. In the second half of the nineteenth century, writers in the English-language press, especially the *Gazette,* frequently disapproved of Carnival, claiming it would die a natural death. The *Sentinel*—a newspaper put out by middle-class coloreds and blacks—usually backed Carnival.[4] This dichotomy occurred precisely because Carnival had become a vehicle of expression for the French Creole population—the former estate owners and slaves, the descendants of the French, free coloreds, and the migrants from the Francophone islands.

In the middle of this cultural pull between British and French allegiances stood the middle class and the elite colored populations. At precisely the time that British law restricted the French elite, it also reduced freedom for the colored middle class. For the English party, once emancipation was fact, there was little to distinguish former slaves from coloreds.

Insofar as their own status was concerned, the coloreds, like the white elite, wanted to put distance between themselves and the emancipated slaves. Often their attitude reflected the prevailing racism of the day. Yet when reacting to a British racism that denied them rights either because of their color or because of their French Creole culture, they sometimes sided with former slaves to oppose discrimination. The nineteenth-century Trinidadian social system can best be understood by examining this complex web of alliances and identities formed out of necessity by the coloreds, the broadening influence of this class in Trinidad, and their role in the formation of basic Trinidadian Creole culture. This culture was not precisely British Creole nor French Creole but Trinidadian Creole.

These highly disparate groups of Creoles came together to develop classic calypso in the early 1900s. The middle class contributed the circumstance (contests, sponsorship of Carnival bands, direct pay-

ment to singers for songs advertising businesses or politicians from
the Labour party). They wrote lyrics or adopted older belairs, calindas, or bongos. Some middle-class Creoles were chantwells for the
fancy masquerade bands or led string bands or small orchestras.
Lower-class Creoles contributed the ambience of Carnival, traditional
music, other chantwells, some of the venues (former calinda yards),
the songs, and much of the audience to the new art.

Between about 1900 and World War I, a complex of Carnival
traditions developed in Trinidad's major towns. Some organizations
of masqueraders and chantwells, called social unions, became respectable. Each social union tended to draw membership from a
single social class or occupational group. They vied with the older,
stick-fighter bands for dominance of Carnival. From both came a
profusion of songs. The chantwells for the large social unions were
the major innovators of calypso at this time—Forbes, Whiterose,
le Blanc. They took the music and style of performance from stick-
fighter bands and produced topical songs that were more acceptable
to officials, Protestants, and other would-be critics.

The calypso tent grew out of calinda yards and casual gatherings of
masqueraders in the process of making their Carnival costumes.
When masquerade-makers paused in their work, they were joined by
hangers-on, and both were entertained by chantwells. In a few years,
tents were major attractions, as singers competed with each other in
their hyperbolical use of English and Patois.

We know what some of this music sounded like, for some of the
records cut in Trinidad between 1912 and 1914 have survived. Jules
Sims recorded calindas in 1914 not unlike those still sung today. In
the same year, Julian Whiterose sang "Iron Duke in the Land," the
first recorded double-tone calypso. Instrumental calypsos were recorded by Lovey's band in 1912 and somewhat later by Belasco and
Merrick.

The first grand Carnival following the end of World War I proved
to be an important one for the development of calypso. The greatest
singers of the time were Henry Forbes the Inventor and Lord Executor. Oratorical calypso reached its peak in popularity, and fancy
masquerade bands reclaimed the streets from the batonniers. From a
Creole perspective, Carnival became the national festival of Trinidad,
and calypso its national music. Carnival tents pulled away from
masquerade camps, and classy chantwells with their oratorical songs

gave way to professional calypso singers and their war songs, ballads, and popular tunes.

By this time, Trinidad had developed a mixed economy, which included plantation and subsistence agriculture, commerce, light industry, oil, American naval bases, tourism, and remittances from Trinidadians living abroad. Trinidad was now among the wealthiest islands in the Caribbean, and its economy supported a relatively large middle class. Some of the Creoles in the middle class and many people in the working class supported the leadership of A. A. Cipriani and the Labour party, as did calypsonians.

Beginning in 1934, recorded calypso gained a firm hold outside of Trinidad. Atilla and Lion went to New York, recorded for the American Record Company and Decca, and appeared on one of the most popular radio shows in the United States. Returning to Trinidad, they were received as heroes.

As calypsos were successfully recorded in Trinidad and New York, calypso tents changed. The professionalism of singers in some tents, such as the one sponsored by Railway Douglas, evolved into a new style of tent, now only loosely affiliated with Carnival masquerade camps. Sponsored by businessmen or by the calypsonians themselves, the best of these new tents were national forums of political and social thought. The new political and social calypsos asserted a code, provided a way to exercise symbols and to air gossip, recent history, and current events. Radio's songs on the "Country Club Scandal" and the "Sedition Law," the new obscene songs, the ballads of Douglas, and the seemingly endless criticisms of the colonial government and of certain elite individuals brought calypso a huge audience and some influence.

This could be called the newspaper effect. Calypso was a medium through which both outside events and Creole daily experiences were filtered. But it was not an unbiased rendering of daily local, regional, and worldwide events. Rather, it usually involved taking a deliberate position on those events. In this way, the community in which the song circulated received information about local news or tidbits of gossip from the perspective of the calypsonian. Such a calypso became not so much a newspaper column but rather a myth fragment. As such, a calypso represented a piece of the Creole's mythological world, an explanation of what that world is, how it came to be, and what it might become.

The mythological world of calypso was a kind of reality. Perhaps all reality is an infinite series of masks, formed into a cylinder so that each mask is the last and the first. Then there is no single reality, because one can always unmask into another. Or maybe reality is that totality encompassed by the circle of masks. Ryunosuke Akutagawa's mystical short story "In a Grove" instructs us about the nature of reality. It is a tale of a robbery of travelers on a road and of a rape of one of them, set in medieval Japan. It is told from the greatly differing perspectives of the witnesses, both living and dead. Each person's view in the story is a mask.

As if they were witnesses in Akutagawa's tale, the calypsonians tell stories. Each tale removes one mask and reveals another. The calypsonian is Legba, the trickster Yoruban god who serves as an intermediary between humans and gods. The calypsonian is beast or dragon, the Carnival devil. Somewhere underneath the devil mask is Humanity. With all the masquerading, stance-taking, story-telling, and image-making, reality is not what one might think. The reality in calypso is Mitto Sampson's story, Atilla's story, Belasco's story, Albany's story, Lion's story, Tiger's story. Together they form a vivid if illusive pattern of calypso, the people who made the music, and the social contexts and processes that underlie individual actions. Although these tales appear as a series of stories, this is a single, composite story, a mythological history. Behind the mask of history there is social process, the movement of water under the motionless surface of the sea, a drama that instructs us about West Indian social structure. In their songs and in their actions, calypsonians reveal how the Caribbean social system was formed, what it was like to live under British colonial rule, how the Caribbean came to be a part of the industrialization of Europe and North America, how Caribbean peoples handled their diaspora, how they developed a new and satisfying culture from patches of older cultures, how they forged an identity, and how they dealt with the stark opposing forces of modern life. This commentary on these quandaries may seem trite at worst, but at best it speaks for all West Indians. Beyond that, it speaks to the modern social predicament.

In the late eighteenth century and throughout the nineteenth century, Patois topical songs (generic calypso) acted in much the same way that gossip functions in small-scale societies: It was an informal mechanism of social control. Although there exists only

legendary evidence, the tales about this period suggest that the mait
kaiso exerted some influence on the estate of Begorrat, an important
French Creole planter of the time. Better evidence is available concerning the importance of topical songs that circulated only within
the slave community, either as a part of protest or in ritual. Still later,
in the second half of the nineteenth century, Carnival songs became
statements concerning the values of the newly freed Creoles. When
Trinidadian institutions became increasingly anglicized, English-language calypso emerged as a forum for discussing the effects of this
British influence first on grass-roots Creoles and their middle-class
backers and, later, on the entire Creole society. Britishness was
praised, on the one hand, as in the songs about the Boer War and
Queen Victoria. On the other hand, social criticism was increasingly
leveled against that same British rule, usually concerning some local
issue. Such issues often involved the shift from agrarian labor to
industrial work (labor strikes), shortages (the water strike), or difficulties of life in the barrack yards. Thus, calypso functioned as a
quasi-legal institution in a society in which there was limited political
expression. On a small island where classes have close, structured
relations, calypso acted to condone, praise, or ridicule certain actions,
thereby giving a measure of accountability.

Changes in calypso in the 1940s again mimicked economic and
political developments. Trinidad boomed in the wartime economy.
North Americans stationed on the island flooded into the tents,
prompting the singers to attend to the soldier's world. Many of the
singers—Tiger, Atilla, Lion, Beginner, Destroyer, Invader—capital-
ized on these developments. Calypsos in Trinidad began to reflect the
interests of the soldiers and tourists as much as they did the interests
of Trinidadians themselves. In the United States, Trinidadians composed new calypsos that reflected American, not Trinidadian, tastes.
Similar developments occurred in England, in West Africa, and
elsewhere.

In the nineteenth century, Trinidadians brought Carnival to the
Paria Peninsula and the interior mining town of El Callao in Venezuela. Around 1900, Lionel Belasco took Trinidadian culture with
him on his tours of South America. Belasco, Wilmoth Houdini, and
Sam Manning were the first Trinidadians to make calypso popular
among West Indians and others in New York. Belasco and Manning
also played an instrumental role in taking calypso to England.

Executor and the second generation of calypso singers—Atilla, Lion,

Tiger, Caresser—led the way in starting a calypso boom in New York
in the late 1930s. Lancelot Pinard, the first nontent singer, took
calypso into motion pictures. Calypso had become more than music
for Trinidad's Carnival, more than a Creole myth.

Changes in the instrumentation that accompanied calypso were
key to the changing function of the music. From Nigeria came the
drums of indentured Africans, and from Venezuela came the string
band. Yoruba and other West African people had settled in and
around Laventille in eastern Port of Spain in the middle 1800s. By the
1880s sacred Yoruba drums and rhythms became part of the jamet
Carnivals. When the drums were outlawed—a law that was not well
enforced— they were sometimes replaced by the tamboo bamboo.
Yet Yoruba rhythms remained in the music of some of the secular
bamboo orchestras. In the first decade of the twentieth century the
changing social climate of Trinidad (especially Port of Spain) was
manifested by a struggle during Carnival and at other festive times
between the more genteel Venezuelan string band—the favored
accompaniment of English-language calypsos and the rising calypso
tent movement—and the grass-roots tamboo bamboo orchestra. This
dialectic was resolved in the 1940s, when the tamboo bamboo gave
away to the "well-tempered" steel orchestra, which overwhelmed the
string band and the colonial life-style it had represented. Yoruban
rhythms flowed into Carnival's new soul, the steel band.[5] The steel
band required new sorts of calypsos, and the lavways and calindas
gave way to road marches composed by Lord Kitchener and the
Mighty Sparrow.

Sometime around 1955—the exact date is not important—Lord
Executor died. Henry Forbes the Inventor was gone, too, as were
Railway Douglas and Chiney Patrick Jones; the first generation was all
gone. For those that loved the old calypso, Carnival Tuesday had
given way to Ash Wednesday. Lord Iere's description of the death of
King Fanto, one of the early singers, provides an appropriate close to
the era:

I could tell about [Fanto's] death and his last song that he sang. [He]
was a chantwell for Red Dragon Band. Around Carnival time, the men
usually climbed coconut tree and cut bamboo [to make a tent]. King
Fanto was playing in a coconut tree. He fell and broke his back.

Surprisingly, on Carnival Tuesday to be exact, while the band were portraying in Charlotte Street after they go into the Savannah competition, King Fanto got up from his bed, tried to walk, and the nurse spot him. He said, "Nurse, I know I'm going to die, but this is my band coming. I would like to see my band for the last [time]." Well, you know, a dragon band usually use horns and bells—loud sound, "Balang!" And your horn blowing. From the time he heard [this loud noise], he knew it was a dragon band coming. As he reached the rail he sang his last melody:

From afar you can hear
King Fanto's voice in the atmosphere
From afar you can hear
King Fanto's voice in the atmosphere
Not a soul to be saved on the day of carnival
When the Dragon appear
Not a soul to be saved on the day of carnival
When the Dragon appear.[6]

Appendix I ✳ Text and Context

> *Nothing can be more delightful to the*
> *conneseur than the quaint manner in which the*
> *chansonnier integrates his clauses, thrusts a*
> *patois phrase into the context slyly to*
> *illuminate a half-hidden meaning. Sneaks in a*
> *colloquialism to sharpen the satire. Inserts*
> *solecisms that make his speech as much a*
> *dialect as any, mispronounces words to mouth*
> *the most fantastic rhythms, strings unfamiliar*
> *sounds together to heighten the effect.*
>
> Alfred Mendes
>
> *In those days . . . English was the thing.*
>
> Lord Beginner

TRANSCRIBED here are the lyrics to songs on phonograph records recorded between 1914 and the early 1950s. Most reflect Beginner's attitude that a calypsonian's sense of good West Indian English should be the language of calypso.[1]

Recorded Calypsos in Context

In selecting lyrics for this section, songs that contain many garbled passages or unidentifiable words have been avoided. This section also contains songs that are not quoted extensively in the text on as wide a variety of subjects as possible. Folklore and political anthropology are no doubt overrepresented in this list. If this were a random sample, many more lyrics about sex probably would be included, as would be songs about men complaining about women. Road marches, although probably not as numerous as indoor calypsos, no doubt were played more frequently. These outdoor songs, however, lend themselves more to musical analysis (or analysis of dance) than to lyrical presentation.

The song texts have been arranged according to the following (overlapping) categories: songs about outdoor Carnival, songs that originated in the tent, vaudeville songs, and other club or show songs.

Many people have helped with the transcriptions. The following people have gone over many of the songs: Steven John, Mike Cato, Gladstone Hutchingson, Mary Clinton, Paxton Rose, and David Sharpe. Ron and Willy Kephart, Maureen Warner-Lewis, Steve Shapiro, Keith Warner, Dick Spottswood, and especially Lise Winer corrected a late draft of the songs. Winer provided many of the Patois translations, and Ron Kephart introduced me to Haitian Creole (*Kreyòl*) orthography, which I have used for spoken French Creole (see the glossary). Maureen Warner-Lewis has helped out with Yoruba terms. I take responsibility for all errors and judgment calls.

French Creole words in the oral texts are spelled according to the Haitian Creole orthography. These words appear in italics.

Each song is transcribed along with some or all of the following information: title, singer (usually as listed on the record and not necessarily the true owner of the copyright or composer of the song), record company, record number, location of recording, date of recording, comments, and lyrics.

Calypsos for the Road

These calypsos were originally sung as calindas, lavways, or road marches or are calypsos whose lyrics evoke the spirit of outdoor Carnival.

1. "Congo Bara," Keskidee Trio (Atilla, Lord Beginner, Tiger), Decca 17257, New York, March 18, 1935.

This is a half-tone calypso based on a calinda, sung mostly in French Creole. As Andrew Carr described him, Congo Bara was a "turnkey with a bad disposition" (1972). The "light" for Congo Bara is ironic. It could be that Congo Bara is dead and the prisoners are, therefore, happy. Yet, as powerful and cruel as Congo Bara was in life, his spirit may be lurking about. The light, then, would indicate Congo Bara's magical power. Another interpretation is that the light serves to show the prisoners the way to freedom now that Congo Bara is dead.

The song begins with pithy comments about Congo Bara and then goes on to tell about the singers themselves. It illustrates quite well

the general principle concerning street calypsos: They tend to consist
of a string of verses that are not always related.

Orchestra leader Gerald Clark's arrangement of this song opens
with an eight-bar rumba, complete with growling trumpet. The effect
of this introduction is to make "Congo Bara" seem more like a cafe
piece than a lavway.

chorus:
Prizonye leve
Mete limyè bay Kongo Bara
(Prisoners, arise
Give Congo Bara some light) [show him the way or cast a spell on
    him]

1. Atilla:
Mete limyè bay Kongo Bara
Mete limyè bay Kongo, se lewa
(Give Congo Bara some light
Give Congo some light, he is the king)
chorus

2. Tiger:
Mete limyè bay Kongo Bara
Kongo Bara ka-plewe pou mwen
(Give Congo Bara some light
Congo Bara is crying for me)
chorus

3. Atilla:
Lamen plen, i fè ti baton-li[2]
Samdi, Madi, i vin pli malewe
(His hand is full, he has made his stick
Saturday, Tuesday, he becomes more unhappy)
chorus

4. Tiger:
Gwan papa-mwen, i mourn *a Dig Martin*
Mama-mwen ka plere pou mwen
(My grandfather mourns in Diego Martin
My mother is weeping for me)
chorus

5. Beginner:

Mete limyè bay Kongo Bara

Judge and jury go' try me for murder [the singer killed Congo Bara
    with magic]

chorus

6. Atilla:

The Greyhound drop me at *Tunapun*

Kongo bay-yo pa fè yo devire

(The bus picked me up at Tunapuna

Congo, give them, don't let them come back)

chorus

7. Tiger:

Mete limyè bay Kongo Bara

Lendi, Madi, djab, mwen dezole

(Give Congo Bara some light

Monday, Tuesday, hell! [devil] I'm sad)

chorus

8. Beginner:

Kongo Bara, Konga lewa

Kongo te metè, i ke mara [?]

(Congo Bara, Congo the king

Congo put, he will [?])

chorus

9. Atilla:

Mete limyè bay Kongo Bara

Mete limyè soti, nou ka-mande

(Give some light to Congo Bara

Give light—we are asking to get out)

chorus

10. Tiger:

Atila, Bigina, epi Tayga

Nou ka-chante ou son Amerika

(Atilla, Beginner, and Tiger

We are singing a song in America)

chorus

11. Beginner:

Mete limyè bay Kongo Bara
Mete limyè ba-i, se lewa, la
(Give Congo Bara some light
Give him light, he's the king)
chorus

12. Atilla:

Kongo Bara, i sick, i dezole
Kongo Bara, i sav mwen danjere
(Congo Bara, he's sick, he's unhappy
Congo Bara, he knows I'm dangerous)
chorus

13. Tiger:

Mete limyè bay Kongo Bara
Mete limyè ba Bara, o
(Give Congo Bara some light
Give Bara light, oh)
chorus

2. "The Bamboo Band," The Black Prince, Decca 17357, Trinidad, March 3, 1938.

This is a road march (half tone). This song is ideal for singing in the streets during Carnival. Its call-and-response form involves alternating lines sung by a chantwell and the rest of the Carnival band. Accompaniment includes that ubiquitous instrument, the bottle and spoon. The bottle, which once held one kind of spirits (gin bottles are favored for use in Carnival), now rings with the spirit of Carnival. Every line of the song is sung by the Black Prince and is followed by a chorus of "You can't beat the bamboo band, you can't!"

1. You can't beat the bamboo band
You can't beat the bamboo band
They're the hottest in the land

2. Everybody breaks away
If you hot on carnival day
We are marching in every way

3. See you with your stick in hand
And the bamboo band at [?] your command
Marching right around the land

4. And then the rum in your head
Want to kill everybody dead
Marching down without any dread

5. The bamboo band gets you brave
Carnival day you bound to live
Want to wake the dead from their grave

3. "Soffie Bellah," Lord Invader, Decca 17429, Trinidad, February 6, 1939.

"Soffie Bellah," attributed to Norman le Blanc, is probably based on a calinda, although the song may have originated as a belair. Perhaps this is le Blanc's ironic claim, expressed in Patois, to "cast a good spell for English calypso." Invader adds his own lyrics to le Blanc's song.

1. *Way ay ay ay ay, Sofi Bèla,*
Mete limyè ba-yo
Mete limyè ba-yo
Mete limyè Inglich Kalipso
(Put a light, give them) [e.g., cast a good spell for English calypso]

chorus:
Way ay ay ay ay, Sofi Bèla,
Mete limyè ba-yo

2. *Way ay ay ay ay, mama*
Listen to the sweet calinda!
chorus

3. Listen to Invader crooning
While you'll hear the bottle beating
chorus

4. Mama, this is glorious morning
So watch how the old mas passing
chorus

5. Mama, I don't like the country
So send me back to the city
chorus

6. Mama I beg you let me go
I want to jump in the band to bongo
chorus

7. Soffie, gal, you know that ent right
I beg you kindly light the light
chorus

8. Why, to put the light for Invader
Because I'm the Lord of mi minor.
chorus

4. "History of Carnival," Atilla, Decca 17253 (British Brunswick 04414), New York, March 15, 1935 (fig. 57).

Scholars sometimes refer to this song to suggest events in the history of Carnival. Atilla sings of his own experiences and about what older singers told him. In the second verse, Atilla sings of the pissenlit (*pisan-nwi*) masquerade, in which a man dressed as a woman with "bloody" menstruation cloths tied around "her" nightgown at the waist. The nightgown was wet, presumably because the person being portrayed was a bed wetter. If this interpretation is correct, then the "half-naked women" are men dressed as women; that is, Atilla refers to the masquerader's role.

1. From a scandal and hideous bacchanal
Today we got a glorious carnival
From a scandal and hideous bacchanal
Today we got a glorious carnival
We used to sing long ago
"*Nou ni yon sèn pou sène-yo*" (We have a seine to catch them, or,
    less literally,
    We have to defend ourselves against people who try
    to stop us)
But today you can hear our calypso
On the American radio

2. Carnival of long ago you used to see
Half-naked women for the *pisan-nwi*
With chac-chac and vira in their hand
Twisting their body as they led the band
You were not safe in your home

57 ＊ Label for a British-release Atilla record from 1935. Atilla sings, "From a scandal and hideous bacchanal / Today we got a glorious carnival." Courtesy of MCA Records.

Through the *nèg jaden* with bottle and stone
But today you can hear our calypso
On the American radio

3. Some of the songsters I can remember
Were Marlborough and Executor
And Black Prince, Hero and Lionel
Edward the Confessor whom I knew well
They used to sing, "Mama Mourio"[3]
Captain Baker was a whopster *bay-yo* blow
(Captain Baker was a good fighter)
But today you can hear our Trinidad calypso
On the American radio

4. Carnival of long ago was real terrible
And the orgies reprehensible
In those days women sang calypso
Like Soki, Mattaloney, and Maribo
They used to walk 'bout with *bouldife* (torch)
I mean, in the days of the *Kannboule*
But today you can hear our Trinidad calypso
On the American radio

5. A prophet has no honor in his own land
The truth of that proverb I now understand
When you sing calypso in Trinidad

You are a vagabond and everything that's bad
In your native land you're a hooligan
In New York you're an artist and a gentleman
For instance take the Lion and me
Having dinner with Rudy Vallee

5. "Mary Ann," Lion, Parlophone MP 114, USDL LP 5505, Cyril Blake's Calypso Serenaders, London, October 9, 1951.

"Mary Ann" was an extremely popular road march at the end of World War II. The lyrics refer to V-J Day, when Trinidadians, along with the Allies, celebrated the official end of the war. Perhaps this song was originally sung during that celebration.

chorus:
All day, all night Miss Mary Ann
Down by the seaside she sifting sand
Strings on her banjo can tie a goat
Water from the ocean can sail a boat[4]

1. V-J Day was bacchanal
The whole island played carnival
People were jumping to and fro
To the rhythm of a red hot calypso
    Hear they singing . . .
chorus [solo by Lion]
    Come up Mr. Coleman! [the guitar player]

2. Port of Spain was really a scene
And pandemonium reigned supreme
A red letter day we can't forget
Young and old, black and white was in the fete
    Hear they singing . . .
chorus [solo by Lion]
    Come up Freddy Grant! [the clarinet player]

3. The whole island was on parade
That was a royal masquerade
There were the black dragon and drum [masquerades]
And the Indian with the hosay coming down [borokit and temple
    masquerades]
chorus [Lion singing solo]
chorus [group]

6. "We Want Sa Gomes," Carnival Vagabonds (Robert Wilky), Decca 17362, Trinidad, March 8, 1938.

Songs of this type—usually lavways (half-tone calypsos)—were used as advertisement. A businessman paid the calypsonian to write and sing about his shop or his product, hoping that the song would catch on and many people would sing it, perhaps at Carnival, thereby providing cheap advertisement. There could be no better subject for a song than Eduardo Sa Gomes, a patron of the singers. In all likelihood this song was sung as a praise, without fee.

leader: Madam who you looking for?
chorus: Yes it is Sa Gomes we want!
leader: The leading man in Trinidad
chorus: Yes it is Sa Gomes we want
leader: In radiophone and gramophone
chorus: Yes it is Sa Gomes we want
leader: He's a man of ability
chorus: Yes it is Sa Gomes we want
leader: In this blessed land of Trinidad
chorus: Yes it is Sa Gomes we want
leader: Don't mind what the people say
chorus: Yes it is Sa Gomes we want
leader: He will treat you in the best of way
chorus: Yes it is Sa Gomes we want
leader: Take a walk down Frederick Street [fig. 58]
chorus: Yes it is Sa Gomes we want
leader: Sa Gomes Emporium you're bound to meet
chorus: Yes it is Sa Gomes we want

The entire set of lyrics is repeated twice, except that the line "He will treat you in the best of way" is sung as "He will treat you with ability."

7. "Netty, Netty," Lion, Decca 17297, New York, February 16, 1937 (fig. 59).

This song could be classified as a lavway, perhaps a leggo. The lyrics describe Lion's way of broaching a censored topic.

1. Christmas night I almost died with laugh
Lying in me bed with a high brown craft
Christmas night I almost died with laugh

58 ✳ Corner of Frederick Street and Queen Street in Port of Spain, early 1940s. The shop of record dealer and calypso patron Eduardo Sa Gomes was located near here. The Carnival Vagabonds sing, "Take a walk down Frederick Street / ... / Sa Gomes Emporium you're bound to meet." Courtesy of Charles Porter.

Lying in me bed with a high brown craft
She heard a gin bottle with a wicked roll [the bottle and spoon]
A tamboo bamboo nearly make her lose control
chorus [as Lion scat sings meaningless syllables]:
Singing, Netty, Netty,
Gimme the thing that you got in your belly!

2. The craft on me bed was very still
And when she heard the gin bottle she got a thrill
And said, "Wake up, darling, wake up, let's make our names,
The tamboo bamboo addling me brain!"
She jump off me bed and nearly burst me blind
Lash me in me face with her body-line
chorus:
Singing, Netty, Netty,
Gimme the thing that you have in your belly!

3. A Patois woman *dit*, Madame Maxwell
"Se sa mwen ka kwiye lave Noèl
You better pull yourself and let me shake me *devire*
Gade dèyè mwen, se sa mwen vle
Ou pa kònèt bagay-la cho
Leze mwen fè manima, avan mwen mò"
(Said the Patois woman, Madame Maxwell,
"That's what I call a real Christmas Eve!
You'd better back off and let me shake my butt
Look at my backside, that's what I want!
You don't know the 'ting hot!
Let me make my moves before I die.")
chorus:
Singing, Netty, Netty,
Gimme the thing that you got in your belly!

4. The craft catch a vap and she start to dance
She said, "Lion this the time to pick our chance."
I said, "Woman, you better stop this stupidness
You always calling me for foolishness."
She said, "I ent care nothing at all!"
She jump out the road and she nightie fall
chorus:
Singing, Netty, Netty,
Gimme the thing that you got in your belly!

8. "Small Island," Lord Invader, Decca 34003 (English issue: M30732), New York, May 21, 1945.

In early 1945, the war in Europe was over. Trinidad's economic boom had come to a halt also, and jobs and consumer products were scarce. Some people found scapegoats on which to blame their economic and social difficulties. The first scapegoat was unemployed young men—from that group sprang the steel band, the mid-twentieth-century equivalent of stick fighters' bands. The other scapegoat was the small islander from the nearby islands, who had migrated to Trinidad in search of employment. In this controversial song, Invader directs his comments at this latter group.

1. No flour, no rice in the land
Believe me too much Small Island

59 * Music for the beginning of "Netty, Netty." Lyrics transcribed by Donald R. Hill; music transcribed by Hewitt Pantaleoni.

Yes they come by the one, the two and the three
Eating our food and they leaving us hungry
chorus:
So Small Island
Go back where you really come from

2. The Grenadians, they's the worst of all!
Hear they talk: "Me not goin' back at all!"

Yes, they land in Trinidad in a fishing boat
Now they wearing they sagacoat [fancy clothes circa the 1940s]
chorus:
So Small Island
Go back where you really come from

3. If ever you meet any Vincentian
They will tell you that "I'm a Trinidadian!"
They improve on their speech and they speaking correctly
And they arguing educationally
chorus:
So Small Island
Go back where you really come from

4. The St. Lucians they are just the same
Now they are making their name in Port of Spain
They will send for their brother, their aunt, and their sister
Their cousin and also their grandmother
chorus:
So Small Island
Go back where you really come from

5. The Barbajans they too blooming bad
Now they get so fresh now in Trinidad
They will live at Arouca and Tunapuna
But their real hiding hole is Arima
chorus:
So Small Island
Go back where you really come from

9. "Rum and Coca Cola," Lord Invader, private tape recorded by John Bessor of Washington, D.C., tape number 3C1, Library of Congress, AFS 12,303 LWO-4395, recorded in Invader's Calypso Club, Port of Spain, Trinidad, March 16, 1950 (figs. 60, 61, and 62).

This was the most popular road march during the early 1940s, dislodging "Mathilda" from that position. The song has a long history in Trinidad, beginning in the 1890s when, as a Martiniquean song, "L'Année Passée" (*Lanne Pase*), it was introduced into the island. Lionel Belasco claimed to have written down the song a few years later, after modifying the tune; band leader Gerald Clark backed him on this claim. Belasco and Massie Patterson published it in a booklet of West Indian songs in 1943. That version of "L'Année Passée" was

transcribed and copyrighted by Maurice Baron.

Probably quite independent from Belasco's publication of this folk
song, Lord Invader (Rupert Grant) modified the tune of the still
remembered "L'Année Passée." Although he claimed that Belasco had
taught him at the time, Invader conformed to the standard procedure
of recycling old tunes with new lyrics. Invader called his new calypso
"Rum and Coca Cola." A songbook, "Victory Calypso," was compiled
by Atilla and Lion and included this song from the Victory Calypso
Tent, whose manager was Mohammed H. "Johnny" Khan. It was
Khan who deposited lyrics with the acting colonial secretary in
Trinidad on March 1, 1943, thereby securing the rights to the lyrics
for himself.[5]

Invader then sang "Rum and Coca Cola" in calypso tents as his
original song. Morey Amsterdam, an American who briefly enter-
tained the troops in Trinidad in 1943, probably heard the song in the
Victory Calypso Tent where Invader performed. Returning to New
York, Amsterdam contacted the music publishing company of Leo
Feist. Amsterdam's "Rum and Coca Cola" was published by Leo Feist,
Inc., with lyrics by Morey Amsterdam and music by Jeri Sullavan and
Paul Baron. Ironically, Paul Baron—not to be confused with Maurice
Baron—had a copy of Belasco's and Paterson's booklet in which the
melody of Invader's tune appeared.

Several claims were filed against Feist et al. in 1947. Lionel Belasco
was represented in his suit by a celebrated lawyer, Louis Nizer. In
court, Nizer pointed out that Paul Baron had access to Belasco's book
containing "L'Année Passée," before Fiest published "Rum and Coca
Cola." However, Baron may not have gotten the song from that
source. It is more likely that Amsterdam copied Invader's version, a
connection also thought plausible by Nizer.

In my opinion, no one had a claim to the tune of "Rum and Coca
Cola"—it was in fact the Martiniquean folk tune. Indeed, Paul Baron's
lawyer had obtained a statement from Lord Executor that said that he
had heard "L'Année Passée" on the streets of Port of Spain during
Carnival in the 1890s; thus, Belasco could not have written it in 1906
as he had claimed. But Nizer's character witness for Belasco, Gerald
Clark, stated that he had seen Executor, and, sorry to say, he was a
bum and quite unreliable.

Eventually, Nizer won his case for Belasco against the publisher,

60 ✳ Sheet-music cover crediting U.S. actor Morey Amsterdam as the composer of lyrics that were set to the tune of a Trinidadian road march.

Leo Feist, Inc., lyricist Morey Amsterdam, and composers Jeri Sullavan and Paul Baron. I do not know what Belasco received in settlement, but it was not the copyright to "Rum and Coca Cola," which Leo Feist, Inc., kept.

Lord Invader had a separate suit against Feist and associates and in 1950 won a $100,000 settlement representing all the royalties to date. Daniel Crowley, a North American anthropologist who spent a

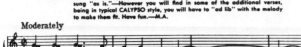

61 * First page of the sheet music for "Rum and Coca-Cola."

lot of time in Trinidad after World War II, said that Invader gave away some of the money to his friends (Lion and Atilla were to get a share but apparently did not) and used the rest to open his Calypso Club in Port of Spain.[6]

Morey Amsterdam appeared on Johnny Carson's late-night television talk show in the late 1970s. Carson said something to the effect that Amsterdam was a man of many talents, not just a comedian; he was the composer of "Rum and Coca Cola." Amsterdam just smiled while the audience clapped.

62 ✳ First page of the sheet music for "L'Année Passée."

The "Rum and Coca Cola" case is significant for several reasons. The Andrews Sisters' version of the song helped maintain Decca Records during World War II when other record companies felt the joint effects of wartime shortages and a musicians' strike. "Rum and Coca Cola" reinvigorated the interest in calypso that had been established in New York in the 1930s. It pushed the appeal of this West Indian music from New York across the United States, Great Britain, and other parts of the world.

The song begins with a spoken introduction, possibly by Bob
Gittins: "Ladies and Gentlemen. It gives me great pleasure to present
to you that distinguished celebrity who goes by the appellation of the
Lord Invader of 'Rum and Coca Cola' fame. And the Lord Invader has
come here to sing you that song which has the world upset—'Rum
and Coca Cola'—in the way it was intended to be sung. The Lord
Invader, Ladies and Gentlemen!"

1. When the Yankees first came to Trinidad
Some of the young girls were more than glad
They said that the Yankees treat them nice
And they give them a better price
spoken:
"They buy"

chorus:
Rum and Coca cola
Go down Point Cumana
Both mothers and daughters
Working for the Yankee dollar

2. I had a little girlfriend the other day
But her mother came and took her away
Self, her mother, and her sisters
Went in a cab with some soldiers
spoken:
"They bought"
chorus

3. I know a couple who got married one afternoon
And was to fly to Miami on their honeymoon
But the bride run away with a soldier lad
And the stupid husband went staring mad
spoken:
"They bought"
chorus

4. They have some aristos in Port of Spain
I know a lot but I wouldn't call name
And indicate, they wouldn't give you a ride

Well you can see them with the foreigners in the night
spoken:
"Drinking"
chorus

5. Mr. Hal Morrow I want you to know
And if you do appreciate this calypso
You have some people there in your company
I sure they appreciate the melody
spoken:
"Singing"
chorus

6. I wonder what is your interested opinion
We haven't got no bad speaking Trinidadian
We never said, "Caca cola" [refers to Amsterdam's song as recorded
    by the Andrews Sisters]
Neither did we say, "Yankee dallah"
spoken:
"We sang"
chorus

[The following verse is extemporaneous.]
7. Now gentlemen I want you to know
It seem as you love this calypso
But I tell you very flat
You look like an American diplomat
spoken:
"Singing"
chorus
from the chorus one person sings:
"Money in the land—Yankee dollar bill"

10. "Nora," Lord Kitchener with Cyril Blake's Calypso Serenaders,
Parlophone MP 102, U.S. Decca DL 8159, London, January 30, 1950.
    This road march is one of Kitch's early hits (fig. 63). The lyrics tell
about an immigrant leaving a strange land (England). It was popular
with many Trinidadian migrants in England and the United States.

    1. Yes, I beg you to leave me Nora
    I goin back to me country

I beg you to leave me
I goin back to me county
I'm tired with London
I can't hear the steel band beating in John John
I'm getting homesick, I'm feeling sad
I want me passage, and I going back to Trinidad
So darling

chorus:
Nora, Nora, Nora [sung by male chorus]
Why don't you leave Lord Kitchener?
Nora, Nora, Nora
I wanna go home to see me grandmother
Nora, Nora, Nora
Darling what is your intention?
You can't fool the Lord
I'm a born Trinidadian

2. She started a crying
When she heard that Kitchie was leaving
These are the things the lady promised me
A Royal Royce car, her father property
But, I told her, "Well Darling
Money nor love doesn't mean anything
I have to go home with no deceit
I have to take up my duties St. Vincent Street"
So darling

chorus:
Nora, Nora, Nora
I beg you to leave Lord Kitchener
Nora, Nora, Nora
Sink or float I gotta see me grandfather
Nora, Nora, Nora
Darling what is your intention?
You can't fool the Lord
I'm a born Trinidadian

3. Miss Nora was angry
Pick up a knife and threaten to kill me
Then, she jumped to my collar

7 **NORA**

Yes, ah beg you to leave me, Nora
Ah going back to me country,
Ah beg you to leave me,
Ah going back to me country
I'm tired with London,
I can't hear the steelband beating in John John
I am getting homesick I'm feeling sad,
Ah want me passage and I going back to Trinidad

So Darling Nora, Nora, Nora, why don't you leave Lord
                                        Kitchener
Nora Nora Nora I want to go home to see me grandmother
Nora Nora Nora Darling what is your intention
Nora Nora Nora you can't fool the Lord I'm a born Trinidadian

She started a crying
When she hear that Kitchee was leaving
These are the things the lady promised me
A Rolls Royce Car, her father property
But I told her well darling, money nor love does'nt mean anything
I have to go home with no deceit
I have to take up my duty, St. Vincent Street.

So Darling Nora, Nora, Nora, I beg you to leave Lord Kitchener
Nora Nora Nora sink or float I got to see me grandfather
Nora, Nora, Nora Darling what is your intention
Nora, Nora Nora you cant fool the lord I'm a born Trinidadian

Miss Nora was angry
Take up a knife and threaten to kill me
Then she Jump to my collar
Stamping her feet and bawling for murder
But I told her quietly, darling my mind is made up already
I am very sorry I cant remain
I have to go to the City of Port of Spain

So darling Nora Nora Nora I beg you to leave Lord Kitchener
Nora Nora Nora I want to go home to see me grandmother
Nora Nora Nora Darling what is your intention
Nora Nora Nora you can't fool the Lord I'm a born Trinidadian

Well Nora was clever She played a trick on the Lord Kitchener
Me clothes in the laundry she has the ticket hidden secretly
But I used my discretion I rent a suit in leaving position
I raise me hand and tell her shye.
On the Flying Dutchman to Piarco

So darling Nora Nora Nora I beg you to leave Lord Kitchener
Nora Nora Nora sink or float I going to see me grandfather
Nora Nora Nora darling what is your intention
Nora Nora Nora you can't fool the Lord I'm a born Calypsoian

63 ✳ Single-sheet copy of a Lord Kitchener road march recorded in 1950. Courtesy of Frances Attaway.

Stomping her feet and bawling for murder
But I told her quietly
"Darling, my mind is made up already.
I'm very sorry, I can't remain.
I have to go to the city of Port-of-Spain."
So darling

chorus:
Nora, Nora, Nora
I beg you to leave Lord Kitchener
Nora, Nora, Nora
I wanna go home to see me grandmother
Nora, Nora, Nora
Darling what is your intention?

Nora, Nora, Nora
You can't fool the Lord
I'm a born Trinidadian

4. Well, Nora was clever
She played a trick on the Lord Kitchener
Me clothes in the laundry
She has the tickets hidden secretly
But I used my discrétion
I rent a suit in leaving position
I wave my hand and told her "*Ay-o!*"[7]
On the "Flying Dutchman" [airplane] to Piarco [Trinidad]
So darling

chorus:
Nora, Nora, Nora
I beg you to leave Lord Kitchener
Nora, Nora, Nora
Sink or float I wanna see me grandfather
Nora, Nora, Nora
Darling what is your intention?
Nora, Nora, Nora
You can't fool the Lord
I'm a born Trinidadian!

Calypso Tents

11. "Three Friends' Advice," Lord Executor, Decca 17298 (fig. 64).

In this song, Executor tells of his journeys through the surreal world of religion. An obeahman is a magician, a person who manipulates the supernatural for practical gain. The Shouters are an Afro-Christian group that sings rhythmic hymns to help bring on possession in order to contact helpful spirits.

This song has been issued in multiple takes, meaning that Executor sang it several times and Decca issued at least two versions of the song. The only significant difference in the takes is the substitution of "tango" for "shango" in some of the verses. It is not known why Executor did this; perhaps he felt that "tango" would have meaning to a New York audience.

1. According to condition, me friends and relation
They gave me their opinion
According to condition, me friends and relation
They gave me their opinion
One said, "Join the Shouters' band"
Another one said, "Be an obeahman"
But to Vio I answer, "No"
"I think I going to learn to dance the Shango"

2. I was advise by a certain friend
Who introduce me then to the Shouters' den
And all the ceremonies that I went through
We sang, "Moses, Moses, take off thy shoe"
I fasted for forty days singing hymn
And then they duck me in the river but I could not swim
Then to Vio I answered, "No"
"I think I going to learn to dance the Shango"

3. In two weeks time, friends, I got so fat
And you can imagine the cause of that
Stew eggs and fried macaroni
That in the meeting the sisters would bring to me
Khaki, serges, palm beach and white
The cork hat and the legging as to lace up tight [white colonial
    attire]
Still to Vio I answered, "No"
"I think I going to learn to dance the tango"

4. Soon after that I draft a different plan
And decided to be an obeahman
Around my neck I had a chaplet
And the beard that I had was like Galbadier [an obeahman]
The shirt on me bosom was a motor-car bag[8]
And the coat on me back was a tickilay rag [a thin piece of cotton
    cloth]
And to Vio I answered, "No"
"I think I going to learn to dance the Shango"

5. Now listen, friend, what I had in me room
Was a grinning skelenton with a face of gloom
A dancing peacock painted in red

64 ✳ Label for Executor's record of a calypso satirizing the world of Trinidadian religion. Courtesy of MCA Records.

With a jumping *krapo* (toad) without a head
Three blind mice and a *makawèl* snake
And a big tar baby to walk and shake
Then to Vio I answered, "No"
"I think I going to learn to dance the Shango"

12. "Gambo Lai Lai before the Court," Lord Executor, Decca 17453, February 8, 1939.

Gumbolailai (*Gònbolele*), son of stick fighter Johnny Zee Zee, was a badjohn known for his flamboyant talk and his habit of fighting police, as in this incident in 1924. "Jules Blades, popularly known as 'Gumbo Lai Lai,' was again the center of attraction yesterday, when he kept up a hideous noise as he appeared before the City Bench, charged by Constable Taylor with being drunk and disorderly at the corner of Prince and Nelson Streets, on the 23rd ultimate."[9] But when called to court, Gumbolailai began to make a "continuous noise," a "promulgation" he said: "I am not a theft. I am not a criminal prostitute, I am not a gambler, I am a free agent; the only single thing I do is to drink my liquer and use my language."

1. *Gònbolele* come back again
Was causing a destruction in Port of Spain
Gònbolele come back again
Was causing all eruption in Port of Spain

From the corner he was told, "Move off!"
He told the police, "I will take (it all?)"
And he was talking his old *angle* (English)
When the police came and took him away

2. *Gònbolele* was dress in his Sunday suit
You could have heard the people said, "He's looking cute"
And on his head he had a panama
And in his mouth he had a grand cigar
You could have seen the smoke coming through his nose
In his washicong [makeshift shoes] you could have seen his toes
And he was talking his old *angle*
When the police came and took him away

3. Now the lady was walking all the way alone
Thinking of the children that she had at home
When suddenly she heard, "Reeto reeto ray"
"Stop your progression woman and don't hesitate"
Se mwen, Gòmbolele, ki mèt angle
(It is I, Gumbolailai, who is master of English)
And the woman said, "*Kite mwen pase*"
(Let me go by)
So he was talking his old *angle*
When the police came and took him away

4. When *Gònbolele* was called he was looking vexed
And he started at once with a curious text
"Non compos mentis comedium"
[Latin: "One is consumed with madness"; that is, the woman's
   crazy]
"I only asked the woman to come along"
"But through her bad propensity"
"I [catch the fire?] with my psychology"
So his language could not prevail
He was given three months in the Royal Gaol

13. "Seven Skeletons Found in the Yard," Lord Executor, Decca
71360, Trinidad, February 26, 1938.
   This song refers to a series of crimes and accidents at Christmastide
and New Year's, 1937–38. Executor muses on the irony.

1. Hideous discoveries and monstrous crime
Always happen at the Christmastime
Hideous discoveries and monstrous crime
Always happen at the Christmastime
For the old year murders and atrocity
Was the New Year's serious calamity
What shocked Trinidad
Those seven skelentons that the workmen found in that yard

2. What marred the Christmas festivity
Was the New Year double catastrophe
When a man and a woman on the ground was found
With blood stains upon the ground
The husband was arrested but they were too late
For the poison he drank sent him to the Gate
That shock Trinidad
Those seven skelentons that the workmen found in that yard

3. In St. James the population went wild
When in the Savannah they found a child
The hair was auburn and complexion pink
Which placed the watchman in the mood to think
"How can a mother despise and scorn
A little angel that she has borne?"
That was more sad
Than the seven skelentons that the workmen found in that yard

4. A lorry was speeding to Port of Spain
When it knock down the cyclist into the drain
It was going as fast as a lightning flash
When the cyclist received the lash
The mother cried out in sorrows and pain
"I am not going to see my boy child again!"
That is more sad
Than the seven skelentons that the workmen found in that yard

5. While the workmen they were digging the ground
The grinning skulls of human beings they found
Feet together and head east and west
Number Five was a watchman among the rest

Number Six had the hands and the feet on the chest

And number Seven the mysterious guest

That shocked Trinidad

Those seven skelentons that the workmen found in that yard

14. "The Lajobless," Lord Executor, Decca 17365, Trinidad, March 1, 1938.

Lajobless (*ladjablès*) is a supernatural creature, a beautiful woman with one foot and one cow's hoof. After dusk, she lures men to some unknown but bad fate. I have met several men who claim to have been lured by lajobless. Their stories are always the same: Lajobless is frightened off but, before leaving, laughs at the man and says that he is lucky that she did not catch him.

1. For a night and a day Narbadeen was lost

Mountain and rivers he had to cross

For a night and a day Narbadeen was lost

Mountain and rivers he had to cross

The Indian laddie had such a fright

He was led away by a woman in white

This is the rumor they heard next day:

"*Ladjablès chaye li ale*"

("The *djablès* carried him off")

2. This is the story of Narbadeen

Of St. James Village, he was highly esteem

With his book in hand he went by a stream

And unfortunately he began to dream

He being a student of human nature

He went to study his literature

This is the rumor they heard next day:

"*Ladjablès chaye li ale*"

3. On the log of wood he sat by the ground

When suddenly darkness came around

Strange whispering came to his ear

Saying, "Go back home, young man, beware!"

But the awful voice of the woman in white

That gave him such a serious fright

That is the rumor they heard next day:

"*Ladjablès chaye li ale*"

4. She led him over mountain, valleys and plain
If he would slide, he surely would break his brain
She led him over many precipice and rocks
That his body should feel some electric shock
There must have been some angel by his side
Or otherwise he would have died
That is the rumor they heard next day:
"*Ladjablès chaye li ale*"

5. She hypnotize him with her magic spell
As though she were a devil from the gates of Hell
Her eyes were large, like goblets of fire
And she said, "Let us climb up higher"
She led him to a room that was like a tomb
There Narbadeen nearly met his doom
That is the rumor they heard next day:
"*Ladjablès chaye li ale*"

15. "Shop Closing Ordinance," Lord Executor, Decca 17308, New York, February 19, 1937.

The Shop Closing Ordinance of 1936 was an attempt by the government to combat the effects of the Depression by restricting the hours that retail stores stayed open to the public. Executor felt it had just the opposite effect—it increased unemployment because poor people, who had to work by day, could no longer shop after work.

1. The New Shop Closing Ordinance
Is an intolerance
The New Shop Closing Ordinance
Is an intolerance
I think that should not be
In a community of wealth and prosperity
Through the passing of the law
After four, bound to affect the poor

2. I was passing when I saw placard against the wall
Posters large and small
Inviting the poor of humanity
To protest unitedly
Oh my, they going to cry
I will tell you why: they can neither sell, nor buy

Through the passing of the law
After four, bound to affect the poor

4. Is the government blind and cannot see
The decrepitude and misery?
Old women and men, girls and boys
Don't rob them of those sparks of joy!
For if they saw the blows, no food, no clothes
On the rum they'll get overdose
So the passing of the law
After four, bound to affect the poor

5. We shall miss the bustle of Charlotte Street
Where wealth and industry meet
The light, the life, the crowd to and fro
To go out to the stores they go
So don't you cast a gloom as a spirit from the tomb
Allow our island to bloom!
Through the passing of the law
Which after four, bound to affect the poor

16. "Death," Lion, Decca 17410, Trinidad, January 31, 1939.

1. To part from life to eternity
The thought makes us all most melancholy
To part from life to eternity
The thought makes us all most melancholy
Though we may be suffering excruciatingly
Still among the living we would rather be
But no solemnity, no grief, no regret
Can make us escape the arrows of death

2. Matters not how severe the world to us may be
How we may be ostracize by society
Groveling in the gutter in abject poverty
Fighting but failing miserably
Still we desperately cling with vice-like tenacity
To prolong our lives interminably
But no solemnity, no grief, no regret
Can make us escape the arrows of death

3. You can be a king, as Nebuchadnezzar
You can be as old as Methuselah
Just as Abraham, our forefather
Wise as Solomon who walk with the Queen of Sheba
However stoical may be your philosophy
Still we quivering at the brink of eternity
But no solemnity, no grief, no regret
Can make us escape the arrows of death

4. The Creator, from the summit of his sapience
Made man in a state of pure innocence
But man disobey most presumptuously
With the implacable wrath of the Almighty
"Dust thou art and unto dust thou shall return!"
So quickly, Lord, and so we all are fated to learn
That no solemnity, no grief, no regret
Can make us escape the arrows of death

17. "The Gold in Africa," Tiger, Decca 17271B, New York, April 2, 1936 (fig. 65).

In the opening years of World War II, calypsonians wrote many songs defending the positions of the Allies and criticizing the Axis powers. Some of these songs were adaptations of old calindas to the single-tone form. Here Tiger refers to Mussolini's takeover of Abyssinia (Ethiopia) and backs Haile Selassie's defense of his country before the League of Nations. He gives Mussolini fatigue or *mepuis* with the line, "I now believe he want Haile Selassie wife." A few years later, Tiger wrote another calypso imploring Trinidad to stay out of the war.

1. Gold, the gold
The gold, the gold
The gold in Africa
Mussolini want from the emperor

2. Abyssinia appeal to the League for peace
Mussolini actions were like a beast
A villain, a thief, a highway robber
And a shameless dog for a dictator

3. He cross the border and added more
The emperor had no intention for war
That man I call a criminal
The man destroy churches and hospital

4. He said expansion he really need
He have forty-five million heads to feed
Why he don't attack the Japanese
England, France, or hang on, on Germany

5. The man want to kill King Haile Selassie
To enslave his territory
They began to cry for food and water
In that burning desert of Africa

6. We have diamond, ruby, and pearl
Platinum, silver, and even gold
I don't know why the man making so much strife
I now believe he want Haile Selassie wife

7. If he want gold as a dictator
Try in Demerara
Venezuela or Canada
Austro-Hungar' or else in America

18. "Yaraba Shango," Tiger, Decca 17269, New York, April 2, 1936.

The Shango religion of Trinidad had its origins in the beliefs of the Yoruba, a people of Nigeria whose customs spread widely in the Caribbean and South America. Similar Yoruba beliefs are found in the Shango group of Grenada, the Lucumí of Cuba, the Candomblé and Macumba of Brazil, and the Santería of Cuba, Puerto Rico, New York, and Venezuela. Shango is the name of the Yoruba god of thunder. One appeases Shango or other guardian gods through propitiation, especially by offering the blood of a chicken or lamb, and by preparing special sacrificial foods. In turn, the Yoruba gods help people in health, in maintaining good relations with the opposite sex, or in life's ventures. Songs to Shango are the sacred equivalent to calypso except that the former implores the gods for successes while the latter comments on conditions as they are or as they are imagined to be. It is no accident that both the Shango ritual, here fancifully described by Tiger, and Shango songs interest calypsonians. Taken

65 ✳ Music for the beginning of "The Gold in Africa," Tiger's calypso deploring the Italian invasion of Ethiopia; later in the song Tiger sings, "I now believe he [Mussolini] want Haile Selassie wife." Transcribed by Hewitt Pantaleoni.

together, Shango songs and calypsos serve the spiritual man and his mundane world. Below is Tiger's translation of the original Yoruba terms, as transcribed by Steve Shapiro and as modified by Maureen Warner-Lewis and myself.

1. I went to see but I did not know
Unfortunately, friend, I find meself in Shango
I went to see, I mean I didn't know
Unfortunately, friend, I find myself in Shango
I mean, the power had me that night
To see me dancing with all my might
And then they're singing:
"*Tina-o, Tina-bo, neebo, adesa, a Tina re ke pa*" (Tina, where are you running from, come back [?]
Ah, Tina, beg pardon of your father)

2. They began to sing, "*Osain no dey*" (Osain is not there[10])
And beat me with a broom called the "shesherey"[11]
I were lying upon the ground
The goblet and the water was passed around[12]
I had a taste of the fowl and the rice
The coocoo and the goat in the sacrifice
Yes! They singing:
"*Tina-o, Tina-bo, neebo, adesa, a Tina re ke pa*"

3. A girl by the name of Mary Walter
Dropped down the candles from the altar
And I mean, the next was Madame Isilaw
That night I made introduction to her
She said, "*Ou pa kònèt mwen danjere*"
I mean, "*Yo pa ka-di ou komen mwen dezole*" (You don't know how I am dangerous
They haven't told you how I am sad)
Yes! They singing:
"*Tina-o, Tina-bo, neebo, adesa, a Tina re ke pa*"

4. They began to sing, "*Eshu kweenambo*" (Eshu, go away)[13]
And the next was, "*Re re re re koko*" (Rejoicing at the departure of Osain[14])
And then they began "*Naniwele*" [song of rejoicing]
By beating the drum they call the "omolé"

A fella had a candle lighting in his mouth
One lash with the cutlass, the goat's head fly out![15]
Yes! They singing:
"*Tina-o, Tina-bo, neebo, adesa, a Tina re ke pa*"[16]

19. "Workers' Appeal," Tiger, Decca 17288, New York, April 7, 1936.

1. Anywhere you go you must meet people sad
They search for employment, none can be had
Anywhere you go you bound to meet people sad
They search for employment, none can be had
They start to drop down dead in the street
Nothing to eat and nowhere to sleep
All kind-hearted employers, I appeal now to you:
Give us some work to do!

2. We are not asking for equality
To rank with the rich in society
To visit their homes in their motor cars
Or to go to their clubs and smoke their cigars
We are asking for a living wage
To exist now, and provide for old age
All kind-hearted employers, I appeal now to you:
Give us some work to do!

3. Many of these persons haven't a meal
They were too decent to beg, too honest to steal
They went looking for work mostly everywhere
But saw signboard mark, "No hands wanted here"
The government should work the waste lands and hills
Build houses, factories and mills
Reduce taxation and then we would be really
Emancipated from slavery

4. The legislator only quarrel and fret
About unemployment but haven't relieve us yet
There is no visions that we can see
To take us out from tribulations and misery
We can't fight physically for we wouldn't prevail
On account of ammunition, cruel laws and jail
But every man was born to be free
From this oppression and tyrannic slavery

20. "King George's Silver Jubilee," Lord Beginner, Decca 17255, New York, March 18, 1935.

The person who wrote the musical arrangement for this recording, probably orchestra leader Gerald Clark, incorporates the tune of "Rule, Britannia," before the first verse.

1. Shout three cheers for his Majesty
In recognition of his Silver Jubilee
Shout three cheers for his Majesty
In recognition of his Silver Jubilee
May his reign be glorious
Happy and victorious
So raise your voices and let us sing
"God save our gracious King"

2. Now folks, you must listen attentively
To the good life of our Majesty
Second son of Edward the Peacemaker
Beloved throughout the British Empire
Born in 1865, he's seventy years old
May his name and prestige never grow cold
So raise your voices and let us sing
"God save our gracious King"

3. In 1910, his father he did succeed
And he has lived up to his ancestral creed
In 1911, with crown and scepter
He was made King at Westminster
He appreciates his subjects' great loyalty
And he's beloved universally
That's why we have all joined wholeheartedly
To keep his Jubilee in our memory

4. In 1914 when the Great War began
He proved himself a soldier and a man
His policy in answering the bugle call
Was, "United we stand, divided we fall"
For he has urged that warfare shall cease
That all nations shall be at peace
So raise your voices and let us sing
"God save our gracious King"

5. It's twenty-five years he's now on the throne
And we can proudly boast he has held his own
So loyal subjects, make preparation
To keep up his Jubilee celebration
Let's hope he'll live for many more years
For him all nations will shout three cheers
Sing, "Rule Britannia, Britannia rule the waves"
"Briton never, never shall be slaves"

21. "The Treasury Fire," Peters, ARC (Melotone M 12705, Banner B-707, etc.), New York, May 17, 1933.

This calypso is labeled as a paseo. The vocalist, Peters, was probably a West Indian who lived in New York; he is not known as a calypsonian. The song is usually credited to Cat, the original Beginner. The lyrics refer to an actual incident. Rum was kept in bond in the treasury, and the fire provided a windfall for spectators.

1. I was asleep when quite suddenly
I heard a fire in the treasury
I was asleep when quite suddenly
I heard a fire in the treasury
I got up in a fearful way
As my mother began to pray
My sister started to clown
Me wife ran down in her blue nightgown

2. We were lying down side by side
When the door was thrown open wide
She sprang up, I told her just to wait
Dorothy, I'm into a funny state
But when the siren began to blow
We sprang through the door like Garvey and Joe
The speed that we made that night
Got me there like a streak of light

3. Rum drinkers from every place
Lamented over that wanton waste
Gumbolailai hadn't a pan
He used for a dipper both of his hand
Loretta put her mouth to the ground
Drank, got drunk that she tumble down

Joe Laughter had so much fun
He laugh so loud that his pants fell down

    4. Rum flowed fast that a boat could sail
A fellow was dipping up with a pail
The flames ascended up like a bird
All sorts of languages you should have heard
French woman shouted, "*Mi dife!*" (Look fire!)
An Indian say, "Am no djanay [?]"[17]
I don't know where the blind man came from
He doesn't see but he smells the rum

22. "Treasury Scandal," Atilla, Decca 17320, New York, February 19, 1937.

    Some calypsos formalize gossip. A widespread theme in Trinidad (and elsewhere for that matter) is that governmental officials are not to be trusted. Atilla castigates an unnamed person responsible for the embezzlement.

    1. I wonder if it's *bòbòl* (fraud)
What they doing with taxpayers' money at all
I wonder if it's *bòbòl*
What they doing with taxpayers' money at all
All around the town you can hear the talk
Two hundred thousand dollars can't walk
People saying it's conspiracy
I mean the scandal in the treasury

    2. It was about just eight months past
That the whole of Trinidad stood aghast
When the government made a declaration
That created a great sensation
In the books of the treasury something went wrong
Two hundred thousand dollars could not be found
And every clerk say, "It ent me fault"
"So it must be a spirit open the vault"

    3. Well, now, the entire population
Are demanding explanation
For when to balance his books the poor clerk fail
They take him to court and sends him to jail

Some say in baccarat [gambling] money loss
Others declare that they buy race horse
That someone stole it we can't deny
For money ent got wings and it cannot fly

4. All of this evidence goes to show
They were bobolising long time ago
In fact it's an opinion of mine
They carry 'way cash a very long time
I'm sure that near everybody know
How they used to burn the notes long ago
Well, this clever culprit he use he head
He keep the bank notes and burn up paper instead

5. Well, I would not have made this song at all
But I ent get nothing in the *bòbòl*
While I, poor Atilla, seeing hell
They carrying away cash and they doing well
For two hundred thousand take it from me
I would make five years quite happily
And when I come from jail what the deuce I care
I'd be living the life of a millionaire

23. "Money Is King," Tiger, Decca 17254, New York, March 18, 1935.

In the third verse, according to Winer, "Tiger . . . imitates a very old-fashioned speech type: '-am' indicates a direct or indirect object following or implied, now rarely found in Trinidad."

1. If a man has money today
People do not care if he has *kokobe* [yaws, a tropical disease]
If a man has money today
People do not care if he has *kokobe*
He can commit murder and get off free
And live in the governor's company
But if you are poor people will tell you
"Shoo, and a dog is better than you!"

2. If you have money to buy in a store
The boss will shake your hands at the door
Call ten clerks to take down everything

Whiskey, cloth, earring, and diamond ring
He may send them to your house on a motor bike
You can pay the bills whenever you like
Not a soul will ask you a thing
They know very well that money is king.

3. A man with a collar and tie and waistcoat
Ask the Chinee man to trust him accra and float
"Me no trust-am," bawl out the Chinee man
"And you better move-am from me frying pan"
"You college man, me no know ABC"
"You want-am accra, gie-am penny"
The worms start to jump in the man's belly
And he cried out, "A dog is better than me!"

4. A dog can walk about and take up bone
Fowl head, stale bread, fish tail, and pone
If it's a good breed and not too wild
Some people will take it and mind as a child
But when a hungry man goes out to beg
They will set a bulldog behind his leg
For the policeman may chock him down too
You see where a dog is better than you

5. If you have money and things going nice
Any woman would call you honey and spice
If you can't give her a dress or a new pair of shoe
She'll say she have no uses for you
When you try to caress her she will tell you, "Stop!"
"I can't carry love in the Chinee shop"
I'm sure most of you will agree that it's true
If you haven't money, dog is better than you.

24. "Warning the Children towards Mother," King Radio, Decca
17289, New York, April 4, 1936.

Mothers are the only women in calypso who are consistently
portrayed in a positive way. This is the archetypical "mother" calypso.

1. Children, the time is rather hard
Don't treat your dear old mother bad
Children the time is rather hard

Don't treat your dear old mother bad
There is a debt we all have got to pay
For treating mothers in a naughty way
You'll never miss the water till the well run dry
Like a mother when she closes her eyes

2. Be kind to your mother from your childhood day
Who always lead you in the correct way
Remember she nursed you to her breast
And for many night she lost her rest
Step by step you gradually grows
Love and behavior to mother you must show
You'll never miss the water till the well run dry
Like a mother when she closes her eyes

3. A mother grieving 'tis hard to see
After raising her child from its infancy
And soon as it reaches a high degree
Give her no "gratuity"
It's rather hard to treat a mother bad
The one that you owes the greatest of regard
So you'll never miss the water till the well run dry
Like a mother when she closes her eyes

4. We know that mothers are kind and brave
To climb any mountain to protect and save
We know she sacrificed to die for love
And to cherish you more than a turtle dove
And when you leave her home going across the sea
She will sigh and cry and count her rosary
So you never miss the water till the well run dry
Like a mother when she closes her eyes

5. Let us kneel and let us pray
And bless our mother day by day
And keep her secrets in our heart
Before the hour of death depart
Her loving face, children, let us keep in memory
As a photograph for all eternity
You never miss the water till the well run dry
Like a mother when she closes her eyes

25. "I Don't Want No Calaloo," Growler, Decca 17409, Trinidad, June 30, 1939.

This is one of many songs about a woman's attempt to control her boyfriend's affections through magical means. Note Growler's tag at the end of the song to identify himself and where the record was cut.

1. Doris, darling, I am so blue
Seems as what the neighbor told me is true
Doris, darling, I am so blue
Seems as what the neighbor told me is true
chorus:
Just give me the raw salt fish
Nothing grinning [?] inside the dish
And gal I must save from you
Lord I doesn't want no more calaloo

2. This kind of love wouldn't do for me
To tie me down in negromancy [necromancy]
I losing me sight, I losing me hair
You getting me deaf, I can't even hear
chorus

3. Why these girls today believe in this thing
Tying down a poor man to get a ring
As soon as you talk 'bout matrimony
The first meal they give you is talkaree [a spicy dish, presumably
    good for hiding potions]
chorus

4. From the day you give me the calaloo
You had me just like your *kounoumounou* (fool)
When she bawl at me, friends, I couldn't talk
And not only that, sometimes I couldn't walk
chorus

5. You men, I am warning you
Be careful when eating crab calaloo
It's a meal you love to partake
But bet your sweet life you will get headache
chorus
This is the Growler!
At Sa Gomes Emporium!

26. "High Brown," Growler, Decca 17423, Trinidad, February 6, 1939.

This song refers to the supposed differences between light- and dark-brown women. In this instance, Growler prefers the darker women as potential mates, although he likes lighter women for prestige.

1. I don't want no High Brown again
You could believe, to come and worry the Growler brain
I don't want no High Brown again
You could believe, to come and worry the Growler brain
I want the Black to call me, "Darling, o' Mine"
Cook and give me meals in time
And when I vex, she must say, "Don't you worry boy!"
Hug me up and call me "Papa Toy-loy" [affectionate name]

2. The High Brown believe in only two thing
Plenty rouge and plenty dressing
Every new fashion dress that they see,
This is the talk, "Honey, buy one for me"
And when you kiss them, this is what they'll do
Charge up with the kids to *mamagay* (trick) you
"Doodoo, darling," and patting your head
Until you catch Mister Jamesie under the bed

3. With a High Brown you got plenty trouble
Don't ask how, they'll have you miserable
They won't wash your clothes, they won't cook your food
And if you speak to them, they want to be rude
And if you hit them, they will bawl for murder
Run in the station for the Super
And when he come, because she pretty and her skin brown
He will rock you, beat you, and carry you down [arrest you]

4. Me darkey will work and give me a help
Buck shoes, flannel pants also with the belt
And pretty rings to wear on me hand
And a Raleigh bike to ride all over the land
She will clean me nails, she will comb me hair
And bet your sweet life, her love is sincere
But the High Brown she only want me money
For she to walk all about and call me *mouki* (fool)

5. You may laugh, this may sound so foolish to you
Young men, every word is candid and true
As soon as you get in with a High Brown
The first thing she tell you, "Let's settle down"
You bound to say, "Yes," and make up your mind
Because she's so fascinating and fine
A pretty face will have you so *bazodi* (crazy)
That you bound to break your neck in matrimony
This is the Growler!
Recording for the Decca!

27. "Fan Me, Saga Boys," Lion, Guild 125, New York, circa May 1945.
These lyrics describe the supposed behavior of the "saga boy," a lower-class male whose garb and behavior were copied from American zoot-suiters of the 1940s. A saga boy dressed in fancy clothes and had little difficulty in getting as many women as he wanted, as Lion noted. The song utilizes images of World War II to metaphorically describe sexual intercourse, which Lion voyeuristically encounters. A piano roll, cut in 1924 and titled "Fan Me Soldier Man, Fan Me," is probably based upon the same lavway as is this song.

1. *Makomè* (girl friend), you have me *basodi* (giddy)
Any more shock give me *malkadi* (fits)
Makomè, you have me *basodi*
Any more shock give me *malkadi*
Just because me blouse ent long
And me pants ent draping with a waist by me shoulders
You wait until I went out on an Xmas evening
And you bring yuh saga in me house romancing
chorus:
Fan me, saga boys, fan me.
I said, "Oh! fan me, saga boys, fan me."
Long live our gracious King
But I kiss me saga boy, Christmas morning.
spoken:
"Hook, line and sinker!"
"She giving me she *koumana!*"
"Wake up, Mr. Clark!" [the orchestra leader]

2. You said I'm wrong, but you do not know
Don't blame the neighbors, for they didn't tell me so

I had me idea and decide to lay me trap
Made me attack and lay wait in the back
I heard a knocking, I saw him entering
The lights went low, I heard a whispering
There was no earthquake, but the place was shaking
You then light the lamp, and you began singing
chorus
spoken:
"And fish is fowl"
"Then fowl is fish!"
"She giving me she koomana!"

3. A hole near the bed, in the partition
Is where I gain my observation
He lock your neck, and you made to gasp a cough [?]
He kiss you in your eyes, and you gave up the ghost
He lock your neck a second time again
Made you content, promise him a fighter plane
In the heat of the battle, made a right about
He mash your corns and you were darn well knocked out
chorus

4. I also saw, though you say I lie
When you hear the facts, sure you can't deny
Same hole through which I gain observation
I even notice some naval action
Because I saw him with his destroyer
While you were getting ready with your mine sweeper
He shot a torpedo at your ship and miss
But dropped his bombs in your captain's office
chorus
spoken:
"Hook, line and sinker!"
"Don't stop at all!"

28. "Radio Trinidad's Tenth Anniversary," Railway (Chieftain) Douglas, probably private acetate or tape, orchestra unknown, possibly recorded in the Radio Trinidad Studios, Port of Spain, Trinidad, 1957.

This is a ballad, of which Douglas was a master without peer. Railway Douglas, as far as I am aware, never made commercial recordings. Two sources remain for his songs: the memories of those who heard them and his only known recordings, the few acetates or tapes that have survived from the 1950s. Thus, the only documentation of his lively artistry is songs composed and recorded when he was well past his prime. This song was saved by Daniel Crowley and is part of the Crowley Collection, Indiana University Archives of Traditional Music. It was written in praise of Radio Trinidad's tenth anniversary and is self-explanatory.

1. We extend to Radio Trinidad most heatedly
Congratulations on your tenth anniversary
The Trinidad Broadcasting Company if you please
Is the most powerful station in the West Indies
Which under competent management
Has an outstanding program arrangement
We prophetize then new name will be
The [?] Broadcasting
chorus:
Hurray Radio Trinidad
Carry on the good service for we're glad
You've won the admiration
Of the entire population

2. To their choice programs tribute must be paid
First we take "Local Talent on Parade"
"Hi Neighbor," "Share the Wealth," "Top of the Morning"
"Sunday Serenade," the popular "Second Spring"
"Pick a Box" with laughter and fun
The exciting Doctor Paul [Anderson?]
"Ten-Twenty Club"—these are just a few
Last but not least is "Dedicated to You"
chorus

3. Of the announcers who take priority
None other but our beloved Sam [Gerney?],
Trum Pado, Bob Gittens, and Frank Hughes
Ken Gordon, Val Douglas all in the news
Radio Trinidad we are told
Is the first radio station in the world
To make a recording while in flight

From a Convair jet plane, what a delight
chorus

4. Radio Trinidad during the past decade
Is first to provide the distressed with aid
For loss of home and in dire poverty
They volunteer free publicity
Remember Lord Executor
Hurricane Janet, the St. Lucia [fire?]
To staff and station may success hang
Under the able management of Michael [Land?]
chorus

29. "Cipriani's and Bradshaw's Death," Houdini, ARC Melotone M 13064, Oriole O 744, and other American Record Corporation labels, New York, July 2, 1934.

Michael ("Mikey") Cipriani was the brother of Captain Arthur Cipriani, leader of the Trinidad Labour party. According to gossip, Mikey and the flyer Leslie Bradshaw had a falling out over the latter's interest in Mikey's wife. Some people suggest that Mikey caused the crash by use of obeah against Bradshaw, even though he, too, died in the accident.

1. We can't forget the tragedy
Of Bradshaw and Cipriani
We can't forget the tragedy
Of Bradshaw and Cipriani
They left Mucurapo air base
The men not knowing what was their fate
It was so stormy and foggy that would cause the tragedy
Sandimanite (without pity)

2. West Indian mourn the tragic end
Of marvelous Mikey and his loyal friend
Leslie Bradshaw who without fear
Ascend the atmosphere
Nobody ever thought, nobody ever dreamt
That it was their fatal attempt
It was so stormy and foggy that would cause the tragedy
Sandimanite

3. When excited crowds at Tobago found
They had seen no plane nor heard no sound
To Trinidad they then telegraph
To find out what detain the aircraft
The reply came that it had sail
And must be in distress through the gale
It was so stormy and foggy that would cause the tragedy
Sandimanite

4. Friends, relatives and government
Their night on expedition they went
To districts where they had seen or heard
The last movements of the Hummingbird
Eventually they found where the flyers died
From a terrible crash down a mountain side
It was so stormy and foggy that would cause the tragedy
Sandimanite

Tent Calypsos: Calypso War

30. "War," Atilla, Lion, Caresser, and Lord Executor, Decca 17328, New York, February 25, 1937.

A war is a battle in song between two or more calypsonians. It is sung in speech tones. Lion mimics the sound of the Carnival character the Midnight Robber in his verse based on robber talk.[18] Such picong (*pikan*) was the highlight of tent performances in the 1910s. This and the subsequent "War Declaration" by Houdini are but two in a long series of recorded duels between Houdini and Executor. This record is common and apparently sold well.

1. Executor:
At last the hour of vengeance is at hand
I am in the land
At last the hour of vengeance is at hand
I am in the land
The Lord Executor's word of command
With my glittering sword in hand
Tell Houdini this is the hour of destiny
In this colony

2. Executor:
Those who boast that Houdini can sing
In my opinion they know nothing
For it's all propaganda, deceit and pretense
He hasn't got the shadow of intelligence
The money that was spent on his slates and books
Has not improved his manners and looks
He has a good inclination but foreign education
In this colony

3. Caresser:
Men boast of their intelligence
While the audience have observed their incompetence
The rattling of their tongue with the music and time
Cannot make Caresser feel that they are sublime
Knowledge have increased understand me well
It was written in a book that others should tell
Tell them seek graduation and then approbation
As a calypsonian

4. Atilla:
From the very first day that I was born
Men like Houdini started to mourn
Monarchs wept and princes cried
When they saw this new star up in the sky
Astronomers in my horoscope state
I'll be proud, grand, illustrious and great
And they name me Atilla the Terror, the Brutal Conqueror
Master mi minor

5. Lion:
The earth is trembling and tumbling
And heroes are falling and all
Because the Lion is roaring
My tongue is like the blast of a gun
When I frown, monarchs I want to bow down to the ground
Devastation, destruction, desolation and damnation
All these I'll inflict on insubordination
For the Lion in his power is like the Rock of Gibraltar

31. "War Declaration," Houdini, ARC (Banner B 750, and other American Record Corporation labels), New York, November 30, 1934.

Houdini consistently gave the impression that he was born in New York, although most scholars believe he was born in Trinidad. His claim of a New York birth may have been a ploy to keep residence in the United States. In this song, which would not have been heard by immigration officers, he refers to Trinidad as home. The "deportation rumor" could have been picong on Houdini by calypsonians in Trinidad, that Houdini was born in Trinidad, not New York as he contended and had been deported to Trinidad. This war chronicles one of Houdini's visits to Trinidad.

1. Cable in the morning send and tell them I am coming
So they better prepare for "war"
Cable in the morning send and tell them I am coming
So they better prepare for "war"
Tell them "murder," "kill," and "slay"
"War declare" at the break of day
On the Lion and Atilla and the Lord Executor
"War declare!"

2. People, listen attentively
I can prove where it is only through jealousy
Songsters dislike Papa Houdini
And I know that it is through my ability
Just listen to the songsters all around the town
How they're criticizing Houdini's song
They have got a wrong conception, I'm a born calypsonian
"War declare!"

3. When I came home 1929
The songsters declare that I must not shine
They follow me all around the town
In every case they're trying to call me down
People, listen attentively
Can't you see it is only through jealousy
That is why they make the scandal about deportation
"War declare!"

4. When you hear me sing my characteristic songs
From the "Book of Auditions" which last so long

The volubility that is lived in me
It is owing to my high class propensity
I am not versed in psychology
But I can sing intelligently
And I can last on my journey to the end of destiny
"War declare!"

Tent Calypsos: Calypso Drama

32. "Women Are Good and Women Are Bad," Lord Beginner and
Atilla, Decca 17266, New York, March 22, 1935.

The duet form is usually credited to Atilla and Lion, but here Atilla
is joined by Beginner. Atilla takes a rare positive stance toward
women.

1. Beginner:
They cause me too much pain
Not me with woman again
They cause me too much pain
I don't want no woman again
I see woman one and all
Always cause a man's downfall
Atilla:
In my opinion
I think they are mankind's consolation

2. Beginner:
Since history began
Woman has been fooling man
I sure you men will agree
They know nothing of fidelity
When you are prosperous they love you and be gay
When your money done they will run away
These things happen to me
That's why I can speak with authority

3. Atilla:
I have heard your song
And I'd like to tell you you're wrong
It's the men that have got no shame

And the poor girls, they weren't to blame
Here is one thing you should know
If a woman is bad, men made her so
For in my opinion
I think they are mankind's consolation

4. Beginner:
Even the mighty King Saul
It was a woman cause his downfall
And Napoleon the Great
Is said that a woman hands met his fate
Turn back the pages of history
See what Cleopatra did to Anthony
Too much sorrows and pain
So never me with woman again

5. Atilla:
Women lose their innocence
In the school of experience
The men lead them astray
And then the vagabonds run away
After so much woe and pain
They'd be fools to play with fire again
Still my opinion
Is that they are mankind's consolation

Calypsos for the Theater

33. "Sly Mongoose," Sam Manning, OK 65008 and Pa R3854, New York, circa December 30, 1925.

This song was first recorded by the Guyanese vaudevillian Phil Madison in 1923 (fig. 66). It was later claimed by Houdini as his own. Lionel Belasco and Clarence Williams once held the copyright. It was originally a Jamaican mento, a topical song similar to the calypso. In the song, a wayward girl is bedded by the "Sly Mongoose," a metaphorical reference to a newspaper reporter. Her father was alleged to be a turn-of-the-century preacher, Alexander Bedward.[19] The mongoose is an animal native to India that was imported into the Caribbean to rid the islands of snakes, rats, and other pests. Unfortu-

66 ✳ Label for the original recording of a song about the wayward daughter of a philandering preacher; a "Sly Mongoose" seduces the girl to retaliate against the preacher's own hypocrisy. Victor trademark courtesy of BMG Music.

nately, it also liked chickens. Bedward himself was notorious for his sexual liaisons with many women, hence he "deserved" to have his daughter seduced by the reporter. In 1921, Bedward was declared to be legally insane and was institutionalized.

1. Listen to the story why Mongoose fled from Jamaica
Listen to the story why Mongoose fly from Jamaica
Mongoose a newspaper reporter
Took bed with the preacher's daughter
Baptize her in his holy water
Sly the Mongoose.
chorus:
Sly the Mongoose, now your name gone abroad
Sly the Mongoose, now your name gone abroad
Mongoose went into Bedward's kitchen
Took up one of his fattest chickens
That's the reason he fly from Jamaica
Sly the Mongoose

2. Sly the Mongoose, now your name gone abroad
Sly the Mongoose, now your name gone abroad
Mongoose fly from Jamaica, fly right on down to Cuba
Wouldn't stop and he reach America
Sly the Mongoose

3. Sly the Mongoose, now the world know your name
Brother Mongoose, now the world know your fame
Mongoose told his high brown mama
Go 'way gal, get another papa
I love your sister a whole lot better
Sly the Mongoose

34. "Caroni Swamp," Phil Madison, Vi 77426, New York, August 8, 1923.

Phil Madison chronicles the scandal about the Caroni Swamp in west-central Trinidad.[20] Developers hatched a scheme to make money by draining the swamp and building a tennis court.

1. A man stood by the Anchor sign
On top of Laventille[21]
And wrote some lines about the swamp
And nothing about the bill
I read those lines with a kind o' smile
Mingled with a tear
Then I thought that such a scheme
Could wreck a millionaire
chorus:
On this swamp, Caroni swamp, oh, this swamp
On this swamp, Caroni swamp, oh, this swamp
The more mud I bail
The more mud I see
Mosquitoes tough like crab and *krapo* (frog)
Stood up an' laugh at me

2. After all the cash is spent
And the island put in pawn
We might sell some seed to get a field
To make a tennis lawn
With all the money 'portioned now
The best thing we could do
As we a'ready have the crabs
Let's plant the calaloo [bush used in a stew]

spoken:
Ah, who say that the Caroni Swamp isn't possible? The scheme is possible! All you've got to do is this: remove the five hills from behind;

put it right along the sea front. Lif' up the swamp, lif' it up and put it where the hills were—dat's the thing!

35. "West Indian Weed Woman," Bill Rogers, Bluebird B-4938, New York, November 19, 1934.

This is a vaudeville song, popularized by Bill Rogers, whose given name was Augustus Hinds. It is a Guyanese shanto, a form mastered by Rogers, who was of Guyanese descent. Songs similar to this one are found in the folk tradition throughout the English-speaking Caribbean.

The "West Indian Weed Woman" is a street vendor whose herbs cure every affliction from gout to loss of love. The song is an anthropologist's paradise: It gives Guyanese names for numerous plants used as cures. Some of the names have interesting derivations. For example, a *jumbie* is a ghost, but a *jumbie bottle* is a plant, possibly named after a special bottle in which one traps a spirit who does one's bidding.

A great start in transcribing this song was provided by a booklet by Tesfa Harris.[22]

1. One day I met an old woman selling
And I wanted something to eat
I say I was going to put a bit in she way
But I turn back when I meet
I thought she had bananas, orange, or pear
But was nothing that I need
For when I ask the old woman what she was selling
She said she was selling weed

2. She had she coat tie up over she waist
And was stepping along with grace
She had on a pair of old clogs on her feet
And was wriggling down the street
Just then she started to name the different weeds
And I really was more than glad
But I can't remember all that she call
But these were a few she had

3. Man Piaba, Woman Piaba
Tantan Fall Back and Lemon Grass

Minnie Root, Gullie Root, Grannie-Back-Bone, Bitter Tally, Lime
   Leaf, and Toro
Coolie Bitters, Karile Bush, Flat 'o the Earth, and Iron Weed
Sweet Broom, Fowl Tongue, Wild Daisy, Sweet Sage, and even
   Toyo

4. She had Cassava Mumma, Coocoo Piaba, Jacob's Ladder, and
   Piti Guano
Fingle Bush, Job's Tear, Piti Payi, a Jumbie Bottle, and White Cleary
Bile Bush, Wild Cane, Duck Weed, Aniseed, Wara Bitters, and
   Wild Gray Root
She even had down to a certain bush Barbajans does call "Puss in
   Boot"

5. When I hear how much bush she had
I left dumb till I couldn't even talk
She started to call from Camp Street corner
Never stop till she reach Orange Walk
The woman had me so surprise that I didn't know what to do
That a girl come and gimme a cuff in me eye
And I didn't even know was who

6. Sweet Broom, Sweet Sage, and Lemon Grass
I hear them good for making tea
Oh well, I hear Zèb Grass and Wild Daisy
Is good to cool the body
The woman tongue was even listed [lisped]
And she was calling out all the time
She even had a little kanwa eye [cast eye]
And the other that left was blind

7. She had Bitter Guma, Portogee Bumboh, Congo Lana, and
   Twelve o'clock Broom
Sarsaparilla, Wild Tomato, Soursop Leaf, and Hafabit Weed
Yoruba Leaf, Sweet Pinpota Bush, White Fleary, and Christmas
   Bush
Scotch and Sandies and even Monkey Ladder and all the rest you
   may need

8. She had Fat Bush, Elder Bush, Black Pepper Bush, French Toyo,
   Qupera, and Capadulla

Tamarind Leaf, Money Bush, Soldier Fork Leaf, Pumpkin Blossom,
  and even Devil Dua
Leeman, Congo Pom, Pingalor, Physic Nut, and Lily Root
In fact the only bush that she didn't got
Was bush in he everyday suit

A Calypso Popular in Clubs in the United States and Britain

36. "New York Subway," Lord Invader, Disc 5009, New York, circa
1946.

1. When I first landed in the U.S.A.
Listen how I got lost on the subway
When I first landed in the U.S.A.
Listen how I got lost on the subway
I had a date with a chick and I went to Brooklyn
But I couldn't find my way back the following morning
I had money yet I had to roam
And still I couldn't get a cab to drop me back home

2. I met a cop and told him I'm a stranger
Lord Invader a calypso singer
I live in Harlem and came here yesterday
But now I want to go home I can't find my way
He told me, "Walk back three blocks" and he further explain
"Go to the subway and take the uptown train"
I got confuse, I was in a heat
I couldn't find my way to One-Twenty-Fifth Street

3. I came out the subway and didn't know what to do
Looking for someone to help me through
You talk about people as bad as crab
Is the drivers who driving the taxicabs
Some passing you empty and yet they wouldn't stop
Some will say they have no gas or they can't make the drop
I had money yet I had to roam
But still I couldn't get a cab to drop me back home

4. I console myself and started to walk
I said that happen to persons who born in New York
So I decided to leave the Jews alone

If they want to see me they must come to my home
Because New York is so big it take a year and a day
For anyone to get accustom to the subway
I had money yet I had to roam
And still I couldn't get a cab to drop me back home

Appendix 2 ✳ Annotated Discography
of Calypso Recordings

THIS discography is a list of some of the classic calypso LPs and CDs that have been issued in recent years. They may be found in large retail shops or ordered directly from the companies. I have included only releases that have excellent notes and lyric transcriptions. Most of the recordings listed here include performers and songs that are discussed in this book.

Calypso Awakenings. Produced by Keith Warner and Ken Bilby. Smithsonian/Folkways CD. The first of a projected series of CDs that reissue the extensive recordings that Emory Cook made in Trinidad in the 1950s, including the first live calypso tent recordings. Due to be released in late 1993.

Calypso Breakaway: 1927–1941. Produced by Dick Spottswood and Keith Warner. Rounder CD 1054. Contains many recordings of calypsos from the 1930s.

Calypso Carnival. Produced by Spottswood. Rounder CD 1071. This recording contains calypsos from the 1930s.

Calypso Ladies. Produced by Spottswood. Harlequin HQ CD 06. Calypsos from the 1930s about women.

Calypso Pioneers: 1912–1937. Produced by Spottswood and Don Hill. Rounder CD/LP 1039. Contains many historic selections, including Julian Whiterose's "Iron Duke in the Land," recorded in 1914, and Bill Rogers's classic mento, "West Indian Weed Woman."

Calypsos from Trinidad: Politics, Intrigue, and Violence in the 1930s. Produced by Spottswood. Folklyric CD 7004. Focuses on songs about the enigmatic Trinidadian labor leader Uriah Butler. An LP issue of the recording (Folklyric LP 9048) may still be found in cutout bins.

History of Carnival: Christmas, Carnival, Calenda, and Calypso from Trinidad, 1933–1939. Produced by John Cowley. Matchbox Calypso Series MDB 905. In addition to the original recordings, the Matchbox calypso packages contain excellent notes and full lyric transcriptions.

Jazz and Hot Dance in Trinidad, 1912–1939. Produced by Spottswood. Harlequin LP HQ 2016; CD HQ 16. A cross section of Trinidadian instrumental music.

Knockdown Calypso: Growling Tiger, High Priest of Mi Minor. Produced by Steve Shapiro. Rounder LP 5006. Tiger still retained his punch in these late-1970s recordings of some of his classic songs. He and Shapiro assembled an all-star backing band, including Chocolate Armenteros on trumpet, Candido on conga, Chombo Silva on violin, and Yomo Toro on guitar and cuatro.

Roaring Lion: Roaring Loud, Standing Proud. Produced by Eddie Grant. Ice LP 930201. Reissue of recordings from the 1930s.

Sir Lancelot: Trinidad Is Changing. Produced by Ray Funk. Heritage LP HT 321. Sir Lancelot continues to perform on several continents. This recording, however, consists of his recording from the early 1940s through the early 1950s, including one of his advertising jingles.

Trinidad Loves to Play Carnival: Carnival, Calenda, and Calypso from Trinidad, 1914–1939. Produced by Cowley. Matchbox Calypso Series MBD 906.

Wilmoth Houdini from the 1930's with Gerald Clark's Night Owls. Produced by Cowley. Folklyric LP 9040. This recording contains some of the rarest of the Houdini and Clark recordings.

Record company addresses:
1. Folklyric
   c/o Arhoolie
   10341 San Pablo Ave.
   El Cerrito, CA 94530

2. Harlequin and Heritage
   c/o Interstate Music Ltd.
   P.O. Box 74
   Crawley, West Sussex RH11 OLX
   England
3. Ice, Inc.
   P.O. Box 2917
   London W11 AUD
   England
4. Matchbox Records
   c/o Flyright Record and Distribution Company Ltd.
   Bexhill-on-Sea
   East Sussex TN40 1HY
   England
5. Rounder Records
   186 Willow Ave.
   Somerville, MA 02144
6. Smithsonian/Folkways
   Office of Folk Life Program
   955 L'Enfante Plaza
   Suite 2600
   Smithsonian Institution
   Washington, D.C. 20560

✳ **Notes**

Chapter I

1. One is advised not to read too much into the term *classic calypso*, which is used here simply to mean Trinidadian calypso of the first half of the twentieth century or its derivatives, the calypso that is the subject of this monograph. Forms of calypso that are not classic include topical songs from other islands that are sometimes called calypso, popular calypso outside of the Caribbean that had no connection to Trinidad's Carnival, and soca or soul calypso, a development of the 1970s.

Some modern researchers have adapted the traditional word *kaiso* to refer to archaic calypso that is authentic, as opposed to *calypso*, which seems to refer to the tourist-oriented music of Trinidad. Yet the word *kaiso* seems always to have been used in several senses. It was an exclamation shouted to give approval to a performance (most frequent use). Newspapers sometimes used *caliso* to refer to calypso, e.g., Carnival songs, although not as frequently as *calypso*. I prefer *calypso* rather than *kaiso* because I want to examine a body of songs that includes all Carnival songs in Trinidad after about 1900 (even those composed in part for tourists), and the mediation of this music to West Indians and others living outside the Caribbean basin.

2. An early reference to *calipso* appears in the *Port of Spain Gazette*, January 20, 1900 (cited in E. Hill 1972:61).

3. *Port of Spain Gazette*, February 5, 1903, p. 5.

4. Lord Beginner, interviewed by Mighty Chalkdust 1975:13.

5. Most tent calypso was not performed in theaters and union halls and other indoor venues until the 1930s; hence, the term *indoor* is metaphorical and refers to the different ambience of these calypsos from the more exuberant street calypsos.

6. Victor Vi 67362, recorded in Port of Spain, Trinidad, September 11, 1914; listed in Spottswood n.d.

7. De 17415, recorded in Port of Spain, Trinidad, February 8, 1939; listed in Spottswood n.d.

8. Charles Jones 1947.

9. Quevedo 1983:44.

10. Steve Shapiro, personal communication to the author.

11. In New York, Houdini and later MacBeth and the Duke of Iron (Cecil Anderson, not Julian Whiterose) seem to have sung many calypsos attributed to other calypsonians.

12. P. Jones, in Cook 1956 and Quevedo 1983:85–93. See song 9, "Rum and Coca Cola," appendix 1.

13. Quevedo 1983:85–93.

14. Only Raphael De Leon, the Roaring Lion, has stressed the French connection. He is correct in pointing to influences often overlooked in the scholar's rush to credit West Africa. However, he overstates his point.

15. D. Hill 1977:359ff.

16. African culture was reinvigorated in Trinidad by indentured Africans brought to the island in the second half of the nineteenth century.

Chapter 2

1. The influence of American Indian culture on calypso is minimal in comparison with the West African, French, and British influences. For that reason, I will not discuss the Indians beyond this note.

Several legendary nineteenth-century singers were said to be Indian. The most important of these was Suricima the Carib, whose story is related in Mitto Sampson (as edited by Pearse 1956a). Next, there are a few references to reputed Arawak Carib singing practices (Elder 1966a:63ff.). Finally, some American Indian musical instruments may have been adapted to resemble Old World counterparts: drums, the quira or gourd scraper, flutes, and maracas.

2. See Wood 1968:32.

3. Here *Creole* means born in the Caribbean. The term glosses an extremely complex mixture of ideas concerning descent, culture, and language. Creole sometimes refers to a people, either of European descent born in the Caribbean, of African descent born in the Caribbean, or people of mixed descent from these groups and born in the Caribbean. This sort of definition emphasizes the newness of these peoples and distinguishes them both from American Indians and from people born in the Old World.

Creole may also refer to the culture of these people. Such a culture includes many different ties to West African and European cultures and also, in contradiction to the definition given above, to American Indian culture. The essence of Creole culture, however, is that it is a Caribbean culture that differs from its parent cultures.

Finally, *Creole* is a language, the Afro-French language of the people of Haiti, Martinique, Guadeloupe, parts of St. Lucia, Trinidad, Grenada and Carriacou, and elsewhere. The languages spoken on the French estates in Trinidad were French (the elite) and Creole (the elite and the slaves). Unfortunately (for this otherwise straightforward analysis here), in Trinidad, this Creole language is usually referred to as Patois, not Creole. In Trinidad, *Creole* more often refers to localized variants of English and is usually not considered distinct from English in the way French Creole is considered separate from French.

In sum, it is normal to refer to many people in Trinidad as Creoles and to their culture as Creole culture. The languages spoken in nineteenth-century Trinidad by Creoles were French, English, French Creole, English Creole, and Spanish.

4. St. Hilaire Begorrat became the right-hand man to Picton, the first British governor of Trinidad. Under the cruel Picton, Begorrat became a magistrate of Port of Spain and, soon, a sadistic torturer and executioner of the leaders of a slave insurrection. He and his father, Pierre, are important characters in legendary accounts about certain slaves who worked for the family as praise singers.

5. The reference here is to the schism between French or Creole planters who backed the French revolution and those who did not.

6. Borde 1797 2:51.

7. The notion of a British people was also undergoing a creolization process at this time. The Scottish and Irish peoples did not accept British rule in the same way the English did.

8. In Trinidad's nineteenth-century press the word *party* is used in several ways. In one sense, it means group, camp, or side. By extension, this usage was expanded in the periodicals to refer to a French party or an English party.

I use these terms because they get at the root of the class structure that developed in the nineteenth century. This class structure, in which the elite was divided into two groups, collapsed into one at the beginning of the twentieth century. The ascent of English-language calypso at that time reflects this important social change.

9. The term *black* is used more today than it was one hundred years ago. I use *black* in the modern sense to refer to people who are mostly of West African descent.

10. See Pearse 1956a:178.

11. See de Verteuil 1984:7–8.

12. The information in this paragraph is based on Brereton 1981:54–56.

13. See Pearse 1956a:180–81. Spanish Carnival predated French Carnival in Trinidad. To what extent the Spanish predecessor influenced the dominant French Carnival is not known.

14. Paraphrased from de Verteuil 1984:57.

15. Ibid.

16. See Pearse 1956a:179.

17. Ibid.

18. See de Verteuil 1984:56.

19. Ibid.

20. Brereton 1981:4.

21. Quoted in ibid.

Chapter 3

1. I have borrowed the idea of the distinction between the yard and the road from Roger Abrahams.

2. This is an extract from the Mighty Tangler's calypso "Good South." Tangler is a Carriacouan who won the Calypso King competition of south Trinidad in 1971 with this song. The lyrics are quoted from Donald R. Hill 1980:9.

3. Labat 1724:16, 153–54.

4. In E. Hill 1972:52–53.

5. See Elder 1966b. Elder notes that before 1901 stick fighters congregated on Easter Monday, August 1, and Christmas Day.

6. Quoted in de Verteuil 1984:50.

7. See Elder 1966a, 1966b.

8. See Elder 1966a:185.

9. *Trinidad Guardian*, March 2, 1919.

10. As Gordon Rohlehr points out (personal communication to the author), it is likely that the author of this article, in spite of his claim, was not a poor stick man. His language is that of an elite person; therefore, he may have been a "gentleman stick fighter."

11. Anonymous, quoted in the *Trinidad Guardian*, March 2, 1919.

12. See D. Hill 1977:318–29.

13. See Elder 1966b.

14. Anonymous, *Port of Spain Gazette*, January 20, 1864; quoted in Pearse 1956a:180.

15. See E. Hill 1972:13.

16. Ibid., 14.

17. John McSwines, February 5, 1845, quoted in Wood 1968:244.

18. Their place on the plantations was taken by East Indian indentured servants and by Creoles from nearby islands. Today East Indians make up more than 40 percent of the island's population. Their population growth between 1841 and the 1930s was very large and centered in the cane-producing areas. Although East Indians have had a major impact on the island economically, socially, and culturally, that influence had not extended far into Carnival and calypso during the period covered in this study.

19. See Brereton 1981:131.

20. Brereton in de Verteuil 1984:49.

21. Brereton 1981:98.

22. See Brereton 1981:98.

23. Kingsley 1889:204.

24. See Wood 1968:240–43.
25. See Carr 1955.
26. See Wood 1968:240–43.
27. See Pearse 1956a:187.
28. See Rohlehr 1984.
29. See de Verteuil 1984:54–65; see also Pearse 1956a:189.
30. See de Verteuil 1984:64–70.
31. See Williams 1962:186.
32. See de Verteuil 1984:72.
33. See the *Hamilton Report* 1881:72.
34. See de Verteuil 1984:74.
35. See de Verteuil 1984:75. Modern attitudes toward the Carnival riot of 1881 reflect one's class or at least one's notions of the elite and the masses. Brereton, Williams, and Rohlehr all take positions that suggest that the riot and the burning of the new barracks in town represent a storming of the Bastille, Trinidadian style. De Verteuil's view is more sympathetic to the French elite.

Those years of turmoil seem to point to an uneasy alliance between the Creole forces—especially the middle-class coloreds and the jamets—and their attempt to anglicize Carnival (and Trinidadian culture generally) while beginning the long process to wrest control of the island from the British.

36. See de Verteuil 1984:76.
37. Ibid.
38. Ibid., 78.
39. Belasco, quoted in de Paur 1961.
40. Anonymous, *Trinidad Guardian*, March 2, 1919.
41. See Carmichael 1961:294; see also de Verteuil 1984:84.
42. Fourteen is de Verteuil's figure (1984:84) while twenty-one is Carmichael's (1961:294).
43. See de Verteuil 1984:86.
44. See de Verteuil 1984.
45. See de Verteuil 1984:88–90.
46. Carmichael 1961:294.
47. The *Hamilton Report*, quoted in E. Hill 1972:59.
48. *Mob* is Carmichael's word (1961:295).
49. See de Verteuil 1984:93–94.
50. Ibid., 95–96.
51. The *Hamilton Report*, quoted in Rohlehr 1984:65.
52. See de Verteuil 1984:100.
53. Ibid.
54. Brereton, in de Verteuil 1984:102–3.
55. Ibid., 103.
56. Ibid., 106.
57. Freeling, quoted in ibid., 107.
58. Ibid.
59. Freeling, quoted in ibid., 108.

60. Ibid., 109.

61. Ibid., 109–10.

62. Freeling, quoted in ibid., 1984:113.

63. Ibid., 114.

Chapter 4

1. See Brereton 1981: 120–22.

2. In Rohlehr 1984:76.

3. See de Verteuil 1984:212 and Brereton 1981:120.

4. See Brereton 1981:120.

5. See de Verteuil 1984:212.

6. Williams 1962: 151–52.

7. See Brereton 1981:122–23.

8. J. H. Collens, in Rohlehr 1984:82.

9. See Brereton 1981:121.

10. Ibid.,144.

11. See de Verteuil 1984:269 and Brereton 1981:142ff.

12. Anonymous, *Port of Spain Gazette*, March 1, 1900, pp 4–5.

13. Anonymous, in *Argos*, quoted in Rohlehr 1984:74.

14. *Re-re* may be a Yoruba word, not a French Creole word, and mean out of control. Then again, it may be Patois for king. Whiterose seems to be boasting in this verse. Transcribed from a Victor 78-rpm record, Vi 67362, recorded in Trinidad on September 11, 1914; see Spottswood n.d.

15. Anonymous, *Port of Spain Gazette*, March 21, 1900, p. 5.

16. Henry Julian, *Port of Spain Gazette*, February 1, 1901, p. 4.

17. "They Couldn't Stop the Masquerade," De 17289, recorded in New York on April 9, 1936; see Spottswood n.d.

18. See Brereton 1981:146–53.

19. Joseph Chamberlain, quoted in Brereton 1981:146–47.

20. Ibid., 148.

21. Quoted in Quevedo 1983:12.

22. These are some of the lyrics of a calypso well known at the time and reported by oldtimers through the 1950s. The lyrics were first recorded by Atilla in Trinidad on March 10, 1938, for Decca (De 17389); see Spottswood n.d.

23. Anonymous [probably Atilla] 1970:42–44.

24. See Brereton 1981:151.

25. Interview in Cook 1956.

26. Anonymous, *Port of Spain Gazette*, March 8, 1905, p. 5.

27. Anonymous, *Port of Spain Gazette*, March 5, 1905, p. 5.

28. Belasco, quoted in de Paur 1961.

29. *Trinidad Gazette,* February 12, 1907.

30. Anonymous, *Port of Spain Gazette*, February 12, 1902, p. 5.

31. Anonymous, *Port of Spain Gazette*, February 12, 1902, p. s.

32. Lyrics of a phonograph record made by Whiterose in Trinidad in 1914, adapted from the text in Spottswood and Hill 1989.

33. After the Dragons were in vogue, they were followed, around 1919, with a spate of tourist Millionaires.

34. This originated as an East Indian masquerade consisting of a horse and rider costume.

35. Patrick Jones, quoted in Cook 1956.

36. Procope 1956:276.

37. Patrick Jones, quoted in Cook 1956.

38. See Procope 1956:275–76.

39. See Procope 1956:277ff.

40. Procope 1956:277.

41. Participant's account, related by Procope 1956:278n.

42. Jones 1947.

Chapter 5

1. Elder 1966a:112–23.

2. Elder 1964:131.

3. Roaring Lion n.d.:180.

4. Jones 1947.

5. Anonymous, *Trinidad Guardian*, February 8, 1899.

6. Anonymous, *Port of Spain Gazette*, January 30, 1903.

7. See Quevedo 1983:35.

8. See Roaring Lion n.d.:191.

9. See anonymous, *Trinidad Gazette*, February 16, 1903, noted in E. Hill 1972:64.

10. Jones 1947.

11. Clerking in one of the major retail stores in Port of Spain was a middle-class job in turn-of-the-century Trinidad.

12. In this instance the term *white* is used as an indicator both of skin color and of social class. A more accurate description would be persons of mostly Northern European descent (mainly French or British) born in Trinidad.

Le Blanc was, for a time, a member of the White Rose Social Union, a band whose members' complexions ranged from white to light brown.

Even in the early 1970s, the range of complexions of the visible members of some bands was limited.

13. Quevedo 1983:35.

14. See Roaring Lion n.d.:181; see also Quevedo 1983:36.

15. In Roaring Lion n.d.:181.

16. Pitts paraphrasing Executor, in Rohlehr 1984:104.

17. Anonymous, *Port of Spain Gazette*, February 27, 1903.

18. Anonymous, ibid., February 10, 1901.

19. Anonymous, ibid., February 5, 1903.

20. What eventually lead to a great reduction in the variety of small masquerades was not the large, fancy masquerade bands, but the steel band. See chapter 10.

21. *Trinidad Sunday Guardian*, February 23, 1919.

22. See Quevedo 1983:36ff; see also Carr et al., in Carr n.d.

23. Atilla, paraphrased in Elder 1966a:112–23.

24. Quevedo 1983:39.

25. Ibid.

26. Jones 1947.

27. E. Hill 1972:65–67.

28. Chalkdust 1975:3. Douglas's tent was near South Quay, where the railroad station was located and where he worked.

29. Beginner identifies Douglas as the head guard for the railroad (in Carr n.d.).

30. Carr 1972.

31. In Rutter 1933:105.

32. Johnnie Walker was more of a vaudevillian than a calypsonian and usually performed in theaters. He took his name from the whiskey.

33. Young Pretender, quoted in Carr n.d.

34. Beginner, quoted in Carr n.d.

35. Chalkdust 1975 (part 2):12–13.

36. Huxley 1934:21.

37. Quevedo 1983:36ff. The Toddy Syndicate was probably the same establishment as the Victory Tent.

38. D. P., *Trinidad Guardian*, January 23, 1941.

39. *Trinidad Guardian*, March 2, 1927.

40. In Roaring Lion n.d.

41. Pretender in Carr 1972.

42. Tiger in Carr 1972.

43. Roaring Lion n.d.

44. Roaring Lion n.d.:195–96.

45. In Roaring Lion n.d.

46. Tiger, quoted in Quevedo 1983:14.

47. Laborite Albert Gomes recollection, reported in Brereton 1981:192.

48. Ibid., 191–92.

49. The rest of this paragraph is based on Brereton 1981:191–92.

50. Wenzell Brown 1947:57.

51. Roaring Lion n.d.

52. Chalkdust 1975:12–13.

53. Jones 1947.

54. Burchhardt 1942.

55. Warner 1982:12.

56. Chalkdust 1975 (part 4):13–14.

Chapter 6

1. Mitto Sampson, in Pearse 1956b.

2. Anonymous, ibid., 253–54.

3. Threat of poisoning was a big concern in those days: the real Begorrat, not the legendary one mentioned here, was involved in the scandalous suppression of

a slave revolt in the early 1800s, a revolt in which poisoning was a punishment rebels inflicted on spies.

4. Mitto Sampson, in Pearse 1956b:254.

5. Mitto Sampson, in ibid., 255.

6. Mitto Sampson, in ibid., 259ff. and de Verteuil 1984:28–34.

7. In de Verteuil 1984:30.

8. Related by Mitto Sampson in Pearse 1956b:259.

9. In de Verteuil 1984:33.

10. This quote is from a taped interview, March 26, 1976. The name of the source is withheld to honor that person's privacy.

11. Huxley 1934:19.

12. Alig 1949:14.

13. Mitchell 1939:61ff.

14. Carr 1972.

15. Lord Beginner, in Carr n.d.

16. Iere, in Carr 1972.

17. Iere, quoted in Chalkdust 1975:13.

18. Lord Beginner, in Carr 1972.

19. Roaring Lion n.d.

20. Quevedo 1983:35.

21. Elder 1966a:113

22. Elder 1964:131.

23. Elder 1966a:113.

24. *Port of Spain Gazette*, February 27, 1903, p. 4.

25. See Jones 1947; see also Carr 1972 and Quevedo 1983:10–11. A chantwell named Cedric le Blanc—no relation to Norman le Blanc—apparently sang in English a generation before Norman le Blanc. It may be that he is discounted by commentators because his songs did not coincide with a broad movement toward English-language calypso.

26. Executor's song, as quoted in Carr n.d.

27. See Quevedo 1983:89–112.

28. Richard, Coeur de Leon, was a crusader; he fought in the Holy Land and later against the Holy Roman Empire. He was killed in battle in France.

29. Lord Beginner, quoted in Carr 1972. A copy is a cheaply printed, single-page transcription of a calypso. Just like British broadsides, copies were sold in the streets by the composers themselves. They consisted of the lyrics only; the calypsonian would sing it for the customer if he wanted.

30. Tiger, quoted in Carr 1972. Le Blanc was past his prime when viewed by the young Tiger.

31. E. Hill, quoting Joseph Belgrave's recollection of one of Forbes's songs, in E. Hill 1972:60.

32. Quevedo 1983:90–92.

33. Quevedo 1983:90. "Me minor" is the key of E minor.

34. See Quevedo 1983:91.

35. Ibid.

36. See Roaring Lion n.d.:184.

37. See Quevedo 1983:91.

38. Roaring Lion n.d.:184.

39. Quevedo 1983:91.

40. Ibid.

41. As recalled by Beginner in Carr 1972.

42. Quevedo 1983:20–21.

43. Quoted in Quevedo 1983:21. The word *kaiso* seems to have been borrowed from the Hausa word for "wow" or "right on!" It has probably always been used as an exclamation yelled out by those who enjoy a chantwell's performance. The phrase "Mait' Kaiso" probably dates from the eighteenth century. Use of the word *kaisonian*, on the other hand, is probably Quevedo's, not Forbes's; the latter probably used *chantwell* or *calypsonian*.

44. Quevedo 1983:22.

45. See Roaring Lion n.d.:184.

46. See Quevedo 1983:93; Roaring Lion n.d. :91; Beginner in Carr n.d.

47. See Quevedo 1983:93.

48. Executor, quoted in Brown 1947:53. The two lines in Patois repeat the two English lines above them.

49. Quevedo 1983:93. Atilla indirectly (and incorrectly) associates class with color here, implying that the lower class is dark skinned, e.g., Afro-Trinidadian.

50. See the Roaring Lion n.d.:91.

51. Quoted in Quevedo 1983:91–92.

52. Pretender, quoted in Carr n.d.

53. Beginner in Carr 1972.

54. As noted earlier, use of the term *kaisonian* probably represented a change made in Executor's lyrics by Atilla or John La Rose, Atilla's editor.

55. Executor's song, quoted in Quevedo 1983:21.

56. "How I Spent My Time at the Hospital," Decca 78-rpm record, De 17420, recorded in Trinidad on March 8, 1938.

57. Iere, in Carr 1972.

58. Gerald Clark, quoted in Nizer 1963:280.

59. Nizer called Gerald Clark as a supporting witness for Lionel Belasco, who claimed he wrote the melody for "Rum and Coca Cola" although it was copyrighted by others. See appendix 1.

60. Crowley n.d.

61. See Pretender, in Carr n.d.

62. Tape recording or 78-rpm record, in Crowley n.d.

63. See Quevedo 1983:96

64. The spellings are given here as they appear on the 78-rpm record labels and may differ from the standardized spellings used elsewhere.

65. E. Hill in Quevedo 1983:viii.

66. Roaring Lion n.d.

67. See E. Hill, in Quevedo 1983:viii.

68. See Roaring Lion n.d.

69. See Roaring Lion n.d.
70. Quevedo 1983:36ff.
71. See Roaring Lion n.d.
72. Tiger, quoted by the Government Broadcasting Unit 1985.
73. See the *St. Georges (Grenada) West Indian*, February 28, 1935.
74. See the *Port of Spain Gazette*, March 5, 1935, p. 11.
75. Quoted in Roaring Lion n.d.
76. Quevedo 1983:146.
77. Ibid., 137–38.
78. Tiger, quoted by the Government Broadcasting Unit 1985.
79. E. Hill, in Quevedo 1983:ix.
80. See Spottswood n.d.
81. Roaring Lion, paraphrased in Gorman 1945.
82. E. Hill, in Quevedo 1983:viii.
83. Quevedo 1983.
84. See Gorman in PM 1945.
85. See Quevedo 1983:104.
86. In Gorman 1945.
87. Ibid.
88. Pretender, in Carr 1972.
89. Gorman gives 1930 as the date, while Quevedo gives 1933 (1983:104).
90. Quevedo 1983:104.
91. Gorman 1945.
92. Quevedo 1983:105.
93. Ibid. No doubt Atilla refers here to calypsonian in the narrow sense: chantwells seem always to have sung for the rich and powerful, even in the days of Gros Jean and Begorrat.
94. Roaring Lion n.d.
95. Pretender, in Carr 1972.
96. Tiger, in Carr 1972.
97. Roaring Lion n.d.
98. In the early 1970s, Lion was still singing in tents in Trinidad. On a more recent trip to the United States, he visited New England, where he lectured to students on calypso. In 1991, he toured England. As of 1993, he continues to sing calypso.
99. Tiger, quoted in Shapiro 1979:2–3.
100. Quevedo 1983:107.
101. Ibid.
102. Tiger, quoted in Shapiro 1979:2–3.
103. Roaring Lion n.d.:104.
104. Tiger, quoted in Shapiro 1979:2–3.
105. Quevedo 1983:107.
106. This information and that in the following paragraphs (until the next reference) has been edited from several interviews with Tiger recorded by the Government Broadcasting Unit 1985.

107. The Shango religion of Trinidad has a Yoruba core of beliefs, which are held in common with many similar religions in the Americas (Shango in Grenada, Candomblé in Brazil, Lucumí and Santería in Cuba, and Santería in New York and throughout the Caribbean basin).

108. The Shouters are a religious group in Trinidad that combines West African religions with Christianity. Their meetings were made illegal by the colonial government in the 1930s. Some of their songs begin as typical Protestant hymns but soon developed into a West African style of call and response.

109. Whe whe is an illegal game of chance, roughly similar to numbers in the United States.

Chapter 7

1. I thank Jim Preston for this idea.

2. Stevens 1910:13–15.

3. Unless otherwise stated, all discographic information on calypsos recorded before 1942 comes from Spottswood's massive discography, n.d.

4. See Osofsky 1961?:130–31.

5. According to John Cowley (personal communication), Lovey's real name was George Bailey. Steve Shapiro lists a "George Baillie" as a member of Lovey's band (1986:3). According to Shapiro, the other members of the band were Egbert Butcher, P. Branch, L. Betancourt, Walter Edwards, Louis Schneider, Patrick Johnson, Cleto Chacha, Donald Black, H. Demile, F. A. Hart, and Eugene Bernier.

6. *Port of Spain Gazette*, August 28, 1914, p. 8.

7. Ibid., February 16, 1915, p. 3.

8. Ibid., February 3, 1915, p. 5.

9. Ibid., February 20, 1915, p. 5.

10. All together, Belasco recorded at least 278 sides under his own name between 1914 and about 1945.

11. Shapiro 1986:2.

12. See ibid., 6.

13. "Sly Mongoose" was not an original song from Trinidad but was sung in the calypso tents during the 1920s as a calypso.

14. Johnny Walker took his stage name from the whiskey.

15. My thanks go to Dick Spottswood for this information.

16. Cat the Beginner wrote many popular road marches in the 1920s. Possibly after his death or retirement from the calypso scene, Egbert Moore took the name "Young Beginner," later becoming known simply as "Beginner." It is the latter Beginner who made records.

17. Sam Manning, Brunswick 7028, recorded March 19, 1928, in New York; in Spottswood n.d.

18. I thank John Cowley for his "best guess" at Houdini's given name.

19. "Mr. Smart" is probably Lionel Belasco, Houdini's partner in many ventures. Indeed, Steve Shapiro thinks that Belasco first selected Houdini for the latter's first recording session (personal communication).

20. Roaring Lion n.d.

21. Shapiro 1986:26.
22. *Trinidad Guardian*, February 16, 1934, p. 2.
23. Quevedo 1983:50.
24. Ibid.
25. Ibid., 51–52. As Errol Hill points out, the language of Atilla's book probably reflects revisions by Atilla's collaborator, Mr. La Rose. (E. Hill 1972: vii).
26. Government Broadcasting Unit 1985
27. Tiger, interviewed by the Government Broadcasting Unit 1985.
28. Ibid.
29. Ibid., n.d.
30. The *Trinidad Guardian*, February 2, 1937.
31. Ibid., February 7, 1937.
32. Ibid., February 2, 1937.
33. Bowles 1940, quoted in Cowley 1985a:93.
34. Alberts 1950.
35. *Billboard*, December 16, 1939, pp. 9–10.
36. Herskovits and Herskovits 1947:350.
37. Ibid., 284.
38. Ibid., 284–85.
39. Waterman (1943:60) outlines some of his ideas concerning Afro-American music, ideas that remained influential for some twenty-five years. Concerning the recorded songs, he wrote:

> The forty-five songs which are presented in musical notation at the end of this study, and on which the analysis is based, are a sampling from the collection of over 325 melodies recorded in 1939 by M. J. Herskovits on the island of Trinidad. . . . The data were found to group themselves in ten categories, these divisions being based on the terminology of informants. The chief groups are the Baptist, Bele, Bongo and Shango. The latter group was found to consist of two general types, the larger group, recorded in Port of Spain by a functioning cult-group, which is accompanied by drums and gong, has been designated simply "Shango." The other Shango melodies that were recorded in the village of Toco, were all songs other than the Port of Spain Shangos were recorded, and were sung by a team which knew them merely from having visited Shango cult-rites. For this reason they are somewhat different in character; they are accompanied only by a box which is used as a drum.

Virtually all the native creole song genres that Waterman mentions have influenced calypso in one way or another, either by wholesale incorporation of the melody and lyrics into calypso or in calypsos composed about the genres that paraphrase passages from them.

40. This section, including table 7–1, is based on Spottswood n.d. It should be mentioned that Spottswood's discography excludes recordings made during this period for the French- and Spanish-speaking markets. Those recordings

deserve studies of their own, although there was a considerable amount of crossover between musicians and markets in the Caribbean music of the period.

Spottswood (1990) has compiled a massive discography of all known ethnic music recorded in the United States until 1942. That discography includes American recordings from the French- (and Creole-) speaking Caribbean (in volume 1) and from the Spanish-speaking Caribbean (volume 4). This work also includes the calypsos and other songs in this study that were recorded in the United States (volume 5).

41. Belasco's orchestra backed many singers. Those recordings are listed under the name of the calypsonian.

42. I base this hypothesis on indirect data from my own research on immigration from Carriacou, Grenada, during this period and project from those data (D. Hill 1977:218ff). For a detailed account of early West Indian immigration to the United States, see Kasinitz 1992: 19–26.

43. The price of thirty-five cents per record was introduced in 1934 by Jack Kapp of Decca. Other labels followed and lowered their prices from the usual pre-depression price of one dollar.

44. The discussion of the markets for calypso records from this point to the close of the chapter is highly subjective and is based on my experience as a collector of original 78-rpm records. Much like an archaeologist making a quick site survey, one gets impressions from buying a record collection that seems to be in the condition left by the original owner. Sometimes one can tell who that owner was. For example, white Americans who bought their records in the 1930s may have favored different sorts of calypsos from those bought by West Indian Americans during the same period. Certain calypso discs turn up over and over in the United States—"Roosevelt in Trinidad," for example—but not as much in Trinidad. From this type of evidence, one can infer information about the original owners.

45. Anonymous, in the *Amsterdam News*, October 16, 1929, p. 9.

46. The name of the newspaper is unknown. The ad was pasted into Gerald Clark's scrapbook, n.d.

47. Walter Winchell, the *New York Daily Mirror*, March 20, 1940.

48. The *New York Telegram*, December 30, 1939.

Chapter 8

1. See E. Hill 1972:40; Crowley 1956; Elder 1966a:109.

2. See E. Hill 1972:40–41.

3. Ibid., 40.

4. Crowley 1956:195–96.

5. Atilla, quoted in E. Hill 1972:41.

6. *Trinidad Guardian*, January 29, 1929.

7. Ibid., February 8, 1929.

8. See E. Hill 1972:69–73; see also Quevedo 1983:46–49.

9. See Quevedo 1983:46–48.

10. Several distinct types of cohabitation existed in Trinidad, although only

the formal Christian (European) system of marriage was legal. As with Roman

Catholic church law, divorce was not legal in Trinidad.

In addition to Christian marriage, there were other types of unions that were legitimate in the eyes of many people, if not in terms of colonial law, including Hindu marriage and Creole cohabitation. Many poor and even working-class Creole couples did not marry until after they had lived together for many years and had children. Before they married, the couple was "keeping." In another sexual liaison, called "friendin," the lovers did not live together. Children of such unions usually lived with their mother.

11. Quevedo 1983:47–48.

12. E. Hill 1972:80.

13. In a recent mid-1980s presentation, Lord Kitchener, singing a song about a pillow fight with his girl friend, is surprised toward the end of the song by another presumed lover or wife. With pillow in hand, she attacks him. Another skit, staged by David Rudder, opens with dimmed lights and a chorus singing "Laventille." Women are seen carrying water from a well. Rudder's song is about the roots of the steel band in the yards of Laventille.

This is not the place to discuss in depth formal drama on Carnival themes written by West Indian playwrights in the vernacular. One such play is Errol Hill's *Man Better Man,* about stick fighting (1964). That play has been performed in the United States, Trinidad, and England. Another more recent play is Earl Lovelace's *Justina Calypso,* which has been performed in Trinidad and which had its American debut at Smith College in 1987. That play concerns identity, concepts of beauty, and larger issues derived therefrom. Its theme is the lavway, "Tobo Justina who go marry to you; For your face like a whale and you jus' come from jail." These plays, in a sense, attempt the same sort of formalization of rich creole culture as Shakespeare's and Johnson's plays did for the vernacular of a creolized people in England some three hundred years ago.

14. Most of this information is from Lion's incisive account: De Leon 1985.

15. Ibid.

16. Gooter, quoted in de Leon 1985.

17. C. G. Errey, in the *Port of Spain Gazette*, February 9, 1918.

18. Lovey, in ibid., February 10, 1918.

19. Anonymous, in ibid., February 2, 1915, p. 2.

20. Anonymous, in ibid., February 9, 1921, p. 4.

21. This section is based on Hicks 1940:17–18. Hicks identifies the jilted man as the boyfriend of the unfaithful woman who left with another man. However, the jilted man was probably the woman's husband, and the other man was probably the inspector general of Trinidad, the head cop on the island.

22. Hicks does not identify this calypsonian, but it was probably Radio.

23. Hicks 1940:18.

24. Quevedo 1983:57–58.

25. Quevedo quoting remarks attributed to Cipriani, in ibid., 57.

26. Ibid.

27. Ibid., 60.

28. *Trinidad Guardian*, February 15, 1934.

29. Chapter 10 will take up the implications of this censorship.

30. Coon song refers to minstrel songs in the United States in the late 1890s and early 1900s. Some were based on southern, African-American melodies but many others were Tin Pan Alley tunes. The lyrics of these songs covered a broad range of topics: romance, supposed behaviors of blacks (coons), and rural themes.

31. De Leon 1985.

32. *Trinidad Guardian*, February 25, 1925.

33. Anonymous, in ibid., November 12, 1921, p. 3.

34. *Trinidad Guardian*, February 21, 1941.

35. See the *New York Sun*, August 24, 1927.

36. D. Hill 1975?

37. See Hill and Abramson 1979.

38. Anonymous, in the *Amsterdam News*, February 6, 1929.

39. Anonymous, in ibid., February 13, 1929.

40. See Nizer 1963:271.

41. This is the opinion of Dick Spottswood, who believes he hears Clark's distinctive guitar runs in several recordings of that era. I am not so sure.

42. Malcolm Johnson, *New York Sun*, April 5, 1940.

43. This article was in Gerald Clark's scrapbook (n.d.). The clipping did not include bibliographical particulars, but it is probably from the *Daily Worker*, the communist newspaper printed in New York, which reported on Clark's orchestra with some regularity.

44. Quoted in the *Trinidad Guardian*, February 24, 1957.

45. Walter Winchell, the *New York Daily Mirror*, April 17, 1940.

46. Although Clark used the name "Dame Lorraine," his Carnival show differed from its namesake. Clark's show consisted of entertainers, a presentation of masqueraders, and a dance. This "Dame Lorraine" dance lasted for many years. Years after Clark retired, it was taken over by Daphne Weekes, who continued until the early 1980s.

47. *Amsterdam and New York Star-News*, January 31, 1942.

48. *Amsterdam News*, May 3, 1947, p. 23.

49. Pretender in Carr 1972. Another version of Pretender's song was developed by the American singer Huddie Ledbetter. Wolfe and Lornell note that Pete Seeger thought that Sir Lancelot was responsible for the song (1992: 244–45).

50. I have not been able to find any other reference to the Cyclone Record Company. This may have been more hype than reality.

51. *Amsterdam News*, November 29, 1947, p. 21.

52. Also at this time, Beryl McBurnie formed a similar troupe in Trinidad that presented an artistic version of Trinidadian popular and folk dance, ritual, and song.

53. Most of the information in this section comes from sources uncovered by John Cowley or from his publications.

54. See Cowley 1986?:2.

55. Al Jennings, quoted in *Melody Maker,* December 7, 1946, p. 5.

56. Al Jennings, quoted in ibid.

57. Cowley 1985a:86ff.

58. Cowley 1985a:91.

59. Cowley 1985b:28–29.

60. Cowley 1985a:85.

61. *Melody Maker,* July 4, 1936.

62. The *Times of London,* June 10, 1938.

63. Cowley, personal communication.

64. Green and Rye 1985:146–48.

65. Cowley, personal communication.

66. Cowley 1986?:3.

67. Cowley and Noblett n.d.:5.

68. Cowley 1989:10–11.

Chapter 9

1. *Port of Spain Gazette,* February 23, 1909, p. 4. Thanks go to Steve Shapiro for some of the particulars about Belasco's personal life.

2. Black Patti was the stage name of Sissieretta Jones, an important African-American concert singer of the late 1800s and early 1900s. She took her name from Adelina Patti, the Spanish-born Italian soprano of the same era. Black Patti toured the southern Caribbean and South America in the late 1880s.

3. This and the other quotes from Belasco, unless otherwise noted, are edited from interviews with Leonard de Paur in the early 1960s.

4. *Port of Spain Gazette,* February 23, 1909, p. 4.

5. Walter Merrick, quoted in Nizer 1963:276–77.

6. Gerald Clark, quoted in ibid., 271–72.

7. The Orinoco ends in the Guiana Mountains. On the other side of the watershed, tributaries of the Amazon have their headwaters. It is not very likely that Belasco sailed that far.

8. Shapiro 1986 and the *Trinidad Guardian,* January 17, 1933, p. 1.

9. Belasco's claim that he put up theaters is probably overstated. He worked for the organization that financed the theaters and he oversaw their construction. Belasco also served as the first manager of many of the theaters.

10. This rumor was often repeated by Trinidadians of Belasco's generation.

11. Personal communication. In the mid-1970s, Bert Belasco was a retired New York City fireman and a betting clerk at the Belmont Race Track.

12. *Trinidad Guardian,* January 17, 1933, p. 1.

13. This section is based on two articles in the *Trinidad Guardian,* January 17, 1933, pp. 1ff. and pp. 7ff.

14. Ibid.

15. Patterson and Belasco 1943.

16. To date, no other evidence has turned up of Belasco's recordings in Canada, France, or Belgium.

17. Nizer 1963:265–328.

18. In the 1950s, Belasco continued to perform but rarely recorded. He was with Gracitia Faulkner when Leonard de Paur conducted a series of interviews in 1961. Their purpose was to publish a song folio, complete with musical transcriptions and brief notes on many of the songs. De Paur would bring the work together based on information Belasco and, to a lesser extent, Faulkner gave him.

In the latter part of his life Belasco seems to have lived on royalties received for the songs he had copyrighted and on income from infrequent tours. He did keep an active interest in the music industry, however. A Scandinavian living in New York in the 1970s who knew Belasco in his late years supported the opinion that few people seemed close to the singer. This man worked writing down scores from tape recordings given to him by Belasco; apparently Belasco did not want to take the time to do it himself.

In early 1967, Belasco completed work on the music for his last project, a play written by a lawyer friend, Joseph Taubman, entitled *The Rajah of the Islands*. The completed play has never been produced. Taubman, incidently, is an authority on copyright law as it pertains to the entertainment industry.

19. Steve Shapiro, personal communication.

20. See Mitchell 1939; Davis and Leiber 1941; *Time* 48:9 (1946):61; E. Hill 1968.

21. E. Hill 1968. John Cowley has reviewed various Christian names that have been associated with Houdini and settles on the one he gave to Hill (personal communication).

22. He told Errol Hill that his father was a marine engineer (1968) and Mitchell that he was a steward (1939).

23. Houdini, quoted in Mitchell 1939:65–66.

24. Roaring Lion n.d.

25. Mitchell 1939.

26. *Amsterdam News*, July 6, 1946, p. 19; July 13, 1946, p. 18.

27. *Amsterdam News*, August 3, 1946, p. 19.

28. Ibid., January 25, 1947, p. 21.

29. Ibid., March 29, 1947, p. 22.

30. Ibid., May 3, 1947, p. 23.

31. Ibid., October 15, 1947, p. 23.

32. Ibid., June 26, 1948, p. 25.

33. John Cowley, personal communication.

34. *Kingston* (Jamaica) *Gleaner*, May 1, 1929, p. 10.

35. Amy Ashwood Garvey is not to be confused with Garvey's other wife, Amy Jacques Garvey.

36. *Amsterdam News*, March 3 and August 17, 1927.

37. Ibid., February 15 and 22, 1928.

38. Ibid., February 20, 1929.

39. *Kingston* (Jamaica) *Gleaner*, May 1, 1929, p. 10.

40. Ibid.

41. Ibid., May 4 (first quote), May 13 (second quote), and May 21 (third quote), 1929.

42. George Tichenor, quoted in Cowley 1986?:8.

43. *Amsterdam News*, December 31, 1930.

44. Quevedo 1983:50.

45. Trinidad *Guardian*, March 7, 1935, p. 2.

46. Quevedo 1983:51.

47. "Guests of Rudy Vallee," written by Hubert Raphael Charles (label credit), Decca De 17389, recorded in Trinidad on March 10, 1938; see Spottswood n.d.

48. *Trinidad Guardian*, March 3, 1935, p. 1.

49. *New York Daily Mirror*, March 25, 1940.

50. *Amsterdam News*, December 6, 1941.

51. Transcription of May 27, 1947, recording broadcast September 5, 1947.

52. *Baltimore Afro American*, September 3, 1949.

53. Most of this information on Sir Lancelot has been researched by Ray Funk, who has assembled many documents and recorded test pressings loaned to him by Pinard.

54. Funk 1988.

55. Sir Lancelot, quoted by Snowden in Funk 1988.

56. Lion says that he gave Sir Lancelot his "Ugly Woman" to sing in the film (Roaring Lion n.d.).

57. Thanks go to Lancelot Pinard and Ray Funk for this copy of Lancelot's résumé.

Chapter 10

1. D. Hill 1977:314.

2. E. Hill 1972:33.

3. Brereton 1981:46.

4. Ibid., 48–49.

5. Quoted in Elder 1966a:96.

6. E. Hill 1972:67.

7. Elder 1966a:97.

8. Quevedo 1983:56–57.

9. Ibid., 58.

10. Anonymous policeman, quoted by Carr in Naar 1975. The quotation starting the next paragraph is also from Carr, in Naar 1975.

11. In Roaring Lion, n.d.

12. In Shapiro 1979.

13. In Chalkdust 1975 (part 4):13–14.

14. Ibid.

15. Quevedo 1983:59.

16. Lion, quoted in ibid.

17. "Sedition Law," recorded by Radio on De 17483 in Trinidad on February 4, 1940; see Spottswood n.d.

18. Spottswood 1987.

19. Brereton 1981:172.

20. Commission report, quoted in Brereton 1981:177–78.

21. Ibid., 196.

22. Ibid., 174.

23. Ibid., 180.

24. "The Strike," Decca De 17371, recorded in Trinidad on March 8, 1938; see Spottswood 1987.

25. Brereton 1981:181.

26. "Miss Marie's Advice," Decca De 17417, recorded in Trinidad on March 14, 1938; see Spottswood 1987.

27. "Where Was Butler?" sung by Atilla, Decca De 17385, recorded in Trinidad on March 12, 1938; see Spottswood 1987.

28. Brereton 1981:171.

29. Ibid., 182.

30. "Mr. Nankiwell's Speech," by Atilla, Decca De 17394, recorded in Trinidad on March 3, 1938; see Spottswood 1987.

31. Brereton 1981:183.

32. "The Governor's Resignation," recorded by Atilla, Decca De 17363, in Trinidad on March 4, 1938; see Spottswood 1987.

33. "Commission's Report," sung by Atilla, Decca De 17350, recorded in Trinidad on February 26, 1938; see Spottswood 1987. In the second line of the last verse Atilla sings "lines of dissertation" when he means "pages" of dissertation.

34. Quevedo 1983:59.

35. Brereton 1981:186.

36. Ibid., 173.

37. This work does not address the real cultural differences between this Creole complex and the East Indian–Trinidadian culture. I suspect that another synthesis will someday occur and combine these very different cultures. A truly national culture in Trinidad and Tobago would be created by such a synthesis.

38. Some scholars feel that the origin of stick fighting (calinda) is unclear (for example, Carr n.d. and Cowley, personal communication). The kind of stick fighting involved in calinda seems to me to have a mostly African origin.

39. "Meet Me Round the Corner," sung by Jules Sims "with bamboo drums," on Victor Vi 67033, recorded in Trinidad on September 11, 1914. "Mama Call the Fire Brigade," sung by Wilmoth Houdini with "bamboo group" on Bluebird B-10647, recorded in New York on January 31, 1940; see Spottswood n.d. and Spottswood 1987.

40. There are many sources for the development of the steel band; the most current is S. Stuempfle 1990.

41. Anonymous, quoted in E. Hill 1972:48.

42. Personal communication.

43. Stephen Stuempfle, personal communication. I thank Steve for his help with this section of the text.

44. E. Hill 1972:48.

45. Roaring Lion n.d.

46. Father Albert Clarke, Memorial Service for Winston "Spree" Simon, St. Matthew's Roman Catholic Church, Brooklyn, New York, May 30, 1976. I thank Jim Murray for his taped copy of the service.

47. *Port of Spain Gazette,* February 15, 1940, p. 7.

48. E. Hill 1972:49.

49. Burkhardt, *New York Times* 1942.

50. E. Hill 1972:49.

51. Burkhardt, *New York Times* 1942.

52. E. Hill 1972:49.

53. Quoted in ibid., 50.

54. Carr et al. :1962.

55. Trinidadian influence has been great in parts of Venezuela, especially in the Paria Peninsula just a few miles from Trinidad, in Maracaibo (where oil fields drew West Indian workers in the late 1930s), and in El Callao, a gold mining center.

West Indians have been in El Callao at least since 1870. They have influenced the local folklore, where a kind of archaic Carnival, not affected by Trinidad's censorship laws of the 1880s, developed. A wave of immigrants from the West Indies in the 1930s changed this Carnival. At that time, certain "Madamas" exerted a great influence over the organization of Carnival. After World War II, many residents left as the gold gave out. Since then, a modern Carnival has been established, one that included the steel band (see Leonel Farfan 1983). I thank Oswaldo Lares (personal communication) and Angelina Pollak-Eltz (personal communication) for bringing El Callao to my attention.

Chapter 11

1. This is Eric Williams's metaphor.

2. Gluckman 1978:131–33.

3. Ortiz 1947:145–63.

4. E. Hill 1972:16–22.

5. Stuempfle 1990:55 (crediting Anthony Prospect) has noted the continuity between Shango (Yoruba) rhythms in drums, the tamboo bamboo, and the steel band.

6. In Carr 1972.

Appendix 1

1. More work needs to be done on calypso in Patois and on the re-afrocreolization of the language of calypso from the early 1940s to the present.

2. An alternate transcription of this line is:

lamé plen, i pèd ti bato-li
[The sea is full (stormy), he has lost his boat]

3. According to Lise Winer, Atilla refers to an old song, "Mama Mourio," about a woman whose daughters go astray, in verse four.

Mama Mourio te tini de ti-fi
Telman yo te . . . yo to ka-janbe baye
Pandan Ma Mourio pa la
Se ti-fi la ka-janbe baye
[Ma Mourio had two daughters
They were so hot/precocious
That they climbed over the barrier/fence
While Ma Mourio was not here
These girls climbed the barrier]

4. According to Winer, the original, obscene lyrics for the last two lines of the chorus are:

And the hair on she *tun tun* (vulva) could tie a goat
The water from she cunny-hole could sink a boat

5. In Cowley, "L'Année Passée," n.d.

6. Daniel Crowley, personal communication.

7. *Ay-o* may be from the Creole *a Du* (à Dieu), meaning "farewell."

8. A motor-car bag is an old paper bag put on the floorboards of a car to protect the upholstery from one's feet. Such a bag gets very dirty; hence, a motor-car bag is a dirty bag used as clothing. I thank Lise Winer for this information.

9. *Port of Spain Gazette*, March 7, 1924, p. 5.

10. Osine is a Yoruba god who is sometimes taken as equivalent to the Christian Satan. "Osine no dey" is a Yoruba chant. The phrase, "Osine no dey" (Osine is not there) probably refers to an incident in which Osine did not possess anyone; i.e., "The spirit of Osine is not present."

11. This is a broom made from the stems of leaves of the coconut palm. It is used to sweep out the prayer house and to beat out evil spirits.

12. Holy water is used to rub the Shango drums.

13. Eshu, also known as *Lègba,* is another Yoruba god that sometimes is translated as the Christian devil. Eshu is the guardian of the crossroads and intercedes between the other gods and man. He is a trickster.

14. The line "Re re re re koko" is from a chant to Osine. This spirit lives in the forest and gathers herbs to be used in medicine. The line may refer to Osine, who is gathering leaves. Thanks go to Dr. Maureen Warner-Lewis for this interpretation.

15. This refers to the sacrifice of the goat. I have seen this done in a branch of Shango called "Norman Paul's Children" in Carriacou. The goat head is put in a boli (a calabash bowl) and held out. Then prayers are given to the relevant god.

16. I am indebted to the Tiger and to Steve Shapiro for their transcription and translation of this song. It is only through using their notes for the Rounder Record 5006, "Knockdown Calypsos by the Growling Tiger," that we are able to crack this wonderful calypso.

17. Lise Winer thinks that "djanay" is a Bhojpuri word. Bhojpuri is an East Indian language.

18. Rohlehr 1984:93–94.

19. Cowley, in Spottswood and Hill 1989.

20. Steve Shapiro, personal communication.

21. This refers to a large advertising sign for Anchor cigarettes that was at the top of Laventille, a district of greater Port of Spain (thanks to Keith Warner).

22. Harris n.d.:38–39.

✳ Glossary

THIS glossary contains significant terms that were used locally in Trinidad during the time of this study. There is no common spelling for many of the English Creole terms. For this reason I have put some of the more common alternate spellings in parentheses. The spelling used in the written text is in boldface.

There are many French Creole or Patois (*Patwa*) words in English Creole. I have put the Patois words in italics to emphasize the difference between that language and English Creole and standard English. As explained by Ronald Kephart (in a personal communication quoted below), the Haitian *Kreyòl* orthography has been used here for Patois words:

> The two principal varieties of Caribbean Creole French, Lesser Antillean [including Trinidad] and Haitian, are not identical in terms of their grammar. For example *ma vini* means "I shall come" in Haitian, but "I haven't come" in Lesser Antillean. However, they do share a basic phonological system, which allows them to be written with a single spelling system. Since Haitian has the most speakers, and also since 1979 has had an official orthography, it seems reasonable to

use the Haitian system for writing Lesser Antillean *Patwa* or *Kreyòl*.
The Haitian system is broadly phonemic and utilizes several French
spelling conventions. The symbols have approximately their most
common English values, except for the following:

a e i o ou	like Spanish a e i o u		
è	like e in set	*fèt*	party
ò	like au in caught (Br)	*zòt*	you all
an en on	nasalized vowels	*mwen*	I/me/my
àn èn òn	vowel followed by n	*kòn*	horn
ann enn onn	nasalized vowel plus n	*senn*	seine net
ch	like sh in sheep	*chak-chak*	maracas
j	like s in measure	*lajan*	money
tch	like ch in cheap	*tchè*	heart
dj	like j in jeep	*djab*	devil

Adja Dja: a Yoruba god; a song of the same name said by calypsonian
Atilla the Hun to be the first calypso

bacchanal (bachanal, bachannal, baccanal, bacchanale, *bakanal*): a wild
party or fete (q.v.); a massive and chaotic public celebration (such as
Carnival); chaos

badjohn: a tough character of the jamet (q.v.) class

Bajan (Bajun, Barbajan): a person from Barbados

bakra: a white person

barrack yard: a partly enclosed area created by adjacent sheds in which
jamet or working-class people lived; sometimes a house of a middle-
class family faced the street and headed two parallel barrack houses

basa basa: trouble

basodee (*bazodi*): crazy, light-headed

batonnier (*batonyè*): Trinidadian stick fighter; see **stick fight**

belair (*bele*): several distinct song forms, all of which were topical and
were popular in the nineteenth century; sometimes still sung today;
several distinct sorts of dances

Big Drum (Big Drum Dance, Nation Dance): an Afro-Caribbean ritual
dance once common in Grenada, Carriacou, and the Grenadines and
brought from those islands to Trinidad

blood hole: a hole into which blood is drained from a wounded stick
fighter

bobol (bobul, *bòbòl*): corruption; theft; smuggling (Carriacou)

body-lines: lingerie; hips

bois (*bwa*): wood, stick

bongo: a song form quite similar to the calinda (q.v.) that is sung at wakes; a dance; la vouez (q.v.)

booboo: an ugly person

bottle and spoon: a percussion instrument in which a spoon is struck against a bottle; the symbol of Carnival

boule de fé (bool de fé, *bouldife*): a torch, a flambeau (q.v.)

bound (*bong*): must

boundary: a very good hit in cricket

breakaway: a Carnival dance also known as a jump-up

bundle: traveling articles in a bag or pouch

bush: the forest; vegetation; a rural area

calaloo (*kyalalou, kalalou*): a soup made from dasheen (q.v.) leaves and okra seasoned with crab or pigtail; a confusion; a mixture

calinda (kalenda, kalendar, calenda, *kalinda*): a seventeenth-century Caribbean dance; stick fighting; the songs of the stick fighters

caliso: a topical song popular in Trinidad in the late nineteenth century and sung by women (one of several song forms which gave rise to twentieth-century calypso); an archaic spelling of *calypso*

call name, to: to gossip about someone

calypso (kalipso; archaic: *caliso, kaiso*): topical songs sung in English, Creole English, or French Patois for the Carnival season in Trinidad either during Carnival itself or for organized shows before Carnival; songs that are of Caribbean origin or mimic calypso songs of Caribbean origin

canboulay (canbulay, cannes brulees, *kannboule;* French: burning cane): an indoor Carnival masquerade on French estates in Trinidad before 1833; a Carnival celebration that began as a commemoration of the abolition of slavery by symbolically burning cane fields; feasting on the Sunday before Carnival, followed by stick fighting

Capitulation: the 1797 treaty by which Spain ceded Trinidad to Britain

carito (cariso): a late-nineteenth-century topical song in Trinidad

Carnival: Afro-Latin celebrations that take place in the week or so prior to the beginning of Lent, especially on the Monday and Tuesday before Lent

carré (*kare, kawe*): a blow struck in stick fighting (q.v.)

Carrera: the island-prison of Trinidad

castillian: a turn-of-the-century ballroom dance popular in the southern Caribbean and in the northern coast of South America

cedula: the first decree of population issued by Charles II of Spain granting Catholics from any nation the right to settle in Spanish colonies and receive land grants; (Cedula de Poblacion) the second decree of population issued by the Spanish in 1783, at the request of French Grenadian colonist Phillipe-Rose Rouse de Saint Laurent, calling for Catholic settlement in Trinidad regardless of nationality and resulting in more massive immigration than the original cedula

chac-chac (shack-shack, *chak-chak*): rattles, maracas

chantwell (chantuelles, chantrel, chantwel, chantwelle, chanter, *chantwèl*): a singer who leads a chorus and who fronts a Carnival masquerade band, a stick fighters' band, or some other Carnival band

cochon (*kochon*): hog

cocobay (*kokobe*): yaws or frambesia, a tropical disease marked by skin lesions

Congo (*Kongo*): in Trinidad, a person displaying physical and mental features thought to be inherited from the people of the Congo (Zaire); a stupid person

coolie (*kouli*): a derogatory name for an East Indian

coonoomoonoo (*kounoumounou*): a fool

copies: calypsos printed on single sheets of paper and sold by the composer in the streets for a penny, replaced after the mid-1940s with calypso songbooks cheaply printed by a singer, a merchant, or a printer

corbeau (*kòbo*): a scavenging bird, *Crotophaga ani*, that is black with a long tail and a parrot-like bill

cork hat: an overseer's hat

craft (craf '): a young woman

crapaud (*krapo, kwapo*): in Trinidad, a large brown toad (*Buffo mannus*); in the islands near Trinidad, an edible mountain frog

Creole (*Kreyòl*): a person born in the West Indies of African and/or European descent; people who have Creole culture; a variant of English that contains many West African and other Indo-European words and grammatical features; English Creole is the informal language of Trinidad, although many Trinidadians also speak standard English. English Creole is to be distinguished from Patois, an Afro-French language that exhibits more independence from French than English Creole does from English. Trinidadian Patois is closely related to Haitian Creole (*Kreyòl*).

cuatro (quatro): in Trinidad and Carriacou, a four-string instrument similar to a ukulele; several different string instruments in Venezuela, Curaçao, Cuba, and Puerto Rico

cuff: a blow, a hit with the hand

cutlass: a machete or long knife used to cut sugarcane or as a general garden tool

Dame Lorraine: a pre-Carnival show popular in Trinidad in the late

1800s and early 1900s that included many double entendres and parodied Trinidadian society; a madame for whom the Dame Lorraine show was named (according to Lionel Belasco)

dasheen (*dachin*): taro *Colocsia esculenta*, a domesticated plant with an edible root and broad leaves

dentist: a stick fighter's blow that could result in a tooth extraction; (the Dentist) Myler's stick fighting name

dingolay, to (tingalay, *dingole*): to have sexual intercourse; to engage in some obscure sexual act

Dimanche Gras (*Dimanch Gras*): Carnival Sunday (Trinidad); Carnival (Haiti, the French Caribbean)

djab djab (job job, jab jab, Djab'la): the devil, a Carnival masquerade

djablès (jobless, lajobless, ladiablesse, *ladjablès*; French: la djablesse, female devil): a female supernatural being who tricks men at night into some unknown but bad fate

do minor: the key of C minor

doodoo (*doudou*; French Creole: sweet, sweet): darling, dear

double tone: a calypso with eight lines of verse

drop, to: to give a free ride to someone in a car, taxi, or bus

fan, to: to have sexual intercourse

fancy masquerade: a Carnival masquerade band involving many people dressed in elaborate costumes based on a nontraditional theme

fancy Carnival: Carnival in which fancy masquerades (q.v.) dominate; such mas' bands (q.v.) became popular from about 1895

fast (fas', *fas*): rude, forward

fatigue, to give (*fatig*): to insult

fete (*fèt*): a party, feast, or pleasant social event

flambeau (*flanbo*): a torch (q.v.) or light made with a bottle filled with kerosene and topped with a wick

giel: the ring in which stick fighting or cock fighting takes place

gonday (gondai): a falsetto exclamation shouted when one gets excited during stick fighting, possibly from the Patois, *bondjen*, "good God"

half tone: carnival songs two lines long with the first line sung by the lead singer and the second line sung as a chorus; many calindas, road marches, bongos, and other litanous songs that are half tone in form

head: penis; see **scratch (a man's) head**

iere: a tropical bird; a symbol of Trinidad

jacket man: middle-class stick fighter; a stick fighter who wore a jacket in the manner of an overseer or a person from the middle class

jamet (*djamèt*): a member of Trinidad's lowest (urban) class; a prostitute or loud-voiced, scandalous woman

jouvay (juvay, *djouve*): Carnival Monday morning; daybreak

juba (ghouba, jouba, *djouba*): an Afro-American dance common in the plantation areas of the New World and dating from the seventeenth century; today in Trinidad, also associated with a dance

jumbie (*djòmbi*): a ghost

jump, to: to join

jump-up: see **breakaway**

kaiso (kayso, caiso, *kayso*): a term possibly derived from the Hausa word for *bravo*; an exclamation shouted while a calypso is being sung; (after about 1971) soulful, natural, or original calypso, calypso that discovers some truth about the Afro-American experience or culture

koomana (kumana, *koumana;* possibly from the French Creole: genitals): sex or love, or, more narrowly, genitals

laja (*lajan*): money

lajobless: see *djablès*

la minor: the key of A minor

lament: in Trinidad, a sad song, especially an African-style song

Land of the Hummingbird: Trinidad

lavway (lauway, la vouez, *lavwe*): a Carnival song for street marching, a road march (q.v.); may also refer to a type of work song or to a bongo (q.v.)

lawa (*lawa, lewa*): king

leggo, to (leggoe, *lègo*): to exhibit reckless abandon; let go, let's go; a road march (lavway), a song for outdoor Carnival; also, in rural Trinidad and Carriacou, the dry season when animals are turned loose

light: a form of magic in which one lights a candle

lignum vitae: *Guaiacum officinale*, a hardwood tree with many uses, some of which are medicinal; penis

limbo: a Trinidadian custom in which dancers move under a stick held by two people or a stand; the dancer goes under the stick as it is lowered until they can no longer continue; originally danced at wakes as a part of the bongo

lime, to: to stand around, to hang out, to stand on a street corner

loogarou (loupgarou, *lougarou*): a witch who has changed from a human into a half-dog or half-donkey (below the waist), with fire coming from its eyes as it flies about menacing people

macafouchet (macafouchette, maquefouchet, *makafouchèt;* Patois: what the fork leaves): leftovers

macomé (*makòmè*): the mother of one's child, e.g., a lover or former lover; a friend; a co-godparent (archaic in Trinidad but in current use in Carriacou)

mait kaiso (maitre kaiso, *mèt kayso*): a master of calypso

make one's name, to: to be successful in sexual exploits; to become locally famous

malkadie (malkidee, *malkadi;* from the French: mal caduc): epilepsy, fits

mamaguy, to (mamaguille, *mamagay*): to mislead by flattery

manima (*manimwa*): doings, carryings-on, one's activities or moves

maribone: wasp; used as the name for a calinda band in the nineteenth century

mas' band: Carnival masquerade band

mash, to: to break, to step on, to hit

mauvais langue (*move lang;* Patois: bad language): one who speaks ill of others

me minor (mi minor): the key of E minor

mento: a topical song from Jamaica

mepuis (*mepwi*): an insulting lyric in a calypso war

mookee (mook, mooke, mookie, *mouki*): a fool

mooma (*mouma*): mother

mount, to: to apply a supernatural quality to an object; to be possessed

name: for a minority of West Indians, particularly those from more isolated areas, the name has almost supernatural significance; some old people of Carriacou, for example, do not refer to others or to themselves directly by Christian names lest use of the name could cause one harm; thus, for some, the name is the essence of a person

name, to call: to gossip about someone; see also **make one's name**

Nation Dance: see **Big Drum**

neg jardin (*nèg jaden*): field slave; a Carnival character who presumably wears the outfit of the field slave

neg (negre, *nèg;* Patois: nigger): a slave, a dark-skinned person; usually considered pejorative, but its usage is complex and it can be an affectionate term; black

negromancy: necromancy

obeah (*obiya*): magic

old mas (ol' mas): casual and inexpensive masquerading on Carnival Monday morning, often in the form of a white t-shirt marked with some cryptic, often lewd, message

old talk: gossip

pan: a percussion instrument made from a 55 gallon oil drum; called a steel drum in the United States

panama: a straw hat

parlor (*pala*): a small shop

party (*pati*): an ethnic group in nineteenth-century Trinidad that more or less hung together as a political faction, as in the English party or the French party

paseo (*pase-u*; Spanish: pasillo): a ballroom dance, possibly of Venezuelan origin, that was popular in Trinidad in the first half of the twentieth century; (especially on phonograph records) an instrumental dance or a calypso

Patois (*Patwa*): in this book, the French Creole language widely spoken in Trinidad in the nineteenth century but rarely spoken today, related to but distinct from French. The Trinidadian variant is basically the same language as St. Lucia Patois and Haitian Creole. Trinidadian Patois is the language of the first generation of calypsos, called *kaiso* (*kayso*) in Patois. Trinidadian Patois is not to be confused with English Creole, which is used to mean the local variant of English.

paylou: a stew of chicken and rice

picong (*pikan;* Patois: thorn): an insult, a calypso of insult

pierrot (*pyewo*): a Carnival character who sometimes shouted speeches, carried whips, or fought with sticks

pissenlit (*pisan-nwi;* Patois: bed wetter): a Dame Lorraine (q.v.) Carnival masquerade

plantain: a fruit like a large banana

play mas, to: to participate in Carnival masquerading

poui (*pwi*): hardwood stick

practice: turn-of-the-century Carnival tent performances, in the masquerade camps, when chantwells and masqueraders prepared their songs for Carnival

pretender: someone who is learning a skill, such as singing calypso, and who feels that he can dislodge the champion

quatro: see **cuatro**

re: the key of D

Red House: the main governmental building in Port of Spain, burned in the riots of 1903 and rebuilt; attacked again in the coup attempt of 1990

rehearsal: see **practice**

resign, to: to retire

road march: Creole English term for lavway (q.v.) that came into widespread use after about 1945

rod of correction: a sword; a phallus

roti: a fast food of East Indian origin consisting of curried potato and chicken or meat wrapped with soft, flat bread

sagaboy: fancy-dressed lower-class male in the style of the American zoot-suiter of the 1940s

sandies: a plant used as medicine

sandimanité (sans humanity, *sandimanite;* Patois: "without pity"): a tag closing a verse in many oratorical calypsos

santapee (*santapi*): centipede

Savannah: the open park in Port of Spain where sporting matches, Carnival competitions, races, and so forth take place; (savannah) any open square, park, or field in a village, town, or city in the Caribbean

science man: magician

scratch (a man's) head, to: to have sexual intercourse

Shango: a Yoruban (q.v.) religion found in Trinidad, Grenada, and elsewhere in the Caribbean; (shango) the songs of this religion; (Shango) the Yoruba god of thunder

shanto: a Guyanese song genre popularized by Bill Rogers

shouter: a member of the Spiritual Baptist church of Afro-Christian origin; noted for the manner in which they sing and undergo possession. While calypsonians use the word *Shouter* to refer to the group, members of the church prefer to be called Spiritual Baptists.

single tone: calypsos with four lines of verse or with one tune

sly mongoose: a wayward girl who becomes a prostitute; a crafty person

small island: in Trinidad, a derogatory name given to migrants from neighboring islands

social union (s.u.): a term for Carnival masquerade bands popular between about the 1890s and the close of World War I

sol: the key of F

soucoyan (*soukouyan*): a female vampire

steel drum: see **pan**

steel band: an orchestra made of pans (q.v.) tuned to different pitches

stick fight: a contest or game played with two or more sides in which two or more men fight against each other in a ring sided by drummers, singers, and onlookers; the purpose of the game is to draw blood from the opponent by hitting him on the head or upper body

sweetman: a man to whom women are attracted; a pimp

syndicate: a loose association of a Carnival band and a calypso tent

talkaree (talkary, talcarrie): a highly seasoned West Indian dish of East Indian origin

tamboo bamboo (*tanbou-banbou*): a small orchestra made up of bamboo tubes that are hit with sticks and struck against the ground to give different notes

taylaylay, to: to carry on; to have sex

tea: a drink made with herbs, leaves, or other bush (q.v.); a thin soup

tent: the place where calypso shows and other indoor Carnival activities are held; a yard covered with a tarpaulin or bamboo fronds or a hall or a theater

tie down, to: to influence through use of magic

tootoolbay: crazy, as in crazy in love

torch (torchlight): flashlight

tut mun (*tout moun;* Patois: all the world): everyone

valse: waltz

vaudeville: American-style variety shows adapted in the Caribbean and in New York by West Indians; popular in Trinidad between about 1910 and 1942

vera (veré, verre, bira, bira, quita): a musical instrument consisting of a metal cylinder with a rough surface across which a metal rod is scraped

Voodoo (*Vodoun*): the folk religion of Haiti that combines West African and Christian customs and beliefs; in Trinidad and outside Haiti, belief in supernatural intervention in one's everyday life

la vouez: see **lavway**

wabeen (*wabin*): a prostitute; a promiscuous woman; a girl

wanga: magic, obeah (q.v.)

war: a singing duel of insults between two or more calypsonians

washicongs: sneakers, rubber-soled canvas shoes

water: urine; vagina

weed: folk pharmacopoeia; bush; (Jamaica) marijuana

weed woman: a vendor of plants used for traditional curing

whe whe (whey whey, *we we*): a game of chance

winin: a carnival dance that mimics sexual intercourse

yard: a living space bounded by a house and outbuildings; a court between rows of barrack ranges (q.v.); normally the domain for women doing their daily chores, sometimes covered with a tarpaulin or sail when fetes, stick fights, and Carnival practices (q.v.) took place

Yoruba (Yaraba, Yarriba): in Trinidad, a group of people who trace descent to southwestern Nigeria; some Yorubas were brought to Trinidad as slaves, others came as indentured workers after emancipation, likely introducing the Yoruban Shango religion (q.v.) or, at the very least, modifying Yoruba religion in Trinidad as it may have existed before 1838

zandoli: lizard

zombie: (Haiti: *zonbi*) a sentient dead body in league with the devil; Grenada: from the Patois *zami* (*zanmi*): friend, a lesbian

Zulu: in Trinidad, a person identified as having certain supposed African qualities

✳ Bibliography

Unpublished Sources

Beginner, Lord
   1972   On stickfighting. Pulsebeat. 610 Radio rebroadcast of interview with
        Bertie Moore. Port of Spain, Trinidad. Tape recording in possession of
        the author.
Carr, Andrew
   1972   *The History of Calypso: Conversations with Great Calypsonians of the
        Past. Transcribed by Donald R. Hill.* Port of Spain, Trinidad: Govern-
        ment Broadcasting Unit (GBU).
Clark, Gerald, ed.
   n.d.   Scrapbook of articles and flyers on the life of Gerald Clark. Original
        held by Sylvia Lynch.
Colcord, Joanna C.
   1940   Selected records of Trinidad calypsos presented to the Archives of
        American Folksong. Second of five items on Music Division microfilm
        no. mx1410441. Washington, D.C.: Library of Congress.
Crowley, Daniel J.
   n.d.   "The Daniel Crowley collection of recordings from Trinidad and
        Tobago." Indiana University Archives of Traditional Music, Blooming-
        ton, Indiana.

n.d.   "L'Année Pasée: Repertoire, Recordings, and Personalities in English-Speaking West Indian Music, 1900–1960." Unpublished manuscript.

Cowley and Richard Noblett

n.d.   "West Indian Recordings in Britain: An Exploratory Discography." Unpublished manuscript.

De Leon, Raphael (the Roaring Lion)

1985   "The Lion Roars." Unpublished manuscript based on a column published in the *Trinidad Evening News* in 1981 and 1982 and edited by Donald R. Hill.

de Paur, Leonard

1961   Interviews with Lionel Belasco and Gracitia Faulkner recorded on tape. (Half of the originals are with Bert Belasco, and the other half are with Leonard de Paur, New York.)

Funk, Ray

n.d.   Sir Lancelot rare sides and acetates. One cassette tape.

n.d.   Sir Lancelot (Lancelot Pinard) preliminary discography and filmography.

Government Broadcasting Unit (Trinidad)

1985   Interview with the Growling Tiger. Port of Spain, Trinidad and Tobago. Radio program.

Herskovits, Melville J.

1939   "Notes to music of Port of Spain and Toco Trinidad." One hundred one 12–inch discs on deposit in the Indiana University Archives of Traditional Music, with copies in the Archives of Folksong, Library of Congress.

Hill, Donald R.

1975?   Interview with Rufus Gorin. Brooklyn, New York.

Kitchener, Lord (Alwyn Roberts)

n.d.   "Nora" (song copy)

Naar, Lillian

1975   Interview with Andrew Carr. Port of Spain, Trinidad.

Spottswood, Richard K.

n.d.   "Discography of West Indian Records, 1912–1945." Unpublished manuscript.

Newspapers and Magazines

Amsterdam and New York Star-News

Amsterdam News

Baltimore Afro American

Billboard

Canada West Indies Magazine

Caribbean Tempo

Chicago Defender

Cleveland Call and Post

Coronet

Down Beat

Ebony

Edison Phonograph Monthly

Esquire

Everybody's Magazine

Holiday

Hue

Hummingbird
Jazz Illustrated
Kingston (Jamaica) Gleaner
Life
Los Angeles Daily News
Los Angeles Examiner
Los Angeles Herald and Express
Los Angeles Times
Melody Maker
Modern Music
Monthly Caribbean Magazine
New York Daily Mirror
New York Daily News
New York Enquirer
New York Herald Tribune
New York Journal
New York Journal and American
New York Post
New York Sun
New York Sunday Mirror
New York Sunday News Magazine
New York Times

New York Times Magazine
New York World Telegram
New Yorker
News Story
Newsweek
Patterson (N.J.) Call
Pittsburgh Courier
P.M.'s Weekly Magazine
Port of Spain Gazette
Record Research
St. Georges (Grenada) West Indian
Time
Time and Tide
Times (London)
Trinidad Evening News
Trinidad Express
Trinidad Guardian
Trinidad Mirror
Trinidad Royal Gazette
Trinidad Sunday Guardian
Vancouver Sun
Variety

Books, Articles, and Dissertations

Abrahams, Roger D.
   1967   "The Shaping of Folklore Traditions in the British West Indies."
          Journal of Inter-American Studies 9 (July).
Akutagawa, Ryunosuke
   1952   "In a Grove." In *Rashamon and Other Stories,* ed. Ryunosuke Akut-
          agawa. New York: Liveright Publishing Corporation.
Alberts, Arthur S.
   1950   *Tribal, Folk and Cafe Music of West Africa.* Booklet and 78-rpm discs
          recorded and edited by S. Albert. New York: Field Recordings.
Alig, Wallace B.
   1949   "Calypso Joe of Trinidad." *Holiday Magazine* (July).
Anonymous
   1970   "A History of Trinidad Calypsoes: From 1908." In *Trinidad Calypso
          Songbook 1970* (possibly written by Raymond Quevado). Trinidad:
          no publication particulars.
Atilla the Hun (see Raymond Quevedo)
Belasco, Lionel
   1939   "Sly Mongoose." Sheet music. New York: Clarence Williams Music
          Publishing Co.
Belasco, Lionel, and Leighla Whipper
   1944   *Calypso Rhythm Songs: Authentic Tropical Novelty Melodies Com-*

plete with Words and Music by Lionel Belasco and Leighla Whipper. New York: Mills Music, Inc.

Bodu, J. M.
  1890 *Trinidadiana*. Port of Spain.

Brereton, Bridget
  1981 *A History of Modern Trinidad, 1783–1962*. London: Heinemann.

Brierley, J. N.
  1912 "Carnival, Familiarly Known as 'Masquerade.' " In *Trinidad Then and Now*. Port of Spain: Franklin's Electronic Printery.

Brown, Wenzell
  1947 "How Calypso Was Born." *Negro Digest* 5 (June):53. Originally a chapter in Wenzell Brown, *Angry Men, Laughing Men*. New York: Greenberg, 1947.

Burchhardt, Rudolph
  1942 "Calypso and Carnival." Article in unknown newspaper, possibly the *New York Times*.

Carmichael, Gertrude
  1961 *The History of the West Indian Islands of Trinidad and Tobago, 1498–1900*. London: Alvin Redman.

Carr, Andrew
  1955 "A Rada Community in Trinidad." *Caribbean Quarterly* 3:36–56.
  1975 "The Calypso: A People's Poetic Platform." *West Indian World* no. 215 (August 29–September 4):12–13.
  n.d. *Trinidad Calypso Is Unique Folk Culture*. Trinidad.

Carr, Andrew, et al.
  1962 *Independence Exhibition: History of Carnival, Calypso and Steelband*. Port of Spain: Trinidad Government Printery.

Chalkdust, Mighty (Hollis Liverpool)
  1975 "History of Calypso with the Mighty Chalkdust (Hollis Liverpool)." Parts 1–4. *Scope* (January 6, 13, and 24 and February 3).

Charles, Hubert (the Lion), and Atilla the Hun
  1943 *Victory Calypsoes 1943 Souvenir Collection*. Trinidad: Caribbee Printerie.

Christopher, Milbourne
  1949 "King of Calypso." *Negro Digest*. Condensed from the *Baltimore Sun*. 7 (January):11–14.

Cook, Emory
  1956 *Calypso Lore and Legend: An Afternoon with Patrick Jones*. Transcription of one 33-1/3-rpm disc. Cook Laboratories. Road Recordings LP 5016.

Cowley, John
  1984 *Wilmoth Houdini*. Notes for one 33-1/3-rpm disc. Folklyric 9040. El Cerrito, Calif.: Arhoolie Records.
  1985a "Cultural 'Fusions': Aspects of British West Indian Music in the USA

and Britain, 1918–1951." *Popular Music.* 5. Cambridge: Cambridge University Press.

1985b "West Indian Records in Britain." *Musical Traditions.* 4:28–30.

1986? " 'Caribbean Carnival': British West Indian Migration to New York and London, the Trinidadian 'Entertainers' View, 1912–47." In *Afro-American Culture, European Perspectives,* ed. R. B. Stepto and J. J. Barnie. Westport, Conn.: Greenwood Press.

1989 "London Is the Place: British Caribbean Music and the British Empire, 1900–1960." In *Black Music in Britain,* ed. Paul Oliver. New York: Open University Press, 10–11.

Crowley, Daniel J.

1956 "The Traditional Masques of Carnival." *Caribbean Quarterly* 4:194–223.

Davis, Hal, and Les Lieber

1941 *Houdini.* Notes for 78-rpm disc record album. Decca album no. 198, 18m series.

de Verteuil, Fr. Anthony

1984 *The Years of Revolt, Trinidad 1881–1888.* Port of Spain.

Elder, Jacob D.

1964 "Color, Music and Conflict: A Study of Aggression in Trinidad with Reference to the Role of Traditional Music." *Ethnomusicology* 8:128–36.

1966a *Evolution of the Traditional Calypso of Trinidad and Tobago: A Socio-Historical Analysis of Song-Change.* Ph.D. diss., University of Pennsylvania. Ann Arbor, Mich.: University Microfilms.

1966b "Songs of the Battling Troubadours of Trinidad and Tobago." *Indiana University Folklore Institute* 3:192–203.

Espinet, Charles, and Peter Pitts

1944 *Land of Calypso: The Origin and Development of Trinidad's Folk Song.* Port of Spain: Trinidad Guardian Commercial Printing.

Farfan, Leonel

1983 "Guyana es . . . Calypso, Convenezuela Vol. 2." Notes to one 33-1/3-rpm disc, TCH Top Hits, Caracas, Venezuela, January.

Funk, Ray

1988 *Sir Lancelot.* Notes for one 33-1/3-rpm disc. Heritage HT321. Crawley, West Sussex, England: Interstate Music Ltd.

Gluckman, Max

1978 *Politics, Law and Ritual in Tribal Society.* New York: New American Library, 131–33.

Gorman, Patricia

1945 "The Lion of Calypso." *P.M.'s Weekly Magazine,* September 16, pp. 5–6.

Green, Jeffrey P., and Howard Rye

1985 "Joe Appleton & Wington Thompson . . . and Eubie Blake, Leon Abbey, George Clapham, Joe Smith, Rex Stewart, and . . ." *Storyville* (October–November).

Hamilton, R. G. C.

1881   "The Causes and Disturbances in Connexion with the Carnival in Trinidad: Despatch to Secretary of State for the Colonies." London, June 13. (Great Britain Public Record Office.)

Harris, Tesfa

n.d.   *The Politics of Caribbean Music.* Toronto: Afro-Carib Publishing Company (?).

Herskovits, Melville, and Frances S. Herskovits

1947   *Trinidad Village.* New York: A. A. Knopf.

Hicks, Albert C.

1940   "Calypso, Songs and Minstrels of Trinidad." *Travel* 76 (December): 16–19, 47, 48.

Hill, Donald R.

1977   *The Impact of Migration on the Metropolitan and Folk Society of Carriacou, Grenada.* Anthropological Papers of the American Museum of Natural History, vol. 54, part 2. New York.

1980   "My Tongue is Like the Blast of a Gun: Politics of Carnival and the Calypso." Abstract in *Latin America Today: Heritage of Conquest,* ed. Hazen, Holloway and Jones. Cornell University Latin Americanist Association Conference Papers, 88–90.

Hill, Donald R., and Robert Abramson

1979   "West Indian Carnival in Brooklyn." *Natural History* 88 (August–September).

Hill, Errol

1964   "Man Better Man." In *The Yale School of Drama Presents,* ed. John Gassner. New York: Dutton.

1967   "On the Origin of the Term Calypso." *Ethnomusicology* 11 (September), 359–67.

1968   "The Gypsy Calypso King Wants to Return." Trinidad Sunday Guardian, February 11, pp. 12–13.

1972   *The Trinidad Carnival: Mandate for a National Theatre.* Austin: University of Texas Press.

Historical Society of Trinidad and Tobago

1932   *Occasional Papers.* Publication nos. 1–. Port of Spain. 1932 to the present.

Houdini, Wilmoth

1946   "Stone Cold Dead in the Market." Sheet music. New York: Northern Music Corp.

Huxley, Aldous

1934   *Beyond the Mexique Bay.* London: Chatto & Windus, 13–22.

Jones, Charles (the Duke of Albany)

1947   *Calypso and Carnival of Long Ago and Today.* Port of Spain: Gazette Printer.

Kasinitz, Philip
  1992 *Caribbean New York: Black Immigrants and the Politics of Race.*
        Ithaca & London: Cornell University Press.
Kingsley, Charles
  1889 *At Last a Christmas in the West Indies.* New York: MacMillan and
        Co.
Krehbiel, Henry E.
  1914 *Afro-American Folksongs.* New York: G. Schirmer.
Labat, Jean Baptiste
  1724 *Nouveau Voyage aux Isles de l'Amerique.* 6 vols. A la Haye: P. Husson
        et al.
Lovelace, Earl
  1987 *Justina Calypso* (play performed at Smith College, Northampton,
        Mass., May 27).
Mendes, Alfred M.
  1944 "If Calypso Is Folksong It Should Be Encouraged." *Trinidad Guardian,*
        February 13.
Mitchell, Joseph
  1939 "Houdini's Picnic." *New Yorker* (May 6):61–71.
Nizer, Louis
  1963 "Talent: The Case of the Plagiarized Song 'Rum and Coca-Cola.' " In
        My Life in Court, 265–328. New York: Pyramid Books.
Ortiz, Fernando
  1947 *Cuban Counterpoint: Tobacco and Sugar.* New York: Knopf. Excerpt
        in Michael M. Horowitz, *Peoples and Cultures of the Caribbean.* New
        York: Natural History Press, 1971.
Osofsky, Gilbert
  1961? *The Making of a Ghetto: Negro New York, 1890–1930.* New York:
        Harper & Row.
Patterson, Massie, and Lionel Belasco
  1943 *Calypso Songs of the West Indies.* New York: M. Baron Company.
Pearse, Andrew C.
  1956a "Carnival in Nineteenth-Century Trinidad." *Caribbean Quarterly.*
        4:175–93.
  1956b "Mitto Sampson on Calypso Legends of the Nineteenth Century."
        Caribbean Quarterly. 4.
Procope, Bruce
  1956 "The Dragon Band or Devil Band." *Caribbean Quarterly.* 4:275–
        80.
Quevedo, Raymond (Atilla the Hun)
  1983 *Atilla's Kaiso: A Short History of Trinidad Calypso* (forward by Errol
        Hill). St. Augustine, Trinidad: Extra Mural Studies, University of the
        West Indies.

Roaring Lion (Raphael De Leon)

n.d.   *Calypso from France to Trinidad, 800 Years of History*. General Printing of San Juan, Trinidad and Tobago.

Rohlehr, Gordon

1984   "An Introduction to the History of the Calypso." Seminar held at the University of the West Indies, St. Augustine, Trinidad, Nov. 24–26, 1983. Published in *Seminar Papers with Recommendations*. St. Augustine, Trinidad: Institute of Social and Economic Research, University of the West Indies.

Rutter, Owen

1933   *If Crab No Walk: A Traveller in the West Indies* London: Hutchinson.

1936   *A Traveller in the West Indies*. 2nd *rev. ed.* London: Hutchinson.

Shapiro, Steve

1979   *Knockdown Calypsos by the Growling Tiger*. Liner notes for one 33 1/3 rpm disc. Rounder record 5006.

1986   "Calypso and Recording from 1912 to the mid-1930s." Paper presented to the Seminar on the Calypso, January 6–10, St. Augustine, Trinidad: University of the West Indies.

Spottswood, Richard K.

1985   *Jazz and Hot Dance in Trinidad, 1912–1939*. Vol. 7. Notes for one 33 1/3 rpm disc. Harlequin HQ 2016.

1987   *Where Was Butler?* Notes for one 33 1/3 rpm disc. Folklyric 9048. El Ceritto, Calif. Arhoolie Records.

1990   *Ethnic Music on Records: A Discography of Ethnic Recordings Produced in the United States, 1893 to 1942*. 7 vols. Urbana Chicago: University of Illinois Press.

Spottswood, Richard K., and Donald R. Hill

1989   *Calypso Pioneers*. Notes for one 33 1/3 rpm disc (or CD) recording. Cambridge, Mass.: Rounder 1039.

Stevens, Walter

1910   "A Trip to South America with Walter Stevens." *Edison Phonograph Monthly* (May).

Stuempfle, Stephen

1990   "The Steel Band Movement in Trinidad and Tobago: Music, Politics, and National Identity in a New World Society." Ph.D. diss., University of Pennsylvania.

Warner, Keith Q.

1982   *Kaiso! The Trinidad Calypso: A Study of the Calypso as Oral Literature*. Washington, D.C.: Three Continents Press.

Warner-Lewis, Maureen

1986   "The Influence of Yoruba Music on the Minor Key Calypso." Paper presented to the seminar on the calypso, January 6–10, St. Augustine, Trinidad: University of the West Indies.

Waterman, Richard A.
  1943   *African Patterns in Trinidad Negro Music.* Ph.D. diss., Northwestern
         University.
Williams, Eric
  1962   *History of the People of Trinidad and Tobago.* Port of Spain: P.N.M.
         Publishing Co.
Wolfe, Charles, and Kip Lornell
  1992   The Life and Legend of Leadbelly. New York: HarperCollins.
Wood, Donald
  1968   *Trinidad in Transition: The Years after Slavery.* London: Oxford
         University Press.

✳ Index

gade Union, Crescent, Iere Bells, Khaki and Slate, No Surrender, Railroad Millionaires, Red Dragon, Royal Britannia, Scottish Highlanders, Shamrock Syndicate, Standard, Sweet Evening Bells, Toddy Syndicate, Trafalgar
Masquerade band. *See* Mas band
Masquerades, traditional. *See* Bad behavior sailors, Bat, Beelzebub, Djab djab, dragon, imps, Job molassie, Judas parody, Lucifer, Midnight robber, Moko jumbie, Pierrot, Pissenlit, Wild Indians masquerade, Yankee band
Mataloney, Lady, 151
Mattaloney, 228
"Mathilda," 9, 234
Matons, Bill, *See* Calypso Kid
Mayaro, 18, 88, 170
McBurnie, Beryl, 298 n.52
McLean, Bert: recordings of, 140. *See also* Bert Mclean's Jazz Hounds
McLean Fitz, 131
McSwiney, John, 32
"Meet Me Round the Corner," 203
Melody, Lord, 181
Mendes, Alfred, 221
Mento (Mentor), 93, 131
Mentor (Lord Mentor), 75, 80, 122
Mentor (merchant), 110
"Mercury Theater," 186
Merengue, 141
Merrick, Walter, 122–24, 140, 159–60, 172, 215
Midnight robber, 58, 137, 149, 268
"Might and You," 143
Mighty Sparrow (Slinger Francisco), 85, 219; photograph of, 84
Mills Brothers, 108
Minerve, James, 173
Minstrels, 156–58
Mirror, 49–50
"Miss Marie's Advice," 199
"Mr. Nankiwell's Speech," 200
Mr. Squash Meets a Girl, 183
Mitchell, Joseph, 90
"Mixed Marriages," 102
Moko jumbie, 58
"Money Is King," 111, 128, 259–60
"Monkey Swing," 136–37
Monrose, Cyril, 124–25, 140–41, 173.

See also Cyril Monrose's String Orchestra
Montserrat (Hills), 34, 43; location of, 13
Mootoo Brothers, 78
Mootoo Brothers Orchestra, 132; photograph of, 134
Moravian Baptist Church, 198
Morrow, Hal, 240
Mussolini, 251–53
"My Indian Girl Love," 99
Myler the Dentist, 5, 31, 151
"My Life of Matrimony," 99
"My Reply to Houdini," 99
"Mysterious Tunapuna Woman," 111
"My Troubles with Dorothy," 99
"My Unconquered Will," 99, 210

"Naniwele," 254
Nankiwell, Howard, 200–201
National Association for the Advancement of Colored People, 142
National Broadcasting Company, 184
National Phonograph Company, 116
Neg jardin (Nèg jaden), 56, 228; outfit, 27–28
Negro Welfare, Cultural, and Social Association (Trinidad), 202
"Nellie Go Out Mi Door," 99
Nelson Street, 245; and the Inventor, 94; location of, 26; tents on, 74, 111
"Netty, Netty," 230; music transcription, 233
New Era, 36
"A New experience that I had gain," 97
Newgate band, 40–41
New London Club, London, 167
"The New Shop Law," 99
New Theatre (San Fernando), 147
Newtown, 171; location on map, 25; and the steel band, 203–4; and stick fighting, 28
New Yorker, 90
New York News, 182
New York City, 1, 122, 165, 174, 191, 197, 235, 238, 245, 252, 270, 294 n.107; Belasco in, 174–75; calypso performances in, 170; and Executor, 97; Houdini in, 177, 179–81; radio in, 184; the recording industry in, 115, 117, 121–29, 135–36, 140–43, 216;